John Ledyard's Journey through Russia and Siberia 1787–1788

JOHN LEDYARD'S JOURNEY THROUGH RUSSIA AND SIBERIA 1787-1788

THE JOURNAL AND SELECTED LETTERS

EDITED WITH AN INTRODUCTION BY
STEPHEN D. WATROUS

THE UNIVERSITY OF WISCONSIN PRESS

The University of Wisconsin Press
1930 Monroe Street, 3rd Floor
Madison, Wisconsin 53711-2059
uwpress.wisc.edu

3 Henrietta Street
London WC2E 8LU, England
eurospanbookstore.com

Printed in the United States of America

Library of Congress Control Number: 66-022855

ISBN 978-0-299-04224-0 (pbk.: alk. paper)
ISBN 978-0-299-04223-3 (e-book)

Preface

This book presents for the first time in unabridged form John Ledyard's available writings about his journey across Russia and Siberia in 1787–88. My aim in editing these papers was to assemble and interpret the accessible information about this remarkable trip undertaken by an American traveler and explorer, and to furnish a biographical and historical setting that would increase the reader's understanding of the journey.

John Ledyard became acquainted with the North Pacific region when he voyaged with Captain James Cook's expedition to the northwest coast of America, Alaska, and Kamchatka in 1776–80. Late in 1786 he set out from Western Europe to cross Russia and Siberia with the intention of reaching the American northwest coast from the west and traversing the American continent on foot. This attempt did not succeed, for reasons which, like some other circumstances of his journey, are still unknown. Nevertheless, the course of Ledyard's journey can be fairly accurately determined and some of its mysteries unraveled by examining letters he wrote from Siberia, his hitherto unpublished journal, and various accounts and documents of others who were in some way involved with his trip.

Ledyard, himself, prepared for publication nothing but his *Journal of Captain Cook's Last Voyage to the Pacific Ocean, and in Quest of a North-West Passage, between Asia & America; Performed in the Years 1776, 1777, 1778, and 1779,* which was printed in 1783. Until recently only a portion of his writings had been published, often altered or abridged. Biographers have romanticized his life and treated it incompletely. Jared Sparks's biography (1828) has rightly been considered the most authoritative, because of the extent of his investigations. Thorough study of Ledyard's journey into Russia and Siberia and careful editing of his writings about it have never before been undertaken.

Problems that were not easy to resolve arose during the research and editing. If official documents, such as orders and letters of the Empress Catherine or of various civil authorities in eastern Siberia, still exist which might tell more about Ledyard's arrest in Irkutsk, they have remained inaccessible. The original journal which Ledyard was able to bring out of Russia has since been lost. Additional observations made in notes and a smaller journal—mentioned by Ledyard in several places—were left behind in eastern Siberia. Only a few letters concerning the journey can definitely be said to be in Ledyard's handwriting. Of the three known copies of parts of his journal, none is in his hand. While the two most important transcriptions of the journal contain much material of similar content, each contains unique material as well. For example, only one account follows the journey eastward across the Russian Empire, while the other provides the sole information about Ledyard's course in returning from Moscow through Poland.

The present volume has two principal parts: an introductory section about Ledyard and his journey, and a section which contains the texts relevant to the journey. In the introductory chapters I have tried to outline the important circumstances in Ledyard's life leading up to the journey, as well as the historical significance of his hopes for the future and of his travels. I have also attempted to throw light on conditions of life and travel in eighteenth-century Siberia and to describe this little-known and remote part of the earth as it was at the time of Ledyard's visit.

Chapter 4, on "The History and Editing of the Papers," discusses among other things the two transcriptions of the original journal which are used as texts and the procedure followed in preparing this edition of the journal for publication.

Among Ledyard's letters I have chosen only those related, directly or indirectly, to the Siberian journey. First in order come the letters in some way connected with his attempts to reach the northwest coast of America with intent to cross the continent, which were written before his deportation from the Russian Empire; then the journal of the trip; and finally the letters related to the Siberian journey which were written after his return to Western Europe. Interspersed among Ledyard's letters are other documents pertaining to the journey. These include miscellaneous letters, recommendations, orders, reports, and so on, written by other people, in particular, letters by Thomas Jefferson. The entire series is numbered and each item is referred to in my introductory chapters and notes by document number.

With the publication of this volume, of *A Journal of Captain Cook's Last Voyage*, recently edited by J. K. Munford in *John Ledyard's Journal of Captain Cook's Last Voyage* (1963), and of most of Ledyard's known letters and reports to Jefferson in *The Papers of Thomas Jefferson*, Vols. 9–14, edited by J. P. Boyd (1954–58), almost all of Ledyard's extant writings are in print. The known exceptions are about twenty-five letters to his cousin Isaac Ledyard, his mother, his brothers, and to other friends, none of which concerns his Siberian journey.

In preparing this book I was fortunate to have the help and guidance of Michael B. Petrovich, of the University of Wisconsin, who first suggested to me the subject of Ledyard's journey and gave me valuable assistance in my research, and of Vernon Carstensen, of the University of Washington, who initially supplied me with photostats of many of Ledyard's writings and made numerous helpful suggestions. The Graduate School of the University of Wisconsin supplied funds to investigate source material in New York City and New England.

I wish to thank the following individuals and institutions for assisting me by providing documents and valuable information:

Chester S. Chard, Kenneth C. Cramer, Louis Gottschalk, Miss Katharine Ledyard Hill, Frank Horlbeck, James Nafziger, Mrs. Viola Stevens, the Library of the Royal Botanical Gardens at Kew, the Sutro Library of the California State Library, the Slavonic Division of the New York Public Library, the Law Library and the Suzzallo Library of the University of Washington, the State Historical Society of Wisconsin, and the University of Wisconsin Memorial Library.

For permission to reprint documents in their possession I would like to thank John D. Ledyard of Cazenovia, New York, the Archives du Ministère des Affaires Étrangères, the Trustees of Dartmouth College, the Trustees of the British Museum, the Harvard College Library, the Manuscript Division of the Library of Congress, the National Archives, and the New-York Historical Society.

My gratitude also goes to the directors of the Glavnoe Arkhivnoe Upravlenie and the Lenin Library in Moscow, the Saltykov-Shchedrin Public Library in Leningrad, and the Tsentral'nyi Gosarkhiv of Yakutsk ASSR, who searched for further Ledyard material for me, although they were, with one small exception, unable to discover any not already known and available to me.

The Archives Department of Dartmouth College, the Houghton Library of Harvard, and the New-York Historical Society furnished photographs used as illustrations.

My mother, father, and wife repeatedly gave valuable assistance and advice in my work.

Throughout the book I have used the Library of Congress system of transliterating Russian words and names, modified by the deletion of diacritical marks except for ë. I have departed from this procedure in the following two instances: in an English context geographical place-names are spelled as in *Webster's Geographical Dictionary;* various Siberian ethnic groups are spelled according to the common usage of both Ledyard and the English language.

S.D.W.

October 1965
Seattle, Washington

Contents

Illustrations

following page 114

Maps

List of Abbreviations

AAE	Archives du Ministère des Affaires Étrangères, Paris.
Beaufoy transcript	Transcript of Ledyard's journal from early autumn 1787 at Yakutsk to mid-April 1788 east of Königsberg. Ledyard Collection, Dartmouth College.
BL	Baker Library, Dartmouth College, Hanover, N.H.
BM	British Museum, London.
Cook Journal	Ledyard. *A Journal of Captain Cook's Last Voyage*, 1783 ed.
Forman transcript	Transcript of Ledyard's journal from June 1, 1787 (N.S.), at St. Petersburg to early autumn 1787 at Yakutsk. John Ledyard's Papers, Cazenovia, New York.
HL	Houghton Library, Harvard University, Cambridge, Mass.
JLP	John Ledyard's Papers. Transcripts of letters and journal in possession of Ledyard family, Cazenovia, New York.
LC	Library of Congress, Washington, D.C.
NA	National Archives, Washington, D.C.
NYHS	New-York Historical Society, New York, N.Y.
PTJ	*The Papers of Thomas Jefferson*, ed. by J. P. Boyd. 17 vols., Princeton, 1950–65.
RA	*Russkii Arkhiv*. 123 vols., Moscow, 1863–1917.

WTJ	*The Writings of Thomas Jefferson,* ed. by A. A. Lipscomb and A. E. Bergh. 20 vols., Philadelphia, 1904–05.
# 1–# 48	Numbered letters and other documents printed in this book.

In addition, works listed in the Bibliography are cited in shortened form in the notes.

INTRODUCTION

1

A Biographical Sketch

John Ledyard in all probability was the first explorer who came to consider himself a native son of the North American continent and a citizen of the young United States of America. Indeed, in the same month that the Declaration of Independence was signed he made his debut as explorer on Captain James Cook's third voyage to the Pacific. During his brief lifespan he embarked upon three exploratory expeditions, of which only the first, the voyage of 1776–80 with Captain Cook to the North Pacific, could be called successful.

Ledyard's effort to reach the northwest coast of America by way of Siberia and Kamchatka in 1787–88 met with disaster. His subsequent expedition to Africa to explore the middle and upper reaches of the Niger River was cut short in January 1789 by his death in Cairo at the age of thirty-seven. Despite his misfortunes, his experiences were unique for a young American. Ledyard was the first American known to have been in the Pacific area and to have seen Hawaii and Alaska, the first to encounter Russians in the North Pacific, and the first to visit Siberia.

John Ledyard was born in November 1751 in Groton, Connecticut. His grandfather, also John Ledyard, had emigrated from Bristol, England, to Long Island in 1717. However, the rest of

Ledyard's ancestors were of Massachusetts Puritan stock.[1] His father, again John Ledyard, was a sea captain engaged in the West Indies trade. To him and his wife, the former Abigail Hempstead, were born six children, only four of whom lived past infancy. John was the eldest of the six. Born three years after him was a cousin, Isaac Ledyard (1754–1803), who was to remain his lifelong friend and correspondent. After his father's death in 1762, young Ledyard went to live at his grandfather's house in Hartford and attended grammar school there. He later worked in the Hartford law office of his uncle, Thomas Seymour, but felt no inclination for this kind of life.

As the eldest son of an eldest son, John would receive a standard portion of the inheritance of his grandfather, still living at the time. However, the deed of inheritance became lost, his grandfather decided to divide up his fortune otherwise, and young Ledyard received next to nothing from the estate. This circumstance threw him upon his own resources in choosing a vocation. Ledyard did not discover his direction in life until on his voyage with Captain Cook he became aware of the tremendous commercial possibilities in the Pacific.[2]

Soon after the death of old John Ledyard in 1771, Dr. Eleazar Wheelock, founder of Dartmouth College and a friend of his late grandfather, urged young Ledyard to come to Dartmouth and train to be a missionary to the Indians. Willing enough to explore this possibility, Ledyard set out in April 1772 for the newly established school in Hanover, New Hampshire. However, he did not long remain a conscientious student. Wanderlust often got the better of him, and he spent much of that year in the wild country north and west of Hanover, learning the languages and customs of the Iroquois. Although Ledyard in his journal only once mentions his encounters with the Indians at Dartmouth (Journal; p. 146), one can conclude from reading his Siberian

1. Augur, *Passage to Glory*, pp. 4–5. For further information on the Ledyard family, see Charles Moore, "John Ledyard the Traveller," *New York Genealogical and Biographical Record*, 7 (Jan. 1876):3–8.

2. For more on Ledyard's early life, see biographies by Sparks, Munford, and Augur listed in the Bibliography.

papers that the knowledge he picked up of Indian vocabulary, manners, and life enabled him to make valid and astute comparisons between what he called "Tartars" of America and of Asia.

True to his restless nature, Ledyard decided by April 1773 that he had had enough of school. Just after the ice had gone out on the Connecticut River, he hollowed out a long dugout canoe and floated away from Dartmouth College.[3] Narrowly missing catastrophe at Bellows Falls, in due time he reached his relatives' home on the banks of the Connecticut near Hartford.

A character sketch of Ledyard during his college days at Dartmouth was later drawn by James Wheelock, son of the founder:

> As a scholar while he was here . . . he was respectable, tho he did not excel—He was gentlemanly, & had an independance & singularity in his manners, his dress, & appearance that commanded the particular notice & attention of his fellow students—I remember when he first came, he came in a sulkey the first carriage of the kind ever on Dartmouth plain, which then, considering the wilderness, the new & almost impassable state of the roads, want of bridges &c displayed in him a fortitude, & something of that spirit of enterprize, for which his after life was so highly distinguished—[4]

Much of the information that the Reverend Jared Sparks collected in 1821–23 from Ledyard's contemporaries at Dartmouth for his biography attests to the eccentricity of character, dress, and action that set Ledyard apart from other students.

Now almost twenty-two, Ledyard still had no definite path or vocation in life. At this impasse, he decided to prove his mettle by succeeding as a divinity student (Congregational). He made his way to Long Island in search of a minister who would take him as an "apprentice" student—but no one wanted him. After also attempting in vain to get a schoolmaster's job, Ledyard

3. Ledyard's memory is preserved today at Dartmouth in the Ledyard Canoe Club. In the summer of 1964 nine of its members set out at Ulm, Germany, to canoe 1,600 miles down the Danube to the Black Sea.

4. Letter to Richard Bartlett, dated Nov. 12, 1821, at Hanover. Jared Sparks MS No. 112, HL; reprinted in *Dartmouth Alumni Magazine* (Feb. 1963), p. 9.

turned to that ultimate resort of many a New Englander before him, the sea.[5]

Late in 1773 he found employment as a sailor on the ship of Captain Richard Deshon, a friend of his father's. Setting out from New London, the ship stopped at Gibraltar, visited the Barbary Coast, proceeded to the West Indies, and returned to New London in late August 1774. The voyage proved uneventful, and there is no reason to stress the effect of this first voyage on Ledyard's subsequent travels.

It was probably not until early 1775 that Ledyard again crossed the Atlantic, bound for England and with no definite purpose in mind other than to look up his grandfather's wealthy relatives in Bristol—also Ledyards.[6] The poor American cousin apparently found little favor with his more prosperous kinfolk, for nothing came of his visit. Some time prior to mid-1776 he enlisted as a corporal in the British Navy. Then he heard of Captain Cook's imminent departure on a third voyage of discovery. His imagination aroused, Ledyard made his way to Plymouth as quickly as possible to investigate the possibilities of employment and of glory and adventure.

Parliament had voted a prize of £20,000 to be awarded to the British commander who should discover a Northwest Passage. Hence the search for a navigable trade route from the Pacific to the Atlantic north of the American continent was the prime objective of Cook's voyage, though any other claims of newly discovered territories would also be welcomed by Crown and

5. Ledyard "tried all over Long Island and Connecticut to get a schoolmaster's job, but was blocked by Dr. Wheelock's refusal to give him the necessary standing of church membership" (Augur, *Passage to Glory*, p. 48).

6. Although Ledyard indicated in a petition to the Connecticut Assembly on January 6, 1783 (reprinted in Lehmann-Haupt, *The Book in America*, p. 88), that he left New York for Falmouth, England, in March 1774 it is more logical to assume that his memory was faulty in this instance, for on September 2, 1774, he wrote his cousin Isaac of his recent return to Groton from his voyage to Gibraltar and the West Indies (JLP). Moreover, another letter to Isaac, though dated January 15, 1773, at Gibraltar, was probably written there on January 15, 1774. Since Ledyard was still at Dartmouth in January 1773, the year was incorrectly transcribed in JLP.

Parliament. After a successful interview with Cook, Ledyard was assigned as a marine to the captain's own ship, the *Resolution,* which had already weathered Cook's second voyage to the South Pacific in 1772–75. On July 12, 1776, the *Resolution* left Plymouth harbor. By mid-September she reached the Cape of Good Hope, and three weeks later her consort, the *Discovery,* commanded by Captain Charles Clerke, joined her there. In late November the ships set out together for the South Pacific Ocean.[7]

Ledyard, in his journal of the voyage, written in early 1783 upon his return to America, recorded his impressions and experiences at such places en route to the Pacific as the Cape of Good Hope, Kerguélen Island, Van Diemen's Land (Tasmania), and New Zealand. In the South Pacific the ships stopped at Tongatabu in the Friendly Islands, Otaheite (Tahiti), Christmas Island (which the expedition discovered on Christmas Eve, 1777), and the Sandwich Islands (Hawaii), which Cook named in honor of the Earl of Sandwich.[8] From these visits Ledyard gained the knowledge which enabled him when in Siberia to draw contrasts in his journal between the customs and appearance of the natives and those of the South Sea islanders. Moreover, of the places where the expedition stopped, four had particular importance for Ledyard's journey through Siberia almost ten years later. These were Nootka Sound, Unalaska Island, Avacha Bay in Kamchatka, and south China.

When Cook's expedition reached Nootka Sound on Vancouver Island in late March 1778, many of the crew obtained furs from the natives to keep themselves warm during the voyage farther north. In Kamchatka and southern China a year later they discovered a bonanza in selling the beaver, sea otter, and wolverine skins they had picked up so casually. Ledyard later wrote in his *Journal of Captain Cook's Last Voyage:*

7. Henceforth all dates on this voyage will be taken from Ledyard's *Journal of Captain Cook's Last Voyage* (1783).

8. John Montagu, Fourth Earl of Sandwich (1718–92), was First Lord of the Admiralty, which sponsored the voyage. In early January 1778 Cook discovered the island of Hawaii, and the expedition spent the rest of the month there.

The light in which this country [Nootka Sound] will appear to most advantage respects the variety of its animals, and the richness of their furr. They have foxes, sables, hares, marmosets, ermines, weazles, bear, wolves, deer, moose, dogs, otters, beavers, and a species of weazle called the glutton [wolverine]; the skin of this animal was sold at Kamchatka, a Russian factory on the Asiatic coast for sixty rubles, which is near 12 guineas, and had it been sold in China it would have been worth 30 guineas. We purchased while here about 1500 beaver, besides other skins, but took none but the best, having no thoughts at that time of using them to any other advantage than converting them to the purposes of cloathing, but it afterwards happened that skins which did not cost the purchaser sixpence sterling sold in China for 100 dollars. Neither did we purchase a quarter part of the beaver and other furr skins we might have done, and most certainly should have done had we known of meeting the opportunity of disposing of them to such an astonishing profit.[9]

The landing at Nootka Sound and the unexpected profits subsequently reaped markedly influenced the members of the voyage, and Ledyard in particular was strongly affected. In this visit lay the seed of two ambitions which dominated the rest of his life: the dream of setting up a fur-trading post and of crossing the North American continent.

The expedition proceeded northward from Nootka, hugging the Alaskan coastline, until Cook finally led his vessels through what is now known as the Bering Strait. Penetrating through loose fields of ice, on August 28, 1778, they reached a latitude of 71° 17′ before turning back. Ledyard stated in his *Cook Journal* that he was informed Captain Cook had with him an account of Bering's discoveries in that region, which "not only much facilitated his own [Cook's] navigation, but deprived him of the honor of being the sole discoverer of the N.W. continent of America, though it must be acknowledged that Bheering's knowledge of such parts as he did explore were incorrect, imperfect and infinitely below the consummate accuracy of Cook."[10]

The first attempt of the expedition to find the Northwest Passage ended, and Cook headed south toward a wintering

9. Ledyard, *Cook Journal* (1783), p. 70.
10. *Ibid.*, pp. 99–100. In all probability, Cook also had knowledge of the recent Spanish expeditions along the northwest coast.

place. En route he was bent on further exploring the environs of Unalaska, which they had named Providence Island on the way north. The ships arrived at this bleak chunk of land in the Aleutian chain on October 2, 1778. Under this date Ledyard later recorded : "I have before observed that we had noticed many appearances to the eastward of this [Unalaska] . . . of an European intercourse, and that we had at this island in particular met with circumstances that did not only indicate such an intercourse but seemed strongly to intimate that some Europeans were actually somewhere on the spot." Among the natives of Unalaska evidence of the use of tobacco, rum, and snuff was found, and Cook's men "observed several blue linen shirts and drawers among them." However, the decisive evidence proved to be the words of a young Aleut chief, Derramoushk, who told Cook about white strangers in the vicinity who had crossed the sea in ships similar to those of Cook.

Eager to follow up this lead, Cook needed a man to verify it and, if possible, gain further information. Ledyard was recommended by John Gore, a fellow countryman and first lieutenant aboard the *Resolution*,[11] to explore the island and to seek out the strangers; this met with Cook's approval. Setting out around October 7, Ledyard was led by his Aleut guides in a two-day journey to the camp of some Russian fur traders. He presented the Russians with small gifts and informed them, as well as he could, that Captain Cook, desiring to meet them, had sent him to show the way. The next day three of the leading Russians and a few attendants accompanied Ledyard back. They spoke—with some difficulty—with Cook, who was well pleased with the success of Ledyard's venture. On October 14 Gerasim G. Izmailov, commander of the Russian expedition in this area, arrived at Cook's ship and exchanged geographical and nautical information with the captain. Izmailov was entrusted by Cook with a letter and chart to the Lords Commissioners of the British Admiralty, which he promised to forward to Okhotsk and overland to

11. Lieutenant Gore, the only other native American on the voyage, was born in Virginia. In contrast to Ledyard, however, he considered himself an Englishman.

St. Petersburg.[12] This was probably how Ledyard first learned of a communications system across the Russian Empire. Izmailov subsequently sent a report of Cook's visit to Major M. K. Bem, Russian commandant in Kamchatka, stating that the two English ships had arrived and that they had communicated by signs only, owing to ignorance of each other's language.[13]

This encounter between English and Russians at Unalaska was the first contact between representatives of those two powerful nations which later became rivals for mastery of the North Pacific. In the person of Ledyard, it was the first contact between the United States and Russia in the Pacific. It was also Ledyard's first contact with a people among whom he would live for over twelve months. The comments in his *Cook Journal* about his experience on Unalaska with Russians and Kamchadals, the first Siberian people he had met, are as interesting and detailed as those written during his Siberian journey.[14]

Leaving Unalaska on November 1, Cook directed his course toward the Sandwich Islands, where he planned to winter, procure supplies, and repair ships. The consequences of what the expedition had hoped would be a pleasant respite were disastrous. Initially friendly relations with the natives took a turn for the worse, and on February 14, 1779, on the beach of Kealakekua, on the island of Owyhee (Hawaii), Captain Cook met his death at the hands of furious natives.

Command of the expedition was now assumed by Captain Charles Clerke. In early March 1779 the expedition made its way north to Kamchatka to procure necessary "European articles," mainly food, clothing, and shoes, since they had learned at Unalaska that Petropavlovsk served as a supply center for the

12. These were delivered in England six months later. For Cook's own account of his stay at Unalaska and his dealings with the Russians, see Cook, *The Explorations of Captain James Cook in the Pacific as Told by Selections from his Own Journals, 1768–1779*, ed. Price, pp. 244–47.

13. Bancroft, *History of Alaska*, p. 213. Bancroft's information was taken from A. Sgibnev, *Morskoi sbornik* (St. Petersburg, 1869), 103 (No. 7): 21, which was inaccessible to me.

14. Ledyard, *Cook Journal* (1783), pp. 91–100. These comments are readily available in the two 1963 editions of his *Cook Journal*.

Russians on that island. On April 26 the ships arrived in Avacha Bay, off Petropavlovsk. There Captain Clerke was able to dispatch home the news of Cook's death, which reached London in January 1780. Almost two months spent in Kamchatka on this first stop and six weeks on a second later in the year acquainted Ledyard with the commercial and shipping connections that linked Petropavlovsk with Okhotsk on the one hand and the northwest American coast on the other. Thus he was ready to count, eight years later, on catching a ship from Okhotsk to Avacha Bay, and from there to North America. Writing of Kamchatka and Siberia for the first time in his *Cook Journal,* Ledyard made the following comment: "This [Kamchatka] is one of the southern circles of Russian Siberia, called thus from its being a place where malefactors of rank from the Court of Russia are exiled: The word Siberia in Russ signifying a prison. . . ."[15] Actually the word "Siberia" comes from Sibir, capital of a sixteenth-century khanate in western Siberia, while the Russian word for prison is *tiur'ma.* Ledyard's error oddly foreshadows the frustration he was to feel during his own experience in Siberia.

The *Resolution* and *Discovery* were the first Western European ships we know to have visited Kamchatka. In spite of Izmailov's advance report to Major Bem informing him of Cook's presence in the North Pacific, panic ensued among the inhabitants of Petropavlovsk when the English arrived. Several years before this time, in 1771, the Polish political exile Maurycy A. Beniowski had led a rebellion on Kamchatka, then escaped by ship to France. When the English arrived, "The general impression," writes Bancroft, "was that the vessels had come at the instigation of Benyovski with hostile intent. . . . runners and messengers were despatched to all the forts and ostrogs to put the garrisons upon their guard."[16] Yet local suspicions were soon eased and the English were able to exchange furs and other

15. *Ibid.*, p. 163.

16. Bancroft, *History of Alaska,* p. 213n. In fact, after the news of the expedition's visits had arrived in St. Petersburg, in 1783 the empress decided to strengthen the defense of Kamchatka by moving the seat of its commandant from Bolsheretsk to Nizhni Kamchatsk.

articles for needed provisions. Wolverine skins brought sixty rubles apiece, and beaver pelts about fifteen rubles each. Ledyard this time had an opportunity for close examination of Russians and Kamchadals in their home surroundings.[17]

The expedition left Kamchatka around the middle of June 1779, heading back toward the Bering Strait in search of the Northwest Passage, but the illness of Captain Clerke and a dangerous leak in the *Discovery* forced its return. The subsequent sojourn at Avacha Bay, during which Clerke was buried and James King, a second lieutenant on the *Resolution,* assumed command, lasted from late August to early October 1779. This period gave Ledyard time to make more extensive excursions around the region and to continue his many-sided investigations.[18]

On October 9 the two ships, now in good repair, left Kamchatka bound for England. By December the expedition had reached Macao and Canton. Whatever furs the sailors and officers still possessed they sold to eager Chinese merchants for twice the price paid in Kamchatka. Here too Ledyard first heard reliable news of the American Revolution. The return voyage from Canton to England lasted about nine months, the ships arriving in Deptford on October 6, 1780. Soon thereafter the Admiralty impounded all diaries and journals kept by the voyagers, among which were all of Ledyard's original notes.

Back in England, still serving as a marine in the British Navy, Ledyard had no desire to fight his own countrymen. Thus he managed to remain in the British service in England until after Cornwallis' surrender in October 1781. Soon after that he was obliged to cross the Atlantic on a British warship. At some point before September 1782 the frigate called at Long Island, and Ledyard was able to detach himself permanently from the British by requesting a week's leave to visit his mother. He was able to salvage from his belongings on board ship the works of Laurence Sterne, whom he much admired and whose style of writing

17. Ledyard, *Cook Journal* (1783), pp. 167–68.
18. *Ibid.,* pp. 182–91.

influenced him somewhat.[19] It is also probable that he brought with him a copy of the anonymous journal of Cook's last voyage which had been printed in London in 1781 and has since been attributed to John Rickman, a second lieutenant on the *Discovery*. At least he had this at hand when he began writing his own account of the voyage.

After paying visits to his mother and friends in the Long Island area, Ledyard had by January 15, 1783, settled down in Hartford to complete the narrative of his recent voyage.[20] The *Journal of Captain Cook's Last Voyage* appeared by mid-1783, dedicated to Governor Jonathan Trumbull of Connecticut and printed by Nathaniel Patten of Hartford. The book was an immediate success, and Patten made a tidy profit; Ledyard at the outset received 20 guineas from Patten for the work. Ledyard, however, had more in mind than book profits and satisfying the curiosity of Americans about the western shores of their continent. The *Cook Journal* was the first step in his project to urge and promote the exploitation by American merchants of the tremendous commercial possibilities on the northwest coast.

During the years 1783–86 Ledyard tried, on both sides of the Atlantic, to find an entrepreneur willing to finance him and provide him with a ship to reach the northwest coast. In the United States, however, from the end of the war on, the state of commercial affairs was becoming worse in the seaports. By the spring of 1784 the glutted market, scarcity of specie, and overextension of credit all combined to produce a serious commercial depression. Although the merchants in Philadelphia and all along the coast were in difficulty, the depression hit the New England states the hardest.[21] It was understandable that during this pe-

19. Augur, *Passage to Glory*, p. 115. According to Augur, "Sterne for a time was to . . . encourage him to use dashes whenever syntax failed him—which was all too often."

20. A letter of that date to Isaac Ledyard written at Hartford describes his recent escape from the British at Huntington Bay, L.I. (JLP).

21. Jensen, *The New Nation: A History of the United States during the Confederation*, pp. 187–91.

riod no one should want to gamble on an expensive and visionary project such as Ledyard's.

Ledyard first tried his luck in Philadelphia with the mercantile house of Blair McClenachan, and visited other shipping firms there, but with no success. He then negotiated with Robert Morris, the financier of the American Revolution. Morris was impressed with the idea, and Ledyard, describing his reaction, wrote: "What a noble hold he instantaneously took of the Enterprize."[22] With a retaining fee from Morris, Ledyard made his way to Boston and procured a ship for the venture. News of the forthcoming voyage to the northwest coast and China was printed in the *Salem Gazette* of August 21, 1783. But at the last moment Morris backed down.

Ledyard then tried to sell his idea to Captain Deshon of New London, nephew of the Deshon with whom he had voyaged earlier; however, this old friend was not quite persuaded. After several futile attempts in New York, Ledyard decided that he might fare better in France. Everyone he approached in America considered his enterprise too risky.

In June of 1784 Ledyard sailed from New London to Cadiz, planning to make his way north from there to Lorient, then one of the busiest ports in France. He had been led to believe in America that he might find support there. By way of Cadiz and Brest, he reached Lorient in September and spent several months there. By February 1785 he had succeeded in the initial steps toward a voyage. He wrote his brothers Thomas and George, "I have a fine Ship of 400 tons, & in August next expect to Sail on another voyage round the world."[23] This prospect too met with failure. The reasons are not known, but the fact that the royally chartered expedition of La Pérouse, spurred by the results of Cook's last voyage, was scheduled to sail from Brest that August

22. Excerpt from a letter to Isaac Ledyard, written in Philadelphia, n.d. (JLP). For Morris' general views on private commercial enterprise at this time, see C. L. VerSteeg, *Robert Morris, Revolutionary Financier* (Philadelphia, 1954), pp. 188–89.

23. Letter dated February 23, 1785, at Lorient; transcript in Jared Sparks MS No. 112, HL.

for the west coast of America may have been among them.

No dated correspondence of Ledyard's exists that indicates exactly when after February 1785 he left Lorient. However, he had proceeded to Paris sometime before July, for in a letter to his cousin Isaac he wrote, "I had the pleasure of being at the Doctor's house [Franklin's] but once only before his departure [from Paris on July 12, 1785]."[24] Succeeding Benjamin Franklin as American minister to France was Thomas Jefferson, whom Ledyard met for the first time probably during the summer of 1785. He must also have become acquainted with the Marquis de Lafayette sometime before July 9, when Lafayette left Paris for Germany.[25] By February of 1786 Ledyard decided to move from Paris to the pleasant suburban town of St. Germain-en-Laye, twelve miles to the west.[26]

A notable event in Ledyard's life between the failure of his venture in Lorient and the first thought he mentions of crossing the Russian Empire (about November 1785; see # 18) was his contract with John Paul Jones to sail to the northwest coast. How Jones and Ledyard met is not known; probably either Franklin or Jefferson introduced them sometime before July 1785. At any rate Jefferson, disturbed at the news of the forthcoming departure of La Pérouse's expedition, threw his support behind Jones and Ledyard. The latter remained in Paris, supported throughout the summer by Jones, while the captain went out to collect his prize money for his successes during the Revolutionary War and to look for suitable ships in Bordeaux and Lorient. Ledyard and Jones planned to fit out two ships, which they hoped Louis XVI would finance, and to set out in October 1785 for Nootka Sound and Alaska via the Horn and Hawaii. After a "factory" on the northwest coast had been set up, Ledyard, with one ship and

24. Letter to Isaac Ledyard dated July [1785] at Paris (NYHS). In this letter Ledyard describes the important sights of Paris at length and relates his various experiences there.

25. # 3. For Lafayette's activities that summer, see Gottschalk, *Lafayette between the American and the French Revolution, 1783–1789*, pp. 179, 266–67.

26. Ledyard to Jefferson, dated February 7, 1786, at St. Germain, in *PTJ*, 9:260–61.

a suitable guard, would spend the summer trading trinkets with the Indians for furs. Jones, with the other ship, would meanwhile try to sell the first load of furs in Japan, Macao, or Canton. He then would return to the "factory" for more furs; and both ships, loaded with sea otter, would proceed to the Orient to exchange them for tea, silk, and porcelain, and return to France. Ledyard estimated a profit of 1000 per cent.[27]

A number of factors prevented the plan from being carried out. Jones could procure no suitable ships for less than 80,000 livres, or treble Ledyard's original calculation. One investor, Dr. Edward Bancroft, grew skeptical upon hearing that the English vessels of Portlock and Dixon were already on their way to the area. Jones had desired the approval of Robert Morris for the project but did not get it. There was delay in Jones's obtaining his prize money. Most important, according to Morison, was the disapproval of the King of Spain, Charles III. Jones's report of the plan to William Carmichael, the American minister at Madrid, had reached the ears of the king, who, considering the entire west coast of America to be his exclusive domain, regarded all attempts of foreigners to trade there as poaching. Thus, Charles's close ally Louis XVI, who, Jones hoped, would provide vessels and assistance, did nothing to further the plan, wishing no French ship to create ticklish problems with Spain.[28]

Others were more successful where Ledyard had failed. In April 1785, Captain James Hanna, an Englishman who sailed from China, collected 560 sea-otter skins at Nootka which he sold upon his return to China for $20,600.[29] In 1786 the ships of two

27. Morison, *John Paul Jones: A Sailor's Biography,* p. 342. A free translation of the document drawn up in French by Jones and Ledyard is given in *Life and Correspondence of John Paul Jones. . . . From Original Letters and Manuscripts in the Possession of Miss Janette Taylor,* pp. 361–63. Ledyard briefly describes these plans with Jones in a letter to Isaac Ledyard from Paris, dated July [1785] (NYHS).

28. Morison, *John Paul Jones: A Sailor's Biography,* p. 342. Lincoln Lorenz in his *John Paul Jones, Fighter for Freedom and Glory* believes the underlying reason for this failure was Jones's basic lack of interest in commercial enterprises (p. 535).

29. A return trip to Nootka a year later was less successful. See Bancroft, *History of Alaska,* pp. 242–43.

former members of Cook's third voyage, the Englishmen Nathaniel Portlock and George Dixon, reached Nootka. Portlock and Dixon were the first to sail from England with the express intention of collecting furs on the northwest coast. Over 2,500 sea-otter skins were obtained and then sold in China for $54,857; the expedition was a resounding success.[30]

American trade with China began in 1784, when the *Empress of China,* sent out from New York, arrived at Canton. Trade with the Orient was to grow year by year, but was conducted under the disadvantage that Americans had few goods the Chinese wanted, and had to pay for their purchases in specie. By 1788 circumstances were to force American merchants into adopting part of Ledyard's plan as their own: the passion for furs exhibited by the Chinese made it clear that furs from the northwest coast were needed to pay for silks and teas in Canton.[31]

Joseph Barrell, a Boston merchant who had read Ledyard's account of Cook's voyage, was able to get the interest and support of five other merchants for a trading expedition. These men, headed by Barrell, appointed John Kendrick to command the *Columbia* and Robert Gray the *Lady Washington.* The two ships reached Nootka Sound in 1788 to collect furs; after Gray and Kendrick exchanged vessels in 1789, they sailed for China where handsome profits were made. Gray, after returning to Boston in 1790, set out again for the northwest coast, and in May 1792 accidentally discovered a great river, which he named the Columbia.

Ledyard's goal of setting up an American fur-trading post on the west coast was not easily achieved. Not until 1811–13 was John Jacob Astor's trading post Astoria established at the mouth of the Columbia River. As Ledyard had envisaged, the furs from the interior and the coast were to be collected at Astoria and taken annually to Canton by a ship which would load up with

30. Bancroft, *History of the Northwest Coast,* 1:173–74; and Howay, "A List of Trading Vessels in Maritime Fur Trade, 1785–1794," *Proc. Trans. R.S.C.,* pp. 111–14.

31. Schafer, "The Pacific Slope and Alaska," in Lee, ed., *History of North America,* 10:34–35.

Chinese goods. One voyage was made in 1812, but improper supplies, mismanagement, and the War of 1812 all contributed to the collapse of Astor's fur post; in 1813 it was sold to the North West Company.

Ledyard, after the failure of his own fur-trading schemes, turned his attention to the second ambition he had conceived as a result of his visit to Nootka Sound: the desire to cross the North American continent. This preoccupied him for his remaining few years of life, and he was to consider his expedition into Africa, made after the unsuccessful attempt to reach the Northwest through Siberia, only a temporary diversion from this main goal.

During his short stay at Nootka Ledyard had experienced a feeling of closeness to home upon again reaching his native continent. In his *Cook Journal* he first recorded his thoughts on the matter under the date April 1, 1778:

> This was the first fair opportunity after our arrival that I had of examining the appearance of those unknown aborigines of North-America. It was the first time too that I had been so near the shores of that continent which gave me birth from the time I at first left it; and though more than two thousand miles distant from the nearest part of New-England I felt myself plainly affected: All the affectionate passions incident to natural attachments and early prejudices played round my heart, and indulged them because they were prejudices. I was harmonized by it. It soothed a home-sick heart, and rendered me very tolerably happy.[32]

Perhaps the desire to seal a bond between New England and Nootka Sound contributed to his ambition to traverse the continent. At all events, he was one of the first to dream of such a crossing, and in all probability was the first to attempt it from west to east. Stirred with the initial flush of American patriotism, he felt that "the American Revolution invites to a thourough discovery of the Continent" (# 10), and came to believe that the

32. Ledyard, *Cook Journal* (1783), p. 71. On the belief in America's continental destiny among such men as Philip Freneau, Thomas Hutchins, and Jefferson in the period 1770–90 see Henry Nash Smith's résumé in *Virgin Land: The American West as Symbol and Myth* (Cambridge, Mass., 1950), pp. 9–12.

destiny of the United States should extend from Atlantic to Pacific. With the collapse of his fur-trading project in September 1785, he seems to have abandoned for a time his hope of reaching the northwest coast via the Atlantic Ocean and Cape Horn. By November of 1785 he was contemplating an attempt to cross the North American continent from west to east by first setting out from France across the Russian Empire to the North Pacific. In February 1786 he wrote to Isaac Ledyard: "In about fourteen days I leave Paris for Brussells, Cologne, Vienne, Dresdon, Berlin, Varsovie, Petersburg, Moscow, Kamchatka Sea of Anadivy, Coast of America, from whence if I find any more cities to New York, when I get there I will name them to you in *propria persona* . . ." (# 4).

While Ledyard was ready to let the matter of getting a passport to travel in Russia wait until he reached St. Petersburg, Jefferson felt that diplomatic procedure was necessary and entered into negotiations that February. Ledyard waited for the outcome in Paris until early August; and then, exasperated by the passage of time, suddenly took off for London. News received from Sir James Hall in London had caused an abrupt turn in his hopes. Sir James, who had recently met Ledyard by accident in Paris,[33] had just found him passage upon a ship leaving England for the northwest coast. In London, Hall gave Ledyard details of the forthcoming voyage and presented him with twenty guineas. The choice of articles Ledyard bought with this money in anticipation of his trek across North America is interesting: "two great Dogs, an Indian pipe and a hatchet" (# 12). It appears that he twice attempted to sail from England, first around August 18 and again around September 20, 1786. Both ventures were ill-fated. In early September Ledyard debated between trying to reach the northwest coast by sea or by land across Siberia (# # 15, 16, 17). On his second attempt to set out by sea, a customs boat halted the ship soon after it had started down the Thames from Dept-

33. Sir James Hall (1761–1832) later became a noted geologist and chemist. He was in Paris on his way home from a geological tour of the continent.

ford and forced it to return. It turned out that certain debts had not been paid up before the ship cleared away.[34]

Ledyard had now made his last attempts to reach the northwest coast by sea from Europe. Although word from Jefferson that the Empress Catherine thought his proposed journey through Siberia "chimaerical" must have reached Ledyard soon before this second failure in England (# # 6, 11), he was still determined to cross the Eurasian continent to Okhotsk and Kamchatka, and set about seeking support for this in London. He secured two main backers, one British, the other American. Sir Joseph Banks, an enthusiastic promoter of exploration and of science, had heard of Ledyard and decided to raise a subscription for him, to which two other British patrons contributed.[35] His other benefactor was Colonel William Stephens Smith, secretary to the American Legation in London, who had previously met him in Paris. Ledyard kept both of them informed by mail of his progress and observations along the way, and through Smith could keep in touch with his cousin Isaac in New York City.[36]

Ledyard set out from London in early December 1786, made his way to Ostend, and proceeded by sea to Hamburg. He was still intent upon traveling with his two dogs, but lost one on his trip up the Elbe River. The fate of the other is unknown. In Hamburg he heard from his innkeeper about an eccentric Virginian, Major William Langborn, who had recently left there for Copenhagen, headed for St. Petersburg, and who like Ledyard

34. According to Sinclair Hitchings, red tape created by the monopolies of the South Sea Company and the East India Company in the Pacific prevented the ship from sailing; see Ledyard, *John Ledyard's Journal*, ed. Munford, p. xlviii.

35. # 20. According to the subscription, Ledyard received 7 guineas, plus whatever undesignated sum W. S. Smith later chose to contribute. James Burney, who knew Ledyard on the Cook expedition, stated in his *Chronological History of Northeastern Voyages of Discovery* (1819) that the subscription raised by Banks amounted to more than £50 (pp. 278–79).

36. Smith probably forwarded the original letters he received from Ledyard to Isaac, and in this way the manuscripts were preserved in America. More than one letter of Ledyard's was forwarded to Banks by Prof. P. S. Pallas of St. Petersburg (# 33). These could not be located in Banks's extant papers.

was an habitual wanderer and walker. This gentleman had reached Copenhagen, but his baggage had not. Anxious to help out a fellow American in distress and eager to find a traveling companion, Ledyard made up his mind to seek Langborn out. He found the major in Copenhagen and requested his company as far as Petersburg, only to receive the reply: " . . . no—I esteem you but I can travel in the manner I do with no man on Earth—" (# 22).

Ledyard had originally intended to reach St. Petersburg via Warsaw, but now that he had already come as far north as Copenhagen, he chose to take the route through Sweden. Thus he proceeded alone to Stockholm. He planned to cross the Gulf of Bothnia to Finland a short distance north of Stockholm. However, the winter of 1786–87 was warmer than usual, the narrow strait between Sweden and the Åland Islands had not frozen over completely, and sledges could not cross. Ledyard then decided upon what was probably the most spectacular feat of his life: he set out on foot to walk around the Gulf of Bothnia to St. Petersburg in the dead of winter. Although he later described this trip with little detail, it appears that he covered about 1,200 miles from Stockholm to St. Petersburg, cutting through the isolated interior parts of Finland in order to travel more directly (# 23). The journey took around eight weeks, which would average about twenty miles a day—a creditable pace in the frozen wastes of Sweden and Finland.[37]

He reached St. Petersburg at some point during the month of March 1787, for his first letter from there, addressed to Thomas

37. Although there is no evidence that Ledyard at times traveled by means of sleigh or sledge during this trek, this possibility cannot be discounted. He probably left Stockholm toward the end of January 1787. According to the Italian traveler Joseph Acerbi, in Sweden at that time there existed no regular conveyance and "no public vehicles . . . for the convenience of common travellers" (*Travels through Sweden, Finland, and Lapland,* 1:5). At Tornio, at the head of the Gulf of Bothnia, Acerbi in 1799 found evidence that "John Stuart, an American" had been there in 1787 (1:347). It seems plausible that Stuart was an incorrect rendition of Ledyard's name. Ledyard probably passed through Tornio in mid-February 1787.

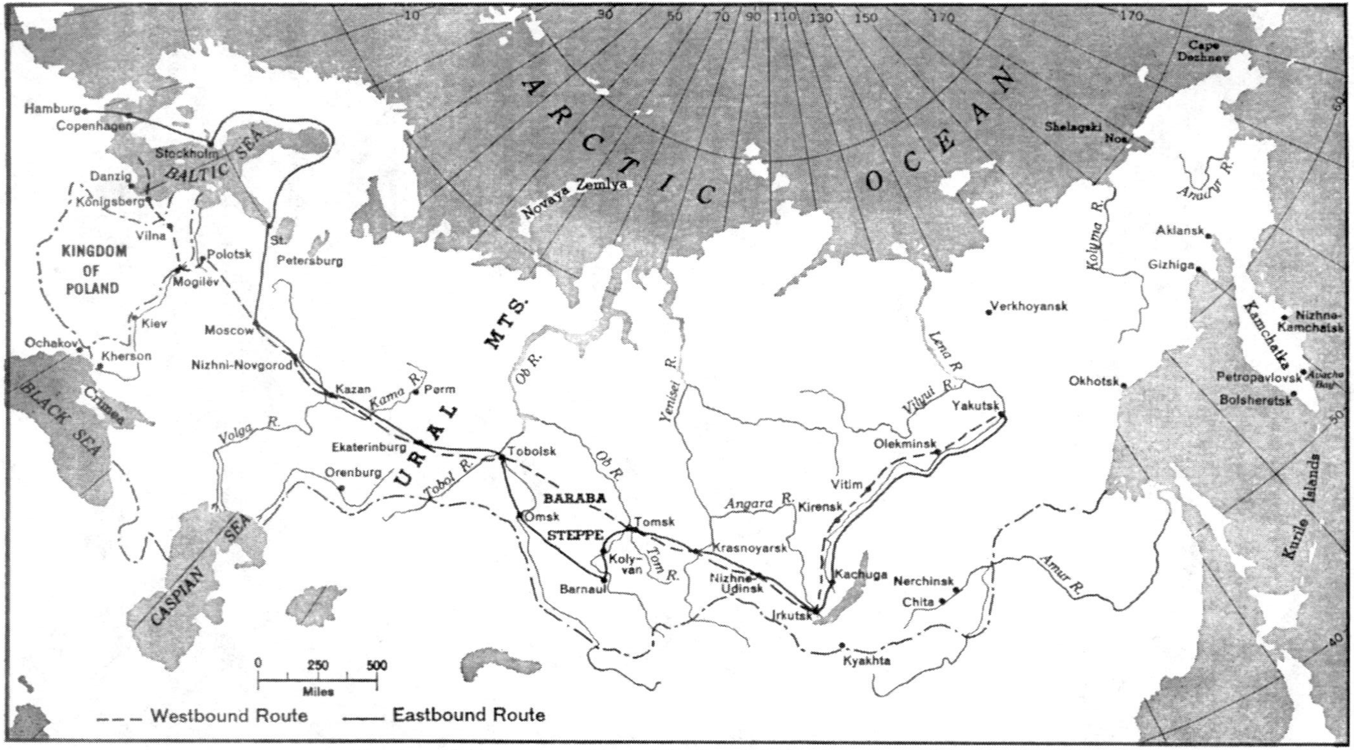

Russian Empire in 1787 and Ledyard's Approximate Route

Jefferson, is dated March 19 (# 23). If Ledyard was following the Julian Calendar (Old Style), then used in Russia, this would have been March 19/30. More likely he was still using New Style (Gregorian), and thus arrived in the Russian capital at least several days before March 8/19.[38] He spent April and May trying to obtain the necessary passport and transportation for proceeding east.

On June 1 (N.S.), traveling in the capacity of a student of natural history, he left St. Petersburg in a kibitka, or covered, horse-drawn coach, accompanied by Dr. William Brown, a Scottish physician who was going on business to Barnaul. According to P. S. Pallas, Ledyard was sent off on his eastward journey as "Messenger," so as "to make him pass without expence" through the Empire (# 33). According to the accounts of Beaufoy and Kippis, Ledyard was able to gain permission to accompany a detachment of supplies which were to be used by Captain Joseph Billings.[39] A former astronomer's assistant on Cook's third voyage and subsequently a captain in the Russian Navy, Billings now headed a scientific expedition commissioned by the Empress Catherine to explore the Kolyma River basin, the Chukotski peninsula, and the islands of the North Pacific. Whether or not Ledyard really traveled part way with supplies (he makes no mention of this in his writings), we shall see that he later encountered his old acquaintance Billings and traveled with him to pick up a shipment of supplies from European Russia.

38. Ledyard wrote in his journal under the date June 1, 1787: "After having been three months in Petersburg, I left it. . . ." If June 1 was written in New Style (Kippis' account indicates that he set off on May 21), taken literally Ledyard's statement would mean he arrived in St. Petersburg about February 18/ March 1. It is also possible to assume that Ledyard's "three months" extended from March 1/12 to May 21/ June 1. This would mean, if he dated his letter to Jefferson in New Style, that he arrived about a week before writing him, i.e. on or about March 12 (N.S.). This date of arrival is the more credible of the two.

39. Henry Hanbury Beaufoy (d. 1795), Whig politician, author, member of Parliament, and supporter of Ledyard's subsequent African venture, suggests that the Portuguese ambassador in St. Petersburg may have been instrumental in obtaining permission for Ledyard to accompany this detachment (# 38). Andrew Kippis (1725–95), a clergyman and biographer of James Cook, was in close contact with Sir Joseph Banks at this time (# 37).

It was with his departure from Petersburg that Ledyard began the journal printed in this book. After a five-day journey Ledyard and Brown reached Moscow, paused briefly there, and set out again on June 8. Passing through Nizhni Novgorod, and following the Volga River, they reached Kazan in good health after a trip of probably five to six days. Although Ledyard gives no further indication of his itinerary until he reached Tobolsk on July 11, his route led from Kazan through the central Urals and the town of Ekaterinburg. After spending several days resting in Tobolsk, the pair set off for Barnaul, on the Ob River, where they arrived July 23, following a nine-day journey through the desolate Baraba steppe.

A bit more than a week later Ledyard bade farewell to his Scottish traveling companion and left for Tomsk, a two-and-a-half days' journey. Reaching Tomsk on August 3, he was detained for a day by a delay in the east-bound mail service, by means of which he was traveling. At Krasnoyarsk, where he spent at least enough time for a meal with the commandant, he crossed the Yenisei River, and reached Irkutsk on August 15.

Here Ledyard spent ten days; was entertained by the governor-general, I. V. Iakobi, and the director of the bank, A. M. Karamyshev; and even took an overnight excursion to Lake Baikal. On August 25 he set out, accompanied by a young Lieutenant Laxmann, and two days later arrived at Kachuga on the Lena River. They exchanged their kibitka for a boat to take them over 1,500 miles downstream to Yakutsk, and got there on September 18. Ledyard pressed to proceed to Okhotsk; but the local commandant, G. A. Marklovskii, urged the dangers of winter travel as reason for remaining in Yakutsk until spring. Although Ledyard protested vehemently, the commandant's will prevailed. It was during the time of waiting in Yakutsk that the greater part of Ledyard's journal was written.

In November Captain Billings arrived with a group of his men, en route to pick up supplies waiting for them at Irkutsk. While in Yakutsk Billings invited Ledyard to lodge at his quarters. With Billings' party was Martin Sauer, an Englishman and secretary to the expedition, who fifteen years later was to publish in English an account of Billings' expedition "narrated from the original papers." Several days behind Billings the naval lieutenant Gavriil A. Sarychev reached Yakutsk. He had been supervising shipbuilding in Okhotsk and also kept an account of the expedition. When in December Billings with a small group set out for Irkutsk, Ledyard joined them, weary of boredom and isolation.[40]

According to Sauer's account (which upon examination is not always accurate), they reached Irkutsk on January 16, 1788, the trip on sledges evidently having lasted less than three weeks. Here Ledyard was arrested and immediately taken off to Moscow by two guards (# 35). During his forced journey westward, he wrote very little in his journal.[41] We know that he left Moscow on March 10 (O.S.), where he had spoken with a "General." Ledyard was then taken to Polotsk, on the Polish border, and then southeast to Mogilëv, where he was questioned by General P. B. Passek. On March 18 (O.S.) he crossed the Drut River into Poland, concluding a stay in the Russian Empire of slightly over twelve months. Reaching Königsberg soon after April 18, he there found someone willing to accept a note on Sir Joseph Banks for five guineas, and with the aid of this sum he regained London by the beginning of May.

Ledyard brought with him out of Russia only part of his writings, an itinerary of his trip down the Lena, and various articles of clothing and trinkets. From London he wrote to Isaac that he would forward to him a reindeer-skin coat, boots, and socks; a cap of Siberian red fox, a Russian cap of white ermine, fox-skin gloves with hare lining, and a reindeer-skin frock from the Kolyma Valley. He sent to Isaac to hold for him the cloak he had

40. Ledyard wrote that Billings arrived in Yakutsk on November 24, while Sauer said November 13. If both dates are correct, Ledyard was using New Style and Sauer Old Style reckoning. Sauer stated that Billings set out from Yakutsk on December 29, while Sarychev gave the date as December 19. (In this case Sauer's date, if correct, may have been New Style.) For Sauer, see # 35. For Sarychev, see *Puteshestvie po severo-vostochnoi chasti Sibiri,* p. 92.

41. The problems of the exact dates of Ledyard's arrest and of his hurried journey west are analysed in Chapter 2, pp. 46–47.

bought in London before setting out; in his own words, he "slept in it, eat in it, drank in it, fought in it, negociated in it" and, in short, traveled twice across Russia and much of Siberia in it (# 39; p. 247). Some of the Siberian garments, trinkets, and carvings sent back by Ledyard are still preserved by his relatives scattered through the United States.[42]

Once again an ambition of Ledyard's was left for others to achieve. The first few subsequent attempts to cross North America, however, were also unsuccessful. In the spring of 1790, Captain John Armstrong of Louisville set out to cross from east to west, but his venture, originally suggested by Secretary of War Henry Knox, was abandoned when reports of Indian disturbances forced him to turn back a short distance above St. Louis. In 1792 Thomas Jefferson, who had championed Ledyard's Siberian journey and whose interest in the Northwest had, for reasons of state, increased since Ledyard's death, initiated a subscription by the American Philosophical Society to send an accomplished French botanist, André Michaux, to explore this region as far as the Pacific Ocean, but Michaux was recalled from Kentucky by the French government because of his involvement in the Genêt affair.[43] Thus the third American attempt to explore the Northwest failed.

The first crossing of North America north of Mexico was accomplished by Alexander Mackenzie, who reached the Pacific at Dean Channel, north of Vancouver Island, on July 23, 1793. It is interesting to note that previous to this, in 1787, Mackenzie had been entrusted by Peter Pond of the North West Company with making a journey in the direction opposite to Ledyard's trip of that year. Pond had made maps of northern Canada and the North Pacific area, and he charged Mackenzie with the duty of

42. Dvoichenko-Markov, "John Ledyard and the Russians," *Russian Review,* 11:218, and information from Prof. Vernon Carstensen.

43. Citizen Edmond Genêt, then French chargé d'affaires in the United States, had instructions from his government to force America to declare war on Great Britain. Since his efforts greatly embarrassed the President, in August 1793 Washington asked the French government to recall him.

presenting a map to the Empress of Russia when he reached her country. Mackenzie "was left by Pond at Slave Lake with orders to go down the [Mackenzie] River, and from thence to Unalaska, and so to Kamskatsha, and then to England through Russia &c."[44] In 1789 Mackenzie made his way down the river which later bore his name, but instead of reaching the Pacific, as he had expected, he reached the Arctic Ocean.

Jefferson's efforts were not to be rewarded until after the turn of the century, when the Lewis and Clark Expedition, which as President he promoted, finally reached the Pacific and explored the Northwest. As Joseph Schafer writes: "Had America done nothing further to strengthen her position, Gray's discovery [of the Columbia] would not have been sufficient basis for our national claim, but by a fortunate combination of circumstances several things were achieved within twenty years after 1792, which established the American hold upon the region of the Columbia. Of these the most noteworthy were the exploration of the river valley by Lewis and Clark in 1804–1806, and the founding of Astoria, with other trading posts, on its banks in 1811–1813."[45]

Ledyard's influence upon each of these three important events in the history of the American Northwest was considerable.

Ledyard's life after the collapse of his Siberian expedition can be briefly described. By May 1788, he was back in London, where he found that his countryman and benefactor William S. Smith had sailed for home just a few weeks earlier. Sir Joseph Banks, however, received the unsuccessful traveler warmly, and soon afterward informed Ledyard of a vast new project of discovery which he had in mind. Sir Joseph was in the midst of organizing an Association for Promoting the Discovery of the Interior Parts of Africa, which was officially formed June 9, 1788

44. Letter of Isaac Ogden to David Ogden of London, dated November 7, 1789, at Quebec, in Wagner, *Peter Pond, Fur Trader & Explorer*, p. 96. See also pp. 17, 29–32.

45. Schafer, "The Pacific Slope and Alaska," in Lee, ed., *History of North America*, 10:38.

(# 38). Writing in June, Ledyard described to his cousin the circumstances in which this group arose:

I must tell you what this African Comittee is. Some few weeks only before my arival now at London a number of Gentlemen had been tallking somewhat in earnest about exploring the Continent of Africa. My arival has made it a reality. An Association is formed & a Comittee balloted from it last week for the management of the affairs of it. The Comittee chosen are a Mr Cerke a Mr *Beaufoy,* Lord Rawdon Sir Joseph Banks & the Bishop of Landaff. The Society consists at present of 200 Members. It is a growing thing, & the King privately promoting & encouraging it will make its objects more extensive than at first thought of. The king has told them that no expence should be spared: the subscriptions are then altered from any fixed sum to such sums as exigencies may require . . . (# 39; p. 249).

The two moving spirits behind the Association at the time of its inception were Banks and Henry Beaufoy. The main problem for the Association, besides gaining members and funds, was obtaining qualified explorers to send out. With a letter of introduction from Banks, Ledyard introduced himself to Beaufoy, who recorded his first impressions of the American traveler as follows:

Before I had learnt from the note the name and business of my Visitor, I was struck with the manliness of his person, the breadth of his chest, the openness of his countenance, and the inquietude of his eye. I spread the map of Africa before him, and tracing a line from Cairo to Sennar, and from thence Westward in the latitude and supposed direction of the Niger, I told him that was the route, by which I was anxious that Africa might, if possible, be explored. He said, he should think himself singularly fortunate to be entrusted with the Adventure. I asked him when he would set out? "To-morrow morning," was his answer.[46]

It is highly probable that Ledyard had for some time desired to explore Africa, witness a remark of September 18, 1787, made in his Siberian journal just after his arrival at Yakutsk: "I have but two long frozen Stages more and I shall be beyond the want or

46. # 38. Beaufoy was perhaps a bit carried away by Ledyard's appearance.

aid of money, until emerging from her deep deserts I gain the American Atlantic States and then thy glow[i]ng Climates. Africa explored, I lay me down and claim a little portion of the Globe I've viewed—may it not be before."[47] Now back in London, he was evidently undaunted by the failure of his Siberian venture. His usual impatience to be on the move had to be controlled, though, until the details of the trip had been arranged.

While in London Ledyard was not able to prepare his notes and journal for publication. An indeterminable portion of his papers remained behind in eastern Siberia after his sudden arrest, and he had neither time nor incentive to edit and publish those writings that he managed to carry back to England, as he had done with his *Cook Journal* in 1783. Just two months after his arrival in England he set off to explore Africa; the Siberian journal was deposited in the hands of one of his sponsors, Henry Beaufoy, to be returned to him if he came back.

The plan of the Association was for Ledyard to travel through Paris to Marseilles, where he would catch a boat to Alexandria. There he would set off up the Nile through Cairo to the town of Sennar, located on the Blue Nile in present-day Sudan. Ledyard hoped, by striking westward from here, to unravel the mystery of the Niger River. Its delta region was known, as was an area around Timbuktu; but the connection between these lower and upper regions was not yet recognized, and the intermediate waters of the long river were still unexplored. As usual, Ledyard set out with little financial assistance, leaving London on June 30. The Association had been formed so recently that many of the pledges of its members had not yet been paid. Secondly, the assistance promised by the king was not given before Ledyard's departure. Thus the five members of the committee were forced to pay Ledyard's expenses out of their own pockets.

47. Journal; p. 167. Ledyard was referring to the "frozen stages" between Yakutsk and Okhotsk and across the North Pacific to America, where he counted on living with Indians without carrying money. "Her deep deserts" refers to the unknown American interior, and "thy glowing climates" to the eastern seaboard.

The first stop of the explorer was Paris, where he arrived about July 4 (# 42). There he gave Jefferson and Lafayette their first news of his deportation from the Russian Empire, and promised Jefferson that if he returned from Africa he would make his way back to America and would set out for the west coast from Kentucky (# 45). After spending a week in Paris, he proceeded to Marseilles, caught a ship sailing for Alexandria, and reached there by August 15.

In Cairo later that month he sought to attach himself to a caravan traveling to Sennar. At this time he submitted detailed reports to Banks and Beaufoy, informing them of his progress and observations in Egypt. He also kept in touch with Jefferson, writing him a letter from Alexandria and two from Cairo.

Ledyard was never to leave Cairo. According to two similar reports, he died a strange death on January 10, 1789. The details of these reports were sent to Thomas Jefferson by Thomas Paine, then residing in London, who transmitted verbatim the news Sir Joseph Banks had received from Henry Beaufoy:

> Mr. Beaufoy presents his compliments to Sir Joseph Banks, and is much concerned that he cannot encourage the hope which Mr. Jefferson entertains that there is no truth in the report of Mr. Ledyard['s] death. The letter which Mr. Beaufoy received from Mr. [George] Baldwin the British Consul at Cairo, and which is dated Alexandria March 4th. 1789 informs him—That a day was fixed for Mr. Ledyard's departure as he was prepared and seemed anxious to set off, but bad weather or other causes occasioned delay as happens to most caravans. Mr. Ledyard took offence at the delay and threw himself into a violent rage with his conductors which deranged something in his system that he thought to cure by an emetic, but he took the dose so strong as at the first or second effort of its operations to break a blood vessel. In three days he was suffocated and died.
>
> This Account is confirmed by a letter from the Compte de Rosette [Carlo Rosetti], the Venetian Resident at Cairo, to Mr. Hunter, an English Merchant who had lived in great intimacy with Mr. Ledyard from the time of their travelling together from Alexandria to Cairo to that of Mr. Hunter's departure for England. This letter is dated Cairo 27th. Jany. 1789 and tells Mr. Hunter "that seventeen days ago poor Mr. Ledyard went to his eternal rest. He suffered himself to be

transported with anger against the persons who had engaged to conduct him to Sennar because they delayed setting out on their voyage for want (as they said) of a fair wind. He was seized with a pain in his stomach occasioned by Bile and undertook to cure himself. excessive vomiting ensued, in consequence of which he broke a blood vessel and died in six days."[48]

Thus, ironically, ended the life of this hardy explorer of continents, whose several goals never came within his grasp. The same restless impatience, quick-tempered determination, and independence of mind which had spurred his journey through Russia and Siberia, and of which Jefferson, Lafayette, and Beaufoy thought so highly, on the other hand often brought him little sympathy and even the outright hostility of others. These traits in his character all contributed, as we shall see, to his misfortunes in Siberia, and they occasioned his death in Egypt. Fate, which had tormented him and hindered his ambitions throughout the best part of his life, had finally caught up with him for good. He died at the age of thirty-seven, his hope to "claim a little portion of the Globe I've viewed" only partially fulfilled.

48. Excerpt from a letter of Thomas Paine to Jefferson dated June 18, 1789, at London (*PTJ*, 15:198). Banks gave Paine a facsimile of Beaufoy's letter.

2

The Siberian Journey Significance and Problems of Interpretation

Few important Americans preceded Ledyard to Russia; none of them left valuable accounts of their stay. The first was Francis Dana, minister of the Continental Congress to St. Petersburg from 1781 to 1783. Fourteen-year-old John Quincy Adams came to St. Petersburg as Dana's personal secretary and translator (of French). Empress Catherine II, however, refused to receive the American minister at court, and Dana finally gave up and left the Russian capital two years after his arrival. As there was no accredited American minister at St. Petersburg from then until 1809, when Adams returned, Ledyard in 1787 was forced to turn to the British and French embassies for assistance. Despite lack of diplomatic recognition, a number of American sea captains and sailors who were engaged in trade visited the Russian capital from 1784 on. By the time Ledyard reached St. Petersburg in the spring of 1787, he could write, "There are 4 American Ships here & 4 more expected . . ." (# 24). John Paul Jones entered Russia in early 1788; Empress Catherine had accepted him into the imperial service as rear admiral to fight in the Russo-Turkish War of 1787–91. He fought at Ochakov and Kinburn on the

Black Sea coast, but left no direct impressions of Russia in his writings.[1]

Although he had received little formal schooling, Ledyard seems to have read a good deal and absorbed much in his peculiar thirst for knowledge. Undertaking his journey through Russia and Siberia on his own and not as a member of a government-sponsored expedition, he was free to write what opinions, sentiments, or objections he pleased, without worrying about censorship by officials or by an expedition secretary who might collect his journal. Ledyard's observations are spontaneous. His journal contains judgments as freely stated and personal as any of that time in any language concerning the state of affairs in the autocratic Russian Empire, and especially in Siberia.

As to the general knowledge of Russia and Siberia that he may have picked up before leaving England for St. Petersburg, he had read at least several travelogues and descriptions of the Russian Empire, such as those of Pennant, Le Brun, and Steller (Journal; pp. 189, 199). Yet as he was to indicate later in some of his letters, his foreknowledge of how he would travel through Russia and Siberia was far from adequate. In his day the Englishman's view of Russia was distorted and fragmentary. "It was incomplete," writes M. S. Anderson, " . . . because it was based on knowledge of only a few areas of a vast country, above all the two capitals and to a lesser extent the Baltic provinces. It was blurred because . . . it had been drawn in the main by men with little or no knowledge of the Russian language."[2]

Ledyard was a shrewd observer in a number of fields. He was highly interested in the peoples of Siberia, "Tartars" as he called them collectively. From his previous observations of American Indians of both coasts, he became convinced that the American continent had been peopled by Asiatic "Tartars," which at that time was a relatively new explanation (Steller had formulated a

1. Jones's letters in French to Prince Gregory Potëmkin and others, written on board the ship *Vladimir* from May to October 1788 and at St. Petersburg in April 1789, have been edited by Frank A. Golder in *John Paul Jones in Russia*, pp. 72–142; translations, pp. 155–215.

2. Anderson, *Britain's Discovery of Russia: 1553–1815*, p. 82.

similar concept forty years earlier).[3] Ledyard was interested in the history, religion, dwellings, customs, facial appearance, and clothing of the Yakuts, Buryats, Tungus, and other Siberian peoples; and in his journal he compared the customs of these "Tartars" and related his observations in Siberia to what he had seen in America and elsewhere in the world. As a son of the Enlightenment, face to face with "noble savages" in a state of nature, Ledyard took every opportunity to study them closely and often compared them with "civilized" Russians. He was especially interested in the causes of difference in skin color among men, in the similarity and historical evolution of customs among different primitive peoples, and in the net effect of European attempts to civilize savages. S. H. Bederman, in examining Ledyard's overall contribution to ethnology, states that "his first-hand knowledge of primitive peoples over the whole world was probably unequaled for his time. It is for this reason that he deserves attention as being one of America's earliest students of culture."[4]

Although an interest in Siberia natives predominated over other subjects in his journal, Ledyard was fascinated by the enormous rivers of Siberia which empty into the "Frozen Ocean." Other geographical features also intrigued him, especially "bottomless" Lake Baikal and the high cliffs along the Lena River. Archeological remains such as burial mounds and mammoth bones astonished him. He perceptively contrasted differences between Western Europe and Asia, in which he included Russia and Poland—differences that we can still see reflected in today's division between East and West.

He was usually less informative, however, about the food, clothing, and life of Russians living in Siberia. In general he mentioned few proper names and wrote next to nothing about the layout or architecture of towns, their administration, or social

3. Stejneger, *Georg Wilhelm Steller,* pp. 289, 298–99. Others such as George Louis Leclerc, Count de Buffon (1707–88), the French naturalist, strongly argued the other way around.

4. Bederman, *The Ethnological Contributions of John Ledyard,* p. 1.

classes. That his knowledge of Russian was sketchy is indicated by his confusing simple Russian once with the Yakut language. (Journal; p. 171). Most officers and men of higher station with whom he had to deal were able to communicate with him in French.

Ledyard's observations in eastern Siberia are less extensive than those of three of his contemporaries, Martin Sauer, Gavriil A. Sarychev, and Jean-Baptiste de Lesseps. His itinerary was more limited, he had neither obligation nor opportunity to record systematically what he observed, and his writings exist only in part. He had intended to travel to Okhotsk and Avacha Bay in Kamchatka as fast as possible, and only forced delays provided time for relatively extensive investigations. It is difficult to determine the amount and content of his lost papers. However, if the well-filled part of his journal written in western Russia and Poland during his return trip to England is taken as an indication of the thoroughness and quantity of the rest of his writings, his observations in eastern Siberia may have been extensive.

Ledyard's trip was to serve as an inspiration for a more successful "pedestrian journey" across Siberia undertaken in 1820–21 by the English sea captain John Cochrane. Moreover, Cochrane began his trip after having offered to undertake for the British Admiralty "a journey into the interior of Africa, which should have for its object the ascertaining of the course and determination of the river Niger." However, he received a negative reply. Then, according to Cochrane, being unemployed, "I determined to undertake a journey, varying only the object and the scene, similar to that of the unfortunate Ledyard, viz. to travel round the globe, as nearly as can be done by land, crossing from Northern Asia to America, at Behring's Streights; I also determined to perform the journey on foot, for the best of all possible reasons, that my finances allowed of no other."[5] Cochrane traveled as far east as Kamchatka, but was unable to reach North America.

5. Cochrane, *Narrative of a Pedestrian Journey through Russia and Siberian Tartary,* I:3, 5–6.

Ledyard's Siberian venture is admittedly less important than were his plans for the American Northwest. Yet he was the first American to travel into Siberia and one of the very few to leave a substantial record of his experiences there. Ledyard's observations contribute toward a better comprehension of the geography, peoples, and way of life at the end of the eighteenth century in a part of the world which has been little known to most Americans at any period of its past. In spite of their limitations they are outstanding in their penetration and outspokenness as well as for the unique circumstances in which they were written. And they have a dash and vigor that such comparable accounts of Siberia at that time as those of Sauer, Sarychev, and de Lesseps cannot equal.

Although a great deal of information concerning the journey can be gained from Ledyard's extant letters and journal and from a number of other relevant documents, various problems of historical importance remain which cannot be fully explained. Frequently one can only conjecture as to the most probable possibility among many in attempting to solve some of these mysteries. As far as the available documents indicate, Ledyard in his letters never described in detail many of the most intriguing and important aspects of his journey: who first conceived the idea of the journey, his winter trek from Stockholm to St. Petersburg, how he gained his passport in the Russian capital, his financial support for twelve months within the Russian Empire, the type of meals and accommodations he received, the immediate circumstances of his arrest in Irkutsk, the nature of his interrogation in Moscow, and so forth. And little more information can be gained from other contemporary sources concerning the shadowy roles of Empress Catherine, her advisers, and possibly of Iakobi, Marklovskii, Karamyshev, and the merchant Shelikhov in bringing about Ledyard's arrest and deportation.

Perhaps the answers to a few of these questions were given by Ledyard in letters subsequently lost or in the missing parts of the journal. Ledyard, however, was usually reticent about matters of his personal experience, no matter what he wrote; he greatly preferred to make abstract speculations and observations of his environment. He imagined that his readers would feel more interest in his opinions and descriptions of what he saw around him than in particulars of his own activities; these he tended to mention only in passing or to put off explaining until a more propitious moment (which usually never occurred, in writing, at least).

Thomas Jefferson credited himself with the original idea not only of Ledyard's proceeding to Kamchatka from Western Europe in order to reach the west coast of America but of his crossing North America as well. In a biographical sketch of Meriwether Lewis, written in 1813, Jefferson stated: "I then proposed to him [Ledyard] to go by land to Kamschatka, cross in some of the Russian vessels to Nootka Sound, fall down into the latitude of the Missouri, and penetrate to, and through, that to the United States. He eagerly seized the idea . . ." (# 47). And in his *Autobiography* (1821) Jefferson wrote: ". . . I suggested to him the enterprise of exploring the Western part of our continent, by passing through St. Petersburg to Kamschatka, and procuring a passage thence in some of the Russian vessels to Nootka Sound, whence he might make his way across the continent to the United States . . . (# 48).

Although no further proof has been found that the idea of crossing Siberia was Jefferson's, no written evidence demonstrates that Ledyard had seriously intended, before meeting Jefferson in 1785, to traverse North America. Jefferson had both read and heard Ledyard's descriptions of Nootka Sound and of Kamchatka;[6] he had also done some vague speculating about the interior of North America in his *Notes on the State of Virginia,*

6. Jefferson had not only seen Ledyard's *Journal of Captain Cook's Last Voyage* (see # 8) but had also been presented at some time between mid-1785 and mid-1786 with a "vocabulary" drawn up by Ledyard and entitled "Comparative view of the Chipeway, Naudowissie & Nootka languages being three of the newest known on the northern continent of America, analogically considered with respect to any other language ancient modern improved or unimproved" (NYHS).

first published in Paris in 1785. He may well have decided that Ledyard, who in his words was "panting for some new enterprise," was just the man to carry out such a trip of discovery across two continents.

Nevertheless, it is doubtful that Ledyard, with his experience at Nootka Sound, his desire to build a fur-trading post on the northwest coast, and his knowledge of Indians in eastern North America, had never before meeting Jefferson thought of crossing the North American continent to the east coast. Furthermore, he knew better than any other American, through his experiences at Unalaska and Avacha Bay, what communications existed between St. Petersburg and Kamchatka, and from there to the coast of Alaska. By his own statement Ledyard was thinking of crossing Siberia as early as November 1785, just after his plans with Jones had collapsed; a year later, on November 25, 1786, he wrote to Jefferson: ". . . I am now going across Siberia as I had once before intended from Paris this time twelve month . . ." (# 18). However, it cannot definitely be proven who first thought of Ledyard's crossing Siberia; and it is not clear how this idea was related in Ledyard's and Jefferson's minds to that of crossing North America.

Jefferson was both the most enthusiastic promoter of Ledyard's journey and his most frequent financial supporter in 1786 during the time of his waiting in Paris.[7] Ledyard regarded him as father, brother, and beloved friend, and wrote him several letters en route which relate his experiences and observations. From Ledyard's remarks in these letters and in his journal it is evident that Jefferson's interest in scientific and philosophical questions had greatly stimulated the curiosity of the already inquisitive traveler.

Still another matter that is unclear is the course of the negotia-

7. On February 15, 1786, according to his account book, Jefferson "lent Ledyard 48f"; on the 20th of that month he received of "M. de la Fayette to be paid to Ledyard on account of Empress of Russia 600f"; on August 4 he "gave Ledyard 132f"; and again on August 7 "gave Ledyard 96f" (*PTJ*, 10: 269). The 600 francs (livres) on Catherine's account was appropriated for Ledyard's use by the empress' special representative in Paris, the Baron von Grimm (see # 6).

tions undertaken by Jefferson to procure Ledyard a passport through the Russian Empire. Jefferson wished to assure Ledyard a passport, the proper letters of recommendation, and the good will of the imperial authorities. According to Jefferson's later accounts, in 1786 (early February) he began negotiations through the Russian minister to France, Count Ivan M. Simolin, for permission for Ledyard to pass through the Russian Empire to America (# # 47, 48). Lafayette, whom Ledyard had met the previous summer, also sounded out Simolin.[8] Of more importance, however, was the fact that during February Jefferson and Lafayette began to deal chiefly with Catherine's special representative at the French court, the Baron von Grimm.[9] On February 9 Jefferson wrote up a formal recommendation of Ledyard's project, which he sent to Lafayette (# 2). The marquis in a letter to Grimm (# 3) forwarded a French translation of this, along with what appears to have been a petition written by Ledyard. Grimm in turn sent all three documents to St. Petersburg.[10] Lafayette also wrote on Ledyard's behalf to his friend and relative, Louis Philippe, Count de Ségur, French ambassador in St. Petersburg.

It was to Grimm that the empress finally stated her decision on Ledyard. On June 17, 1786, she wrote: "Mr. Ledyard would do well to take another route than that of Kamchatka, because, as far as this [Billings'] expedition is concerned, there is no longer a way to reach it. Besides, everything that has been written about

8. Lafayette also spoke with the Marquis de Castries and wrote to the Count de Vergennes on February 8 about Ledyard, hoping that France too might support the venture (# 1); both of the latter however hesitated to encourage the project. See Gottschalk, *Lafayette*, p. 267.

9. Friedrich Melchior, Baron von Grimm (1723–1807), "conseiller d'état" and confidential correspondent of Catherine II; publicist, critic, and minister from the Duchy of Saxe-Gotha to Paris.

10. Information obtained from personal correspondence with Louis R. Gottschalk. Ledyard's petition (or propositions) may perhaps be the document translated into Russian which is mentioned by Golder as located in 1917 in the Petrograd State Archives: "(Date?) Memoir written by a man who was with Captain Cook, urging closer trade relations between China, Japan, Kamchatka, and America" (Frank A. Golder, *Guide to Materials for American History in Russian Archives*, 1:14). I have been unsuccessful in tracking this document down. Also see Gottschalk, *Lafayette*, pp. 267–68.

this [Ledyard's] expedition is completely false and a chimerical dream: there never has been a party on foot, and it all comes to the expedition of Captain Billings and of the personnel selected by him and Pallas. Let the American have the money you have given or promised him; but don't throw my money out the window in the future: I do not know those people at all and have had nothing to do with them up to now." (# 6). Apparently Grimm had suggested that Ledyard catch up with and accompany Billings' expedition as far as Kamchatka, and in the meantime had given Ledyard 600 livres (25 guineas) out of a fund allotted to the baron by the empress.[11] Billings' expedition however had left St. Petersburg the preceding October.

Before learning of Catherine's final decision on Ledyard, Grimm must have pressed the issue further, for on July 23 the empress wrote him crisply: "I have told you all I had to say about Mr. Ledyard" (# 7). Neither Grimm nor Lafayette had heard this news when the latter wrote Jefferson on August 2 referring to a sum he had himself advanced to Ledyard above what Grimm had advanced, "which of course the Empress will Reimburse if She Accepts of the proposal. In the mean while Baron de Grimm advises our friend Ledyard not to Throw a way Any other opportunity that might offer" (# 9). Ledyard did jump at the next chance, whether or not he knew of the baron's advice, and left for London soon after August 8 in hope of sailing on an English vessel to the northwest coast of America. News of Catherine's definite refusal probably did not reach him until after his failure to set sail on or around August 18. Jefferson wrote Ledyard on August 16, 1786: "I saw Baron de Grimm yesterday at Versailles, and he told me he had received an answer from the

11. See n. 7 above. At that time roughly 24 livres (in actual coin, 24 francs) equaled a guinea. Grimm's most recent annual subsidy from the empress, 60,000 livres, had been remitted to him on July 22, 1785, through the imperial court banker, Sutherland. See *Sbornik, imperatorskago russkago istoricheskago obshchestva,* 23 (1878):704 and 44 (1885):833. Apparently in Grimm's transaction with Ledyard Lafayette served as the middleman; according to doc. # 9, Lafayette later forwarded another 25 guineas (600 livres) to Ledyard under Grimm's name.

Empress, who declines the proposition made on your account. she thinks it chimaerical" (# 11).

We have fragmentary information on how Ledyard finally acquired the passport without which he could not travel into the interior of Russia.[12] When he arrived in St. Petersburg in March 1787 the empress was on a lengthy tour of the Ukraine and the Crimea. In her suite was the French ambassador, the Count de Ségur, whose absence from the capital hardly helped Ledyard. Since his letters of recommendation were all in English, he applied first to the British Embassy (# 23). Besides probably taking with him Colonel Smith's letter of introduction (# 16), it is likely that he also carried a letter from Sir Joseph Banks recommending him to Professor Peter Simon Pallas, since the eminent naturalists were acquainted with each other and both belonged to the Royal Society of London. Pallas subsequently accompanied Ledyard to the French Embassy, where a letter was dispatched to Ségur in the south regarding Ledyard's application for a passport (# # 23, 24). In spite of these efforts, it was not until mid-May that Ledyard finally reached the right person: an unnamed officer who was a favorite in the circle around Grand Duke Paul offered to obtain a passport from "the Chancellor" and apparently succeeded, for on June 1 Ledyard set out from St. Petersburg.[13]

It is difficult to determine what financial support Ledyard received during his journey, in addition to the subscribed sum that he started out with from England.[14] It appears that money came and went easily with him; yet at times he was too poor to

12. Russia was the only country through which Ledyard ever traveled that required a passport for travel in the interior. Prior to World War I, only two countries, Russia and Turkey, required passports for foreigners.

13. This reference to "the Chancellor" is puzzling, for Russia had been without an official chancellor since 1763. At the time of Ledyard's visit, Count Ivan Osterman held the post of vice-chancellor. The matter is further complicated in that the rank of *kantsler* (chancellor) was the highest of all positions of government civil service in the Table of Ranks. This person may have been one among many "chancellors" then in St. Petersburg.

14. See # 20, and p. 20, n. 35.

pay the postage of a letter. In Hamburg he drew a sum on the credit of William Smith, which presumably enabled him to reach St. Petersburg. There he was able to obtain twenty guineas, this time on the account of Sir Joseph Banks. This transaction was probably made through W. Porter & Co., Merchant Bankers in St. Petersburg, sometime in March.[15] From then on until he drew on Banks again in Königsberg on his return trip, we have little information as to Ledyard's sources of funds. He may have received something through Pallas or other benefactors in St. Petersburg. In Moscow, at the beginning of his trip, Ledyard mentioned the fact that he lost fifty rubles (Journal; p. 203); and at some time in eastern Siberia he had enough ready cash to purchase a cap, coat, and gloves totaling over 100 rubles (roughly 20 guineas). Thus he must have received some financial support from Russians during his east-bound journey, besides being carried "from place to place without any recompence" (# 36).

The order for Ledyard's arrest and banishment remains a mystery. All that we know about it for certain is the date it was issued, as noted by Catherine's personal secretary, A. V. Khrapovitskii, in his diary on December 18, 1787 (O.S.): "It is ordered to send back the American John Ledyard, making his way from Okhotsk to America, from that place . . ." (# 34). There are several possibilities as to who instigated the order. It is certain that Catherine learned sometime after her return to St. Petersburg in July 1787 that Ledyard had received a passport, though she may not have heard of it before late November (# 32). After consultation with her closest advisers, she may then have ordered his arrest. This is the most probable explanation.[16]

15. Banks, *The Banks Letters,* ed. Dawson, p. 682. Here a letter of William Porter to Banks dated April 10, 1787, is described which inquires as to Ledyard's financial position; Porter's partner in St. Petersburg, Brown, had already made small cash advances to him.

16. John Quincy Adams, who knew Catherine and Russia as well as any other American of his time, later recorded in his memoirs under the date February 3, 1831: "There was nothing in this dishonorable to the Empress Catherine, who certainly acted by the advice of her counsellors, who could have no personal motive for opposition to the undertaking of Ledyard, and

It is also possible that in Irkutsk Ledyard's activities and intentions aroused suspicion. Sparks has suggested that Governor-General Iakobi, backed by jealous fur merchants, was instrumental in bringing about the arrest. According to Sparks' calculations, at the same time that a letter could have been dispatched to St. Petersburg urging Ledyard's arrest, Iakobi might have sent a letter ahead of the traveler to commandant Marklovskii at Yakutsk, alerting him and asking him to detain Ledyard—as the commandant subsequently did.

I am convinced that a plan was concerted at Irkutsk [writes Sparks] to send him back, very soon after his arrival in that place. . . . In effecting this point, some management was necessary, as he had a passport from the Empress, with a positive order to the Governor-General to aid him on his way. This order could not be countermanded, nor the passport of the Empress treated with disrespect, till intelligence could be sent to Petersburg, and influence there used with the Empress to procure the annulment of her grant of protection, and Ledyard's immediate recall. Time was requisite to bring this scheme to an issue, and the first thing to be done, in the train of manoeuvres, was to throw obstacles in his path, and retard his progress. This was begun in good earnest at Irkutsk, where he was detained several days longer than he desired, waiting, as he was told, for the post.[17]

As far as Iakobi's delaying Ledyard is concerned, all we know is that on Monday, August 23, Ledyard was "informed by the Viceroy [Iakobi] that the post will not be ready until Wedenesday" (Journal; pp. 161–62)—and on Wednesday accordingly Ledyard left Irkutsk. Whether he had been originally scheduled to leave that Monday or not is mere conjecture.

Iakobi's attitude toward Ledyard was outwardly nothing but cordial. His regard for Ledyard is mentioned twice in the journal and is also indicated in a letter of introduction that he wrote for

---

who was individually as ambitious of philosophical fame and as eager for the progress of discovery as Mr. Jefferson himself" (C. F. Adams, ed., *Memoirs of John Quincy Adams,* 8:310).

17. Sparks, *Life of John Ledyard* (1864), pp. 369–70. Moreover, Sparks believes that the empress had given Ledyard "a royal passport for proceeding unmolested to Kamchatka" (p. 365).

Ledyard to take personally to Marklovskii (# 28). Ledyard wrote in his journal on August 16, the day after his arrival in Irkutsk: "Our conversation was merely respecting my going with the Post, which he granted me and besides that told me I should [be] particularly well accomodated—wished me a good and successful voyage,—and that my travels might be productive of information to mankind" (p. 154).

It is doubtful that Iakobi secretly urged Marklovskii to keep Ledyard in Yakutsk. He could have held him longer than two days in Irkutsk had he wished; and if Marklovskii had ulterior motives of his own in detaining Ledyard, the inclement weather certainly served as a satisfactory pretext. It is not impossible that Iakobi sent a dispatch to St. Petersburg informing the empress of Ledyard's whereabouts and his suspicious designs. But an urgent dispatch to Catherine would probably have reached her by the end of September, and the order for arrest was not issued until December 18. Khrapovitskii's diary entry suggests that the empress and the authorities in St. Petersburg believed Ledyard to have reached Okhotsk; that they had received no assurance he would be detained in Yakutsk and had no idea he would actually be in Irkutsk at the time of his arrest.[18]

Besides the possibility that Iakobi, or perhaps Marklovskii, may have urged Ledyard's arrest, Sparks' suggestion that jealous fur merchants were involved deserves consideration. Ledyard recorded on August 18 that in Irkutsk he "Went this morning to see a Merchant owner of a Vessel that had passed from Kamschatka to different parts of the Coast of America. Shewed some Charts rudely discriptive of his voyages. . . . [He] has a Vessel of his own at Ohotsk. which leaves that Country for America next Summer, and offers me a passage in her" (Journal; pp. 158–59). This merchant must have been Grigorii I. Shelikhov, who had just returned from Kodiak Island off Alaska and was in Irkutsk from

18. Perhaps Catherine believed that there was still a chance of catching him beyond Okhotsk, either waiting for a ship in Petropavlovsk or, as "one of the Expedition," having attached himself somewhere to Billings and his men.

April 6 to early December 1787.[19] Perhaps, however, Shelikhov had second thoughts about Ledyard. If Iakobi or other officials, such as the director of the Irkutsk bank, whom Ledyard later termed the "scoundrel Karamyshev" (Journal; p. 196), did not suspect that Ledyard was a potential security risk to Russia's American colonies and fur trade, Shelikhov certainly might have. He may have tipped off Iakobi, who supported his interests in the North Pacific; he may have written to his business partner, Ivan Golikov, then in European Russia, who could have advised someone in court circles; or he may himself have informed somebody in circles close to the empress' ear of Ledyard's suspicious intentions.[20]

A point of interest, though of little help in determining how Ledyard's arrest was ordered, is that on November 26 (O.S.) Catherine mentioned Ledyard again to Baron von Grimm, for the first time, so far as we know, in over a year. "You were wrong, if you don't mind," she wrote, "to strike off my accounts the very small expenditure for the American, Ledyard . . . . Regarding Ledyard, discovery for others is not always discovery for us, in view of the difference in languages, manners, and customs . . ." (# 32). Thus she must certainly have heard before late November of Ledyard's being in Siberia and feared the consequences of the discoveries he might make for England.

A statement of Sauer's envelops the matter in even denser mystery. Writing of Ledyard's arrest in Irkutsk, Sauer relates: ". . . a secretary belonging to one of the courts of justice came in, and told us, with great concern, that the Governor-General had received positive orders from the Empress, immediately to send one of the Expedition, an Englishman, under guard to the

19. G. I. Shelekhov, *Rossiiskago kuptsa Grigor'ia Shelekhova stranstvovanie*, p. 56; V. Grigor'ev, *Grigorii Shelikhov: istoricheskii roman*, p. 167. According to Efimov's charts no Siberian merchants sent out vessels from Okhotsk in the summer of 1788; only in August 1790 did Shelikhov send out two more vessels (Efimov, *Iz istorii russkikh ekspeditsii na Tikhom okeane*, p. 308).

20. It is certain that Shelikhov did not personally inform the empress; his journey to St. Petersburg, undertaken in December 1787, did not bring him to the capital before December 18.

private inquisition at Mosco . . ." (# 35). According to Sauer, the order of arrest treated Ledyard as a member of Billings' expedition. Whoever in St. Petersburg wrote the order, however, could not possibly have known that Ledyard had temporarily joined the expedition so recently. Ledyard did not even meet Billings and his men until November 24 in Yakutsk (Ledyard's date), and did not formally attach himself to the expedition at least until December 19 (Sarychev's date), when he set out for Irkutsk—one day after the order was issued in St. Petersburg. Furthermore, the empress knew that Ledyard was not an Englishman.

Catherine, of course, gave the order for Ledyard's arrest; but it is as yet impossible to determine who advised her on his activities and whereabouts, or perhaps urged her to take this measure.

Despite Sauer's account, Ledyard left no indication in his existent writings of a "private inquisition" in Moscow, though he did speak with a "General" there. To determine how long he spent in Moscow relates directly to another problem: where the city of "Neeshna" was located. On March 12 (N.S.) Ledyard wrote in his journal: "I am on my Road to Poland & 220 Versts from Moscow—". A few lines below he noted, "I am at the City of Neeshna . . ." (p. 200). This might be taken to mean that Ledyard had left Moscow and was already approaching the Polish border. Yet there is no city with a name resembling Neeshna 220 versts west of Moscow. In addition Ledyard wrote a few lines farther along that he had traveled in an open kibitka for more than twenty days. It is hardly possible that in little over twenty days he had left Irkutsk, gone through an "inquisition," and then traveled 220 versts beyond Moscow.

It is more probable that "Neeshna" was Nizhni Novgorod, some 400 versts east of Moscow, and that March 12 was New Style.[21] According to his journal, Ledyard left Moscow on March

21. At the beginning of the 18th century the traveler Le Brun (de Bruyn) wrote: "Les Russiens nomment ordinairement cette ville Niesna ou Nisen; d'autres Nisi-Novgorod, ou la petit Novgorod." *Voyages de Corneille le Brun par la Moscovie*, p. 80.

10, at the "time of the equinoxes with them," in other words, March 21 (N.S.). This supposition would leave nine days between the time he was in Nizhni Novgorod and his leaving Moscow—long enough for an interrogation in Moscow.

Furthermore, from this assumption an approximation of the date of Ledyard's arrest in Irkutsk can be made. Sauer gives the date as February 24, but if Ledyard's own dates are assumed to be correct it appears that the arrest was actually some time before this, be Sauer's date either by Old or by New Style reckoning. Over twenty days before March 12 (N.S.) would have been at least some time before February 21 (N.S.).[22] This seems plausible in that Ledyard later wrote his cousin from London that his journey from Irkutsk to the Polish border took six weeks. As Ledyard entered Poland on March 18/29, the evidence thus points to his arrest having occurred between February 16 and 20, 1788 (N.S.)

What were Catherine's reasons for expelling Ledyard from the Russian Empire? Ledyard was never told why he was deported; he was a prisoner for over six weeks, without ever knowing what crime he was supposed to have committed. All he knew was what he later wrote to his cousin: "The motives of the Empress in arresting me are found upon examination to have been a mixture of jealousy envy & malice" (# 39; p. 243). Sauer, however, claimed upon finding Ledyard under arrest, "He [Ledyard] then began to explain his situation, and said that he was taken up as a French spy, whereas Captain Billings could prove the contrary . . ." (# 35). This statement is the sole evidence for Ledyard's being arrested as a French spy. It is probable that Sauer's memory was somewhat faulty, for Ledyard was arrested a year before the French Revolution, and could hardly have been spying in Siberia in the service of the French monarchy, of which Catherine had no fear.[23]

22. Or February 10 (O.S.). This calculation includes Leap Year's Day, 1788.

23. There is also the remote possibility that Ledyard was accused of being a spy for the French naval expedition of La Pérouse. However, La Pérouse did not land at Kamchatka until September 1787.

Another explanation of doubtful validity has been advanced by Sarychev, the naval lieutenant in Billings' expedition. Sarychev, who last saw Ledyard in Yakutsk, later asserted that Ledyard had challenged the commandant at Yakutsk to a duel and had made a general nuisance of himself; that subsequently he had been arrested in Irkutsk for disorderly conduct: ". . . the Commandant wrote to the Governor-General and complained about this impudent Englishman. As a result of this, on his arrival in Irkutsk he was sent off to Petersburg as a troublemaker."[24] Sarychev, however, had left Yakutsk in early January 1788 for the mouth of the River Mai and did not meet Billings again until June 12 in Yakutsk, where he first could have learned of Ledyard's arrest.

There is also Ségur's account of the reasons lying behind Catherine's decision. In a letter to Lafayette written thirty-five years after Ledyard's journey, Ségur stated:

I have no longer any letters in my possession relative to the celebrated traveller Mr. Ledyard. I remember only that in compliance with your request I furnished him with the best recommendations at the court of Russia. He was at the first very well received, but the Empress who spoke to me on the subject herself, observed that she would not render herself guilty of the death of this courageous American, by furthering a journey so fraught with danger as that he proposed to undertake alone across the unknown & savage regions of the North western America. She consequently issued her prohibition; however as the custom of passports for the interior, as practiced with us, is unknown in Russia he succeeded in effecting his passage across the empire but having reached Kamschatka & essaying there to embark in opposition to the order of Govt, he was arrested & reconducted to the European frontier. Possibly this pretext of humanity advanced by Catherine only disguised her unwillingness to have the new possessions of Russia on the western coast of America seen by an enlightened citizen of the United States. The above however were the reasons she advanced to me.[25]

24. Sarychev, *Puteshestvie po severo–vostachnoi chasti Sibiri,* p. 92n. See also # 36.

25. From a translated copy of Ségur's letter to Lafayette, written in French on August 10, 1823; Jared Sparks MS No. 112, HL.

Ségur was wrong about certain facts, having been in the south with the empress when Ledyard was "very well received" in St. Petersburg, where Ledyard spent two months trying to obtain an internal passport. Yet Ségur, although in no position to know how far east Ledyard had really been, saw through Catherine's pretext to her probable motives for having Ledyard arrested.

Another questionable explanation of the arrest has come by way of Professor Pallas, who mentioned Ledyard's fate to Edward D. Clarke when this English traveler and mineralogist visited him in St. Petersburg in January 1800. Pallas told Clarke that "the sudden recall of the unfortunate Ledyard . . . it is said, would never have happened but through the jealousy of his own countrymen, whom he chanced to encounter as he was upon the point of quitting the eastern continent for America, and who caused the information to be sent to Petersburgh which occasioned the order for his arrest."[26] Catherine might have felt she had to placate Ledyard's friend Professor Pallas with such a fiction as this concerning the reason for his arrest.

A present-day student of Ledyard's Siberian journey, Eufrosina Dvoichenko-Markov, has also taken into account the turbulent political situation at the time "because it gives us a different perspective on the forces and circumstances which Ledyard had to contend with." After mentioning that in August 1787 Turkey had declared war upon Russia, she goes on to say: "As to Siberia, Russia was still under the impact left after the famous uprising, organized by the exiled Pole Beniowski, who in 1771, under the pretext of supporting the Grand Duke Paul against Catherine the Great, fled with a group of exiled Russians from Kamchatka to France on a captured Russian ship. . . . Catherine the Great feared that knowing the way to Kamchatka he would return with

26. Clarke, *Travels in Russia, Tartary, and Turkey,* Vol. 1, sec. 1, p. 10. Could Billings have been one of Ledyard's "own countrymen, whom he chanced to encounter," and who requested his arrest? Billings met Ledyard in Yakutsk on November 24 (Ledyard's reckoning). Even if Billings had sent a dispatch that very day, it would have taken three and a half weeks just to reach Irkutsk, in other words, on or about December 18. Even if Ledyard's date were New Style, it could not have reached Petersburg by December 18.

the help of his protectors, and from 1771 to 1787 Russia secretly fortified Kamchatka."[27] This statement suggests that Ledyard's intent to visit Kamchatka and the outbreak of war with a Turkey backed by Western powers helped prompt Catherine's order. Even though Cook's expedition had been received with hospitality in 1779, St. Petersburg still maintained a suspicious attitude toward foreign intrusions in the Kamchatka area. However, it is difficult to believe that a Westerner in eastern Siberia could in any way affect a Russo-Turkish war fought in the Balkans. Although Ledyard's arrest was linked with foreign politics, the most important reasons were other than those suggested by Dvoichenko-Markov.

Of all the varied suggestions offered as to the reason for Ledyard's arrest, that of Sparks, that it was to protect Russia's American colonies, is the most plausible. His explanation needs correction only by replacing his reference to the "Russian-American Company" (which was not formed until 1799) with "Shelikhov's company": ". . . the head-quarters of this company were at Irkutsk, and it could not have escaped the sagacity of its conductors, that a foreigner, visiting their stations at the islands, would make discoveries, which might be published to their disadvantage, both in regard to the resources of traffic, and to the cruel manner in which the traders habitually treated the natives, in extorting from them the fruits of their severe and incessant labors. To obviate such a consequence, it was necessary to cut short the traveller's career, before he had penetrated to the eastern shores of Asia."[28]

Fear of Ledyard's publishing unfavorable reports about the Russian colonies on the northwest coast (Catherine was always sensitive to foreign public opinion) was probably subordinate to anxiety lest foreign powers, especially England, attempt to wrest

27. Dvoichenko-Markov, "John Ledyard and the Russians," *Russian Review* (1952), 11:220–21. Because Catherine had illegitimately acceded to the throne in 1762 through the murder of her husband Peter III, she feared any movement that supported the only legitimate heir to the throne, her son Grand Duke Paul.

28. Sparks, *Life of John Ledyard,* pp. 369–70.

this region away from Russia's control. This apprehension had suddenly mushroomed after the unexpected visit of Cook's expedition to the North Pacific in 1778–79. Ledyard, although an American, was associated in Russian minds with this expedition which threatened Russia's mastery of the North Pacific. Khrapovitskii noted, as he mentioned in his diary the order for Ledyard's arrest, that "he was a naval cadet with the famous Cook" (# 34).

The Soviet historian Okun has pointed out that "The Russian government was seriously disturbed by Cook's voyage to the coast of America, and it was not out of mere curiosity that Catherine immediately ordered L. I. Golenishchev-Kutuzov to translate into Russian the great navigator's journal which had just come off the press. James Cook . . . had recorded on the map all the places he visited under new English names, thereby laying claim to England's 'primogeniture' in the matter of these discoveries. . . . Thus he renamed 'Nootka' Cape King George, Chukotski Peninsula—Cookshaven, and so forth."[29] That Governor-General Iakobi took a lively interest in keeping the English out of the North Pacific we know from his secretly ordering Shelikhov's clerks, who were to set out for Alaska in 1787, to raise the emblems of the Russian Empire in those localities "where in 1784 an English vessel had been and the crew had made a rich haul."[30]

The empress herself viewed this rivalry with the English with concern. Because of "encroachments on the part of English traders on trade and hunting in the Eastern Sea," she had issued, on December 22, 1786, a year before the order for Ledyard's arrest, the following statement proposed by her ministers A. R. Vorontsov and A. A. Bezborodko: "To Russia must indisputably belong: 1) the American coast from 55° 21′ extending northward . . . ; 2) all the islands situated near the mainland and the peninsula Alaska that were discovered by Bering and Cook . . . ; 3) all

29. Okun', *Rossiisko-amerikanskaia kompaniia,* p. 15.

30. *Ibid.* This was probably Captain Hanna's ship, which reached Nootka Sound in 1785; see p. 16 above.

the islands . . . called the Fox Islands and the Aleutians. . . ."[31] Vorontsov and Bezborodko considered Cook's discoveries invalid and insisted on the necessity of informing all maritime powers that Russia could not allow foreign vessels to touch at any of the harbors in the above-named regions. To put teeth in this policy, the two ministers drew up a plan in late 1786 for dispatching a squadron of four ships, commanded by Capt. G. I. Mulovskii, from the Baltic to the North Pacific to protect Russia's possessions in that area. This project was never effected because of the outbreak of the war with Sweden and Turkey and the expense involved in supporting such a fleet.[32]

There is no dearth of evidence that Russia was intent upon keeping foreigners out of her American territories. Russian authorities considered a foreigner's presence in this area a threat to Russia's claims in the North Pacific. Ledyard's connection with Captain Cook made him more suspect than ever. Thus, both the conception and execution of Ledyard's journey through Siberia and his arrest and subsequent deportation were to a great extent determined by his association with Cook's expedition to the North Pacific—to Alaska, Kamchatka, and Nootka Sound. Catherine's warning to Baron von Grimm that Ledyard would make discoveries for "others" and not for herself and Russia must be kept in mind (# 32).

31. Okun', *Rossiisko-amerikanskaia kompaniia,* pp. 17–18.
32. *Ibid.,* p. 18.

3

Siberia in the Eighteenth Century

As background for following Ledyard's journey through Siberia, I shall here briefly summarize general developments and conditions throughout this vast subcontinent during the eighteenth century, focusing principally on eastern Siberia, where Ledyard spent six months of his stay in the Russian Empire, and on the decade of the 1780's. Only a half century before Ledyard's time did the Russian government first dispatch scientific expeditions to study the resources, peoples, wildlife, and geography of this enormous region and to explore its farthest limits. By his day the knowledge of Siberia's boundaries had been well established, the existence of the Bering Strait proven, and Russian exploration and colonization were proceeding into northwest America.

It is not hard to gather material on the achievements of exploration and scientific research in Siberia during the eighteenth century. More difficult is to determine conditions of daily life and migratory travel among the common people. Moreover, material on the natives is often easier to come by than on the Russian inhabitants. In general, information is readily available for three chief periods of Siberia's past. Historians, both Russian and foreign, have frequently dwelt on the fascinating epoch of Muscovite expansion into Siberia and to the Pacific in the seventeenth century. Numbers of travelers, exiles, scientists, and explorers have left a large body of literature that contributes to a comprehensive description of Siberia in the nineteenth century. And Soviet historians and memoir writers have recently turned their attention to Siberia at the time of the Bolshevik Revolution and the Civil War. In spite of information on various aspects of Siberia gathered by eminent explorers and scholars in the eighteenth century, there remains a relative dearth of astute observers and chroniclers of daily life.[1]

Among the native Siberian population in the eighteenth century five major Uralian and Altaic ethnic groups stood out: those of Samoyed and Finno-Ugrian stock and those of Turkic, Mongolian, and Tungusic origin, respectively. The Samoyed tribes and those of Finno-Ugrian descent such as the Ostyaks and Voguls inhabited the northwestern parts of Siberia. Tribes of Turkic origin generally populated the southwestern borderlands, with the notable exception of the Yakuts, who lived primarily in the middle region of the Lena River valley. The Kalmyks and Buryats were the most numerous among the Mongol peoples. Largely through Tibetan Buddhist and Chinese influences the Buryats, who inhabited the region around Lake Baikal, possessed the most advanced customs, laws, and social life of all the native peoples of Siberia. The Tungus, a relatively numerous and varied people, who were also quite culturally advanced, inhabited a wide region extending from the uplands of the Tunguska tributaries of the Yenisei to the Pacific. Scattered ethnic groups of ancient Siberian origin (Paleoasiatics) inhabited the most distant fringes of the subcontinent. Chukchi and Yukagirs dwelt in northeastern Siberia; Koryaks and Kamchadals lived in northern

1. Walther Kirchner has described the problem thus: "Characteristically our sources for the seventeenth century are more productive than for the eighteenth century. . . . Siberia in the eighteenth century had developed into a giant organism, constantly growing and getting more complicated, for the understanding of which we have needed far more numerous and varied statements. Firsthand accounts, more continuous and richly flowing, are just not available in proportion to the growing significance of Siberia" (*Eine Reise durch Sibirien*, p. 9).

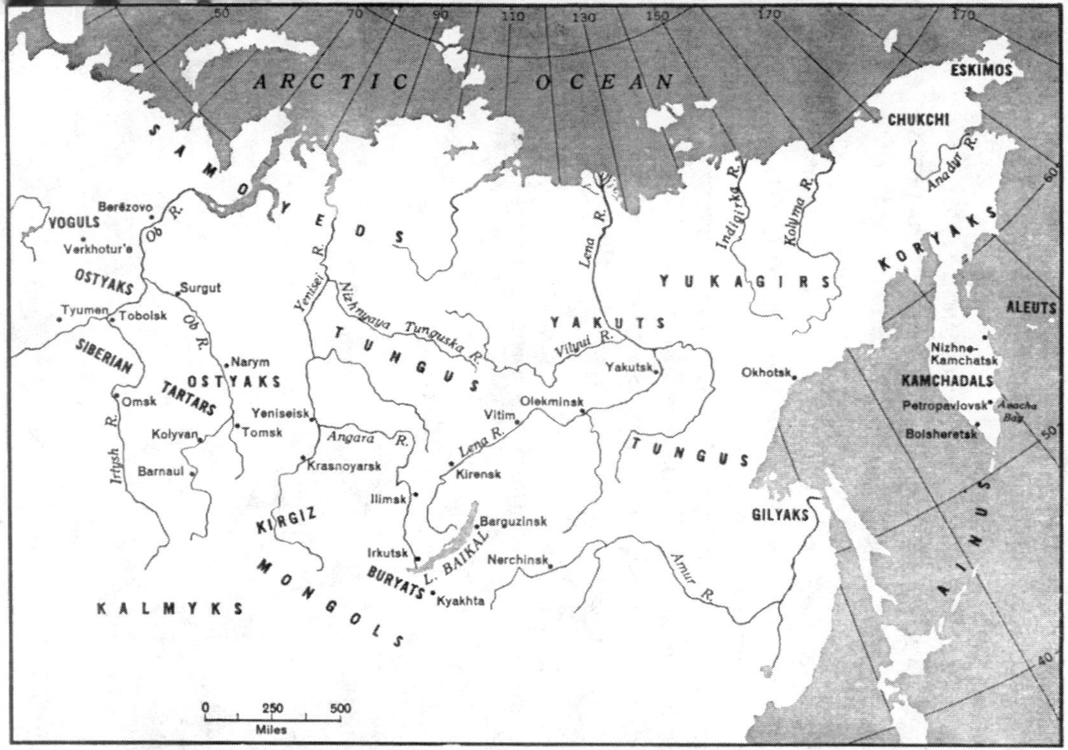

Eighteenth-century Siberia, Showing Important Towns and Native Peoples

and southern Kamchatka, respectively; and Ainus (Kurilians) inhabited the Kurile Islands.[2]

As early as the twelfth century Russians from the commercial city of Novgorod had traded with western Siberian natives, and by the late 1400's the lands of Novgorod extended as far north and east as the lower Ob basin. The initial thrust of Muscovite Russia into Siberia began over two hundred years before Ledyard's journey, when the Cossack freebooter Yermak, with the aid of firearms and 800 men, conquered Sibir, capital of the Siberian Tartar khanate, in 1581.[3] With this conquest the ice was broken, and soon afterwards a rash of eastward expansion ensued, in which Russian entrepreneurs, searching for valuable furs, pressed onward from one river valley to the next, finally reaching the Pacific. The first Russian town in Siberia, Tyumen,

2. The census of 1782 (the Fourth *Reviziia*) gives the breakdown by peoples which is closest to our period. The figures here indicate only taxable "souls" (working males) and cannot be assumed to be precise.

Peoples	*Tobolsk province*	*Kolyvan**	*Irkutsk*	*Total*
Tartars	17,931		—	17,931
Ostyaks	13,751		—	13,751
Samoyeds	3,109		—	3,109
Bukhartsy	2,720		—	2,720
Tungus	1,610		13,149	14,759
Voguls	1,257		—	1,257
Yakuts	299		43,004	43,303
Buryats	—		49,239	49,239
Kamchadals	—		1,537	1,537
Koryaks	—		823	823
Lamuts	—		819	819
Yukagirs	—		335	335
Alyutary (Aleuts)	—		215	215
Kurilians	—		132	132
Others	487		—	487
Unspecified		11,818	—	11,818
Total	41,164	11,818	109,253	162,235

* No breakdown by peoples.

The natives comprised about 29% of the 552,000 taxable souls in Siberia in 1782. The total native population was roughly 400,000. See V. M. Kabuzan and S. M. Troitskii, "Dvizhenie naseleniia Sibiri v XVIII v." (Movement of the Population of Siberia in the 18th Century), in Akademiia nauk SSSR, *Sibir' XVII–XVIII vv.*, pp. 155–56.

3. Sibir was located across the river from present-day Tobolsk. From the 15th century on, the phrase "the land of Siberia" (*Sibirskaia zemlia*) was used in the Russian chronicles.

located just east of the Urals, was built in 1586. Along the Ob River the *ostrog* (walled fort) of Tobolsk was founded a year later; farther to the east, Tomsk was established in 1604. Krasnoyarsk in the Yenisei basin followed in 1628; and still farther east, Yakutsk in 1632. By 1648 the ostrog of Okhotsk had been established on the Pacific Ocean, and that year the Cossack explorer Semën Dezhnev reputedly sailed around the easternmost tip of Siberia from north to south. Thus, Muscovite lands in less than seventy years were extended across Siberia to the Pacific, even before a foothold on the Baltic could be permanently obtained.

The second half of the seventeenth century saw the Russians penetrate into the region of Lake Baikal and beyond into the Amur River basin. In 1661 the ostrog of Irkutsk was established; with its command of the Angara River valley below Lake Baikal, it soon became an important trade center.[4] By 1697–99 Vladimir V. Atlasov had discovered and described the peninsula of Kamchatka, and in 1703 the fort of Bolsheretsk was established there.

Tsar Peter I (1682–1725) did not show much interest in Siberia until the latter part of his reign; his attention was usually directed toward the expansion of his western and southern borders. However, at the very end of his life Peter commissioned the Danish navigator Vitus Bering to settle once and for all the question of a water passage between Asia and America. Although Bering did not completely solve the mystery, in 1728 he sailed through the strait that has since borne his name. This expedition was the first of a number of explorations of the Siberian subcontinent undertaken to areas which during Peter's reign had scarcely been known.

Soon after Peter's death in 1725, governmental authorities began to wonder what lay within Siberia itself. In the early 1730's the St. Petersburg Academy of Sciences organized a scientific

4. Irkutsk was originally founded in 1652 as a *zimov'e* (wintering station) on an island close to the mouth of the Irkut River for the purpose of collecting tribute from the Buryats. In 1661 it was transferred to its present location and made into an ostrog. In 1686 it became a town and center of a *voevodstvo* (province).

expedition to describe systematically the vast region from the Urals to the Pacific. Johann Georg Gmelin, an accomplished natural historian from Tübingen, was designated leader of this venture; scholars and scientists from France, Germany, and Russia accompanied him. The expedition left St. Petersburg in 1733; Gmelin himself did not return until ten years later. This spurt of exploration and research in the second quarter of the century was succeeded by another between 1767 and 1774. At this time Catherine II sent out the celebrated expedition led by the German natural scientist Peter Simon Pallas, which explored much of western Siberia and traveled as far east as Irkutsk and Kyakhta.[5] Its task was to observe and describe the geography, geology, flora and fauna, natural resources, and the life and customs of the natives. The last of the important scientific expeditions of the century took place in 1785–94, when the Englishman, Captain Joseph Billings, was appointed by Catherine to conduct investigations of northeastern Siberia, to chart the Arctic shoreline from the Kolyma River to East Cape on the Chukotski peninsula, and to explore the northwest coast of America.

All these expeditions reflected the spirit of their age by gathering much information about strange lands and peoples; they contributed far less about regions and towns already settled by Russians. One gets from their accounts a one-sided, often idyllic picture of a land inhabited by industrious settlers and noble savages. That Siberia in the latter half of the century was undergoing severe social and economic changes affecting the lives of both Russian and native inhabitants these investigators often overlooked.

Siberia was in fact slowly becoming an organic part of Russia. It had been regarded solely as a colony in the seventeenth century, and was exploited by voevodas (governors), absolute dictators of vast provinces who had come from European Russia and stayed only long enough to reap immense fortunes before

5. Peter Simon Pallas (1741–1811) was born in Berlin; in 1767 he accepted the post of professor of natural history at the Academy of Sciences in St. Petersburg along with the leadership of this expedition.

leaving voluntarily or being expelled from their posts. In spite of good intentions, the central government of the tsar during the 1600's was unable to keep a close check on the voevodas, who were free to develop their own ways of tyrannizing the local population. Although Tsar Peter's large-scale administrative reforms did not penetrate into Siberia for the most part, Peter did concern himself with bringing Siberia under more centralized control. In 1708 the several voevodas were placed under a single official, the governor-general; two years later Peter made Siberia into a single province (*Sibirskaia guberniia*). In 1719, however, Peter subdivided the governorship into five regions (*provintsii*). The net result of these changes was that Siberia came under the despotic rule of one governor-general rather than of several voevodas.

At the beginning of the reign of Catherine II, who ruled from 1762 to 1796, a change developed in the government's attitude toward Siberian administration. On the one hand, the empress and her advisers became increasingly aware of Siberia as a political and administrative problem in itself and began to realize that its conditions were different from those of European Russia and should be dealt with separately. With this view went a tendency to regard Siberia as still a colony of Russia. Yet to reaffirm the prestige of the central government Catherine insisted on making the rule of law prevail in Siberia and on subjecting local officials to more effective supervision. In 1763 she abolished the Siberian *prikaz,* the government office which had been concerned with Siberian affairs since 1637. Siberia was now to be called a "realm" (*Sibirskoe tsarstvo*). In the early 1780's she reorganized the system of local administration by creating three provinces, officially called *namestnichestva* (vicegerencies), modeled on the reorganized system of local administration begun in European Russia in 1775. Thus in 1782 the province of Tobolsk was established, and in 1783 those of Kolyvan and Irkutsk were set up. The namestnichestvo of Irkutsk, for example, was divided into four regions (*oblasti*): Irkutsk, Yakutsk, Okhotsk, and Nerchinsk, each headed by a commandant. Each oblast' was in turn further subdivided into districts (*uezdy*).[6] Catherine's Siberian policies were generally unsuccessful and acute administrative problems continued to press until 1822, when Governor-General Michael Speransky, at the behest of Emperor Alexander I, remodeled the entire administrative structure with a wholesale set of reforms.

The vast land of Siberia traditionally provided a haven for political and religious refugees, runaway serfs, and for enterprising merchants and fur traders. Since Muscovy's conquest of Novgorod in the 1470's, Siberia had served as an asylum for refugees from European Russia. During the 1700's inhabitants of Russian origin were a heterogeneous mixture: despotic officials, wealthy merchants, emigré Cossacks from the Don and the Dnieper regions, fur trappers, political exiles, convicts, agricultural settlers, and persecuted Old Believers.[7] Mazour has gone so far as to say that in Siberia "all social barriers were dissolved."[8] Certainly a good deal more social fluidity existed there than in European Russia.

A Decembrist exile, N. V. Basargin, wrote favorably of the Russian settlers whom he observed while traveling in 1826 to his place of confinement: "The farther we moved on in Siberia, the more that country gained in my estimation. The common people seemed to me much more free, more clever, even more educated than our Russian peasants and especially more so than the peasants of the landlords. Here they have better understood human dignity, and have valued man's rights more highly. Later I more than once happened to hear from those who visited the United States and lived there that Siberians have much in common with Americans in their manners, customs, and even in their way of life."[9] An anonymous Polish political exile who spent some time

6. See Ledyard's listing of these in his journal, p. 161.

7. Old Believers had fled religious persecution since the Church Schism in the 1660's, and many found freedom of worship in the relatively isolated parts of Siberia. In the 1760's a number of them settled in the Baikal region, and with diligence they transformed an agriculturally backward area into a flourishing granary.

8. Mazour, *The First Russian Revolution, 1825*, p. 240.

9. Basargin, *Zapiski N. V. Basargina*, p. 94.

in western Siberia in the 1770's described his impressions as follows: "We had heard much about Siberia as a deserted and thinly populated country; actually we found everywhere abundance, prosperity, and villages populated with a people more humane than in Russia."[10] The Englishman, Martin Sauer, traveling with the Billings expedition, felt, "The Siberians throughout are more industrious and independent than any Russian peasants, [and] live more comfortably. . . ."[11] These comments indicate that conditions among the Siberian peasantry differed considerably from those in Russia, and especially those of Russian serfdom.

The chief way the structure of Russian society in Siberia differed from that in European Russia was the lack of a traditional landed nobility. The Russian nobility had played no part at all in the settlement of Siberia in the seventeenth century, and except for voevodas and *deti boiarskie* (officers descended from petty nobility), members of this class had never lived there. Since Siberia escaped the nobility, which as a class had military obligations in European Russia and enjoyed positions of privilege there, Siberia accordingly escaped serfdom. Of the social groups, the upper administrative officials and the merchants were by far the most powerful and privileged. Consequently, by the late 1700's a sharply antagonistic relationship had developed in Siberian towns between the increasingly wealthy merchant class and the class of local administrative officials. Although the officials represented political and "legal" authority, they regarded the wealth and economic power of the merchant class with suspicion and envy.

Siberian officials were quite unlike civil officials in European Russia, who, since the implementation of Peter's Table of Ranks, could become members of the hereditary nobility by government service and promotion to the eighth rank, and who strove to keep in step with Catherine's "enlightened" court in St. Petersburg. In

10. From "Poliak-konfederat v Sibiri" (A Polish Confederate in Siberia), *RA* (1886), Bk. 1, p. 289.

11. Sauer, *Account of a Geographical and Astronomical Expedition*, p. 9.

the lower echelons Siberian officials were for the most part a poor, uneducated group who had to struggle hard to keep their families alive and whose intellectual horizon was limited. They were hardly suited to assume leadership of whatever intellectual and social life existed at the time. Many of these local officials had been born and bred in Siberia and still had the common Siberian distrust of things intellectual. To all officials, irrespective of their rank, were given broad powers to interfere in the daily life of the people, and many of them took advantage of their position to fill their own pockets and allow free play to their whims, just as their predecessors had done in the seventeenth century.

The Russian merchants especially lived in the world of seventeenth-century Muscovy, and many of them were in fact Old Believers. Remaining extremely conservative, they still thought only in terms of privilege, monopoly, and special rights.[12] Most of them could read and write; some were familiar with Oriental languages and customs, a knowledge necessary for the foreign trade they conducted. Beyond this, however, they had no intellectual interests. Although many Irkutsk merchants became quite wealthy, they lived as their Muscovite forefathers had, in a few small, dark rooms at the back of their homes, which they also used as places of business; they slept on boards and trunks, ate coarse food, and preserved the old Russian and Oriental custom of keeping their women out of public places as much as possible.

The merchants, with their financial success and influence, were the only social class outside that of administrators that might have played a political role on the local level, as did the provincial nobility in Russia. Yet though the St. Petersburg government was never anxious to favor the Siberian merchant class with political and economic privileges, as it did the Russian nobility, geographical and economic conditions favorably influenced the growth and predominance of the merchant class in Siberian

12. Raeff, *Siberia and the Reforms of 1822*, p. 32; Shchapov, "Sibirskoe obshchestvo do Speranskago," *Sochineniia*, 3:669–70.

society. Abundance of furs and proximity to China permitted the development of commercial exchange with the Chinese and the increasing success of merchants who traded with them. The presence of a Russian population scattered over a huge expanse of barren region made necessary the procuring of large amounts of provisions and supplies. This presented fine opportunities for traders and was an important cause of what Shchapov called the eventual "supremacy of the rich merchants."[13] Toward the end of the eighteenth century this economic empire spread still farther when the merchants of Irkutsk began to supply the distant Russian dominions in northeastern Siberia, America, and the Kurile Islands with various goods.

The stronghold of the Siberian merchant class was Irkutsk. Here, around 1800, an oligarchy of rich and powerful merchants flourished and dominated society. Their influence radiated out to the farthest corners of northern Asia. By this time elections to the Irkutsk Duma and the magistracy were fully dependent upon the wishes of a few of these merchants. According to the historian Shchapov, born in 1830 in a village not far from Irkutsk, most of the means of livelihood were concentrated in the hands of the merchants, and especially of those in Irkutsk.[14]

Nomadic groups of Cossack frontiersmen had inhabited Siberia since Yermak's conquest of Sibir and had sought furs, silver, and other forms of wealth. During the early 1700's, however, they became occupied with agriculture, trade, or handicrafts; they were formed into military "hosts" along the frontier or in the interior and were available to the high command of the imperial army in case of war or emergency. Later in the century the Cossack military formations fell into serious decline. If any opportunity arose to make a living elsewhere than on their posts or otherwise than in the government service, the Cossacks took advantage of it. Many of them fled into the countryside or settled

13. Shchapov, *Sochineniia,* 3:653.
14. *Ibid.,* p. 657.

in towns, leaving their posts to take up trapping or trading. Consequently, "state peasants" were impressed into fulfilling the military and police duties of these Cossacks.

As most of the land in Siberia belonged to the state, almost all those who worked it became state peasants; by 1719 over 50 percent of the Russian population in Siberia was of this category. Most of Siberia's settlers had come voluntarily. However, in the seventeenth century the Muscovite state had fostered Siberian agriculture as a means of supporting local soldiers and officials; and since that time political criminals had been exiled primarily for the purpose of agricultural colonization. Attempts to meet the urgent need for agricultural labor to help feed the growing Siberian towns were made throughout the eighteenth century. From the early 1700's on, the obligation of state peasants in Siberia to work a parcel of state land was replaced by the obligation to deliver a fixed quantity of grain to representatives of the state, a change which allowed the peasants more freedom in their activities. A further increase in the peasant population of Siberia occurred in the 1770's as a result of the brutal crushing of the Pugachëv peasant uprising in the Volga region by the government. Many serfs refused to return to their former owners and fled to Siberia.

By the time of Catherine II the demands of trade and the then current idea of the French Physiocrats that agriculture was the primary source of all wealth resulted in a new stress upon agricultural expansion into Siberia; the country came to be regarded as an area of vast agricultural potential. The major problem in carrying through this policy was lack of labor, and so development of agriculture went hand in hand with a policy of colonization and settlement. Serfdom in Russia had never been so widespread and so politically and economically entrenched as it was during Catherine's reign; consequently, to settle peasants in Siberia, the government resorted to compulsory colonization. Along with these attempts went the first efforts at surveying this vast territory—a prerequisite for permanent, orderly, and stable peasant settlement by either Russians or natives.

Along the southern fringes of Siberia, wheat, rye, barley, flax, and vegetables were common crops, while sheep and cattle provided wool, meat, milk, and butter. For beverages the peasants made beer and kvass, a fermented drink prepared from rye bread and malt. The following description of Siberian agriculture was given by the exiled Alexander N. Radishchev, traveling eastward to Ilimsk in 1791: "The agriculture of this country is vast, but I would not say that it is in a flourishing condition. Excluding the years of dearth, the land produces well, but the soil is quite unfruitful. Fertilizers are hardly known, but the fields would have great need of them. The immensity of the land allows one to pass up improving it and always to cultivate virgin lands elsewhere. . . . In many places the peasant lives in abundance; the old inhabitants are often wealthy from raising grain and cattle, but lack money from the absence of markets; the colonists are for the most part poor."[15] In the north fishing and hunting were common pursuits; the economy of many native tribes was centered around the domesticated reindeer, which could provide, if so desired, transportation as well as milk, meat, and clothing. The circulation of money had always played a minor role in Siberia's subsistence and barter economy, especially in the northern areas.

Along with the increasing but inadequate growth of agriculture came the exploitation of mineral riches. The development of local mining industries east of the Urals was concentrated principally in the Altai and upper Ob area and east of Lake Baikal. Important silver mines in the Altai area around Barnaul and Kolyvan were opened in 1738–39 by A. N. Demidov; mines in this region also yielded gold, lead, salt, and copper. In 1764 Siberia received the right to make its own copper coins from ore extracted from the Kolyvan mines. In the trans-Baikal region at Nerchinsk and at Chita, state factories run with forced and penal labor smelted silver and, to a lesser degree, gold, iron, and pig iron.

15. Letter of Radishchev to A. R. Vorontsov, dated at Tomsk on August 23, 1791, in *Polnoe sobranie sochinenii,* 3:389–90.

In the seventeenth and eighteenth centuries the destiny of Siberia was shaped by one all-important factor: the fur trade. The dominant motive for Russia's steady expansion eastward, across the Urals to the Pacific Ocean and to the shores of North America, had been the acquisition of the pelts of fox, sable, sea otter, and beaver. Trade had in general been the traditional occupation of settlers in Siberia. In the 1600's handsome profits could be acquired from selling to the great princes and boyars of Muscovy pelts collected as tribute from the natives. After the treaty of Kyakhta in 1727, the Russians opened up a regular source of gain through commercial exchange with the Chinese at Kyakhta[16] of furs for various Oriental articles. By the period of Catherine II, wealthy Siberian merchants were having the Alaskan coast combed for new supplies of furs to replenish Siberia's diminishing stock.

Because of the depletion of fur-bearing animals in Siberia, many hunters and trappers (*promyshlenniki*) migrated to the towns and, as small businessmen, bought and sold various goods transported from Russia and from fairs within Siberia. Well-established merchants, especially those of Irkutsk, affected by the fur scarcity, turned increasingly toward Central Asia and China in an effort to expand trade opportunities. Capital which they had built up in the China trade they now expended in financing expeditions to America. The most famous of these enterprising merchants was Grigorii Ivanovich Shelikhov, a Ukrainian by birth, who in 1781 founded the Northeastern-American Company together with the merchant Ivan Golikov and his nephew, Captain Mikhail Golikov. That year Shelikhov sent out Gavril Pribylov to the Alaskan coast to collect furs. After an eight-year voyage Pribylov returned with 2,270 sea otter pelts, 8,000 fox skins, and 31,000 seal furs. Shelikhov netted over 250,000 rubles from this single venture.[17]

16. For a contemporary description of Russian-Chinese trade and of Kyakhta, see Coxe, *Account of the Russian Discoveries between Asia and America* (1787), pp. 297–350.

17. Bancroft, *History of Alaska,* p. 185n.; Efimov, *Iz istorii russkikh ekspeditsii na Tikhom okeane,* pp. 308–9.

Although other Siberian merchants, such as Pavel Lebedev-Lastochkin, formed companies in the America trade, Shelikhov came to dominate this whole area of commerce, with the result that in September 1788 the empress granted him exclusive control over the region then occupied by his company.[18] While the central government since the time of Peter had not usually favored the merchant class, Catherine was aware that her interest in securing these territories in the North Pacific in the face of recent English advances, and Shelikhov's interest in commercial profits and economic power, were at one. In 1794, the year before his death, Shelikhov organized a second association, the Northern Company, to establish permanent settlements in America. Out of this grew the well-known Russian-American Company, founded in 1799 by decree of Emperor Paul I.

Russia's penetration to the distant coast of America not only had a pronounced effect upon the affairs of wealthy merchants in Irkutsk but influenced the lives of certain common people. "Throughout the vast expanse from Irkutsk to Okhotsk," writes Okun, "there were found at the end of the eighteenth and at the beginning of the nineteenth century, though not in large numbers, the so-called 'idle people' [*guliashchie liudi*]. Runaway peasants, small merchants and artisans who had lost everything—they were all trying to reach the distant borderlands, attracted by the chance to escape from the watchful eye of the authorities and by rumors of enrichment. It was from among these people that workers for the Russian colonies in North America were recruited. . . ."[19]

Irkutsk was not only the administrative and political center of eastern Siberia but the economic capital as well. All sea otter and sable shipments from the Aleutian Islands and Kamchatka were consigned there for sorting. Sauer, passing through Irkutsk in the mid-1780's, described its economic life as he saw it:

18. Bancroft, *History of Alaska,* p. 309. Okun interprets this decision of the empress as somewhat less far-reaching for Shelikhov at that time (*The Russian-American Company,* p. 28). Regarding Catherine's interests in the Pacific, see Okun', pp. 16–17.

19. Okun', *Rossiisko-amerikanskaia kompaniia,* p. 166.

The shops are in the heart of the city, an elegant square pile of brick building, under piazzas which support warehouses. The butchers' shops are in the eastern extremity. . . . Near this is the fish-market; also a bazar, or renok [*rynok:* market], for vegetables, corn, bread, butter, flour, pedlary, and wooden ware. The latter is a place of resort of the Burati, who hawk about sables, martins, otter, and other furs. . . . The merchants are numerous and affluent; and a considerable trade is carried on with the Chinese. . . . Here the assortments of furs are made, which are brought from America, and the northern parts of the empire, in the following manner: The inferior and worst coloured sables, the fox skins, from the Aleutan islands; the second sort of sea otter, river otter, &c. are allotted to China. Such as are defective and weak in the hair, as also inferior sorts, are sent to the fair at Irbit; and the very best are sent to Mosco and Makaria, where they meet with ready purchasers among the Armenians and Greeks.[20]

Before 1700 the settlement of Siberian towns had proceeded slowly and their population had remained quite small; Yakutsk for example counted 610 inhabitants in 1662, and in 1675 only 609.[21] However, in the eighteenth century, while new agricultural settlers were being brought in or came voluntarily, within Siberia migrants streamed continually away from the land. The easy rewards of trade drew many people away from agriculture, mining, and hunting, and brought them to the towns. Because of the decreasing sable population many hunters and trappers left the outlying districts to settle in towns. An increase in urban population around 1700 was brought about by the influx not only of peasants from Russia and promyshlenniki but also of rich Siberian peasants, exiled *raznochintsy* (men of some education belonging to no definite class), and merchants from European Russia, who came primarily from the northeastern Pomor'e region, formerly controlled by Novgorod. All of these migrants were lured by the attractive possibilities that trade and commerce offered in Siberian towns. Although many of the raznochintsy and the peasants registered themselves in the town records

20. Sauer, *Account of a Geographical and Astronomical Expedition,* pp. 14–15. The town of Irbit is located just east of the Urals; the monastery Makar'ev on the upper Volga was the site of an important trade fair.
21. Shchapov, *Sochineniia,* 3:646.

as petty bourgeois (*meshchane*) or as guild artisans (*tsekhovany*), the urban lower classes for a long time had no real social structure and were a chaotic mixture of all sorts of people.[22]

Administratively, Siberian towns were divided into three categories: "populated" towns, which were actually cities; towns with medium-sized population; and the still smaller "underpopulated" towns. Those in the first category usually had an elected council (*gorodskaia duma*) and a mayor. The departments of police, economy, and justice were separate. Towns in the other two categories had progressively less functional division of power, and broader authority proportionately fell into the hands of fewer officials.[23]

With their varied and unstable population, it was difficult for Siberian towns to set up any well-organized forms of municipal and economic life. Many urban inhabitants lived in poverty and backwardness and suffered from the burden of town taxes. Floods, fires, and famines often took their toll. Difficult economic conditions sometimes produced a reverse movement of petty bourgeois and artisans to the outlying districts. This uncoordinated migration to and from the towns was viewed with displeasure by the administrative authorities, who desired more stable social conditions. Thus, toward the end of the eighteenth century, local officials were authorized by the Municipal Statute (*Gorodovoe Polozhenie*) to transfer peasants from town to country and petty bourgeois from country to town.[24]

Because Siberia's early expansion and colonization followed existing water routes, towns were generally located on large rivers or bodies of water. In the eighteenth century even the largest of them were little more than overgrown, unplanned villages, easily open to devastation by fire and flood. While some houses and public buildings were constructed of stone, often in

22. *Ibid.*, p. 650.
23. On the administrative structure of Siberian towns in the late 18th and early 19th centuries see Raeff, *Siberia and the Reforms of 1822,* pp. 80–83.
24. Shchapov, *Sochineniia,* 3:651.

the popular Russian baroque style, the usual material was wood. Only in the early 1800's did stone structures become common in the larger towns.

In eastern Siberia, Irkutsk had the largest population and was the administrative and commercial center; Yakutsk commanded passageway both to northeastern Siberia and to the Pacific Ocean; Okhotsk was the principal port on the Pacific, from which all naval enterprises to Kamchatka and Alaska set out; Petropavlovsk, in southern Kamchatka on Avacha Bay, was established in 1740 and soon became the economic and shipping center of Kamchatka. Practically all trade with China passed through Kyakhta on the Chinese border below Lake Baikal. Nerchinsk, a "factory" town famous for its silver mines, gave its name to the treaty which in 1689 established the Russo-Chinese border, cutting off Russia from the Amur valley, eastern Siberia's natural route of access to the Pacific.[25]

In western and central Siberia important towns were Tobolsk, Tomsk, Kolyvan, and Barnaul. The first three were administrative centers of provinces (*gubernii* or *namestnichestva*) at some time during the 1700's. In fact Peter I had Tobolsk made administrative capital of all Siberia after his reform of 1708. In ecclesiastical affairs Tobolsk was the seat of the Metropolitan of Siberia. Kolyvan (adjacent to present-day Novosibirsk), established in 1726, became an important manufacturing and mining town. Barnaul, which grew out of a silver-smelting plant established in 1738, became a town in 1771 and served as the administrative center of the Altai mining district. At the end of the seventeenth century over 60 percent of the Russian population lived in western Siberia, and much of that in Tobolsk district. By 1795, however, over 60 percent of the total Russian population in Siberia lived in the central and eastern areas.[26]

It is difficult to obtain accurate information on the number of

25. After 1689 Okhotsk became Russia's main outlet on the Pacific; control of the Amur was not regained until the 1850's.

26. Levin and Potapov, eds., *Narody Sibiri*, p. 9; Kabuzan and Troitskii in Akademiia nauk SSSR, *Sibir' XVII–XVIII vv.*, p. 153.

inhabitants in Siberia or its towns during the 1700's. Toward the end of the seventeenth century the Russian population became larger than the native population. According to the data of the Siberian prikaz in Moscow, in 1697 in 19 out of 20 Siberian districts there were 36,915 Russian adult males and 27,300 native adult males. Counting females and children, there may have been about 150,000 Russians and 125,000 non-Russians.

Adult Russian Males in Siberia in 1697[27]	*No.*	*%*
Peasants	25,965	70
Military and civil officials (*sluzhilye liudi*)	8,829	24
Townspeople (*posadskie*)	1,093	3
Clergy	376	1
Unidentified	652	2
Total	36,915	100

According to one estimate, by 1783 the total number of Russians in Siberia had increased to 1,059,850 persons.[28]

Adult Russian Males in Siberia in 1782[29]	*No.*	*%*
State peasants	297,698	77
Monastery peasants	17,266	4
Serfs (private peasants)	3,097	1
Townspeople and merchants	27,241	7
Officials (*dvoriane*) and clergy	43,916	11
Total	389,218	100

Rough figures are available for some towns in the 1780's. In 1786, Sauer reported, there were in Tobolsk approximately "2300 houses and 23 churches, chiefly of wood." The next year Tobolsk

27. Levin and Potapov, eds., *Narody Sibiri*, p. 124. I have calculated the percentages. Because of their wandering habits, *promyshlenniki* and traders were excluded from this count, as were the "idle people." Properly speaking, the *sluzhilye liudi*, or service gentry, constituted a broad group which had received land from the state in return for military or civil service.

28. *Entsiklopedicheskii slovar'*, 58:807.

29. From the census of 1782 (Fourth *Reviziia*); in Kabuzan and Troitskii, Akademiia nauk SSSR, *Sibir' XVII–XVIII vv.*, p. 153. I have calculated the percentages.

suffered a devastating fire but was "rebuilt on a regular plan; the streets wide, with churches, and a great number of houses, of brick."[30] The trading center of Tomsk had 2,000 houses before a terrible fire in 1773 destroyed half the city; thirteen years later the town had about 1,500 houses.[31] According to Sauer's reckoning, in 1786 Irkutsk contained "2500 houses, chiefly of wood, 12 stone churches, a cathedral, and two monasteries; beside which, there are several public buildings, an hospital, an inoculating house, a seminary for the study of divinity, a public school, a library and collection of curiosities; also a theatre. . . ."[32] Irkutsk could also boast a school of navigation and geodesy. Sauer calculated the number of inhabitants as about 20,000. Yakutsk in contrast contained 362 dwellings, five churches, and a cathedral, and Okhotsk only one church and "132 miserable wooden houses."[33]

It is difficult to determine the extent of intellectual life in Siberia in the eighteenth century. Most sources indicate that the level of education and cultural activity was uniformly low. Speransky in 1819 wrote of Siberia to his daughter, ". . . there is no place for the life of a higher civic education. . . . There is almost no intellectual conversation at all in society."[34] Shchapov, with his usual dogmatic approach, also viewed the whole situation darkly. He felt that the intellectual development of Siberian society had not risen high enough for people to feel critical of the "bourgeois aspirations of the merchant class, the despotic monopoly of the officials, or the dark ignorance and passive servility of the masses. The only intellectual interests and ideas

30. Sauer, *Account of a Geographical and Astronomical Expedition,* p. 7n.

31. Letter of Jakob Fries of 1776, printed by Kirchner, *Eine Reise durch Sibirien,* p. 77; Sauer, *Account of a Geographical and Astronomical Expedition,* p. 9.

32. Sauer, *Account of a Geographical and Astronomical Expedition,* p. 14. The "inoculating house" was for smallpox vaccination, which had recently been introduced in Siberia.

33. *Ibid.,* pp. 27, 40.

34. Letter of June 14, 1819, dated at Tobolsk, in "Pis'ma M. M. Speranskago k ego docheri iz Sibiri" (Letters of M. M. Speransky to His Daughter from Siberia), *RA* (1868), No. 11, p. 1685.

of the majority of Siberian society were inspired by bourgeois motives or represented the chaotic mixture of pre-Petrine ideas with Chinese-Asiatic ones."[35] Furthermore, the Russian Orthodox clergy generally were not strong civic leaders, nor did they effectively raise the moral and spiritual level of the Christian population, both Russian and native.

In spite of Irkutsk's variety of religious, educational, and medical institutions, the civilian governor of that province in the early 1800's, N. I. Treskin, complained that in Irkutsk society "there was an absolute wilderness, almost no education at all," a situation to which peasants and townfolk alike were indifferent.[36] Sauer felt, however, that the schools and theater had a positive influence. And those in Irkutsk who could afford it could obtain for their children private tutors, who were generally "Poles, Swedes, French, and some of the Jesuitic order. . . ."[37] Ledyard's acquaintance in Irkutsk, A. M. Karamyshev, headed a small coterie of literati and intellectuals. Members of this group read and discussed the works of Lomonosov, Derzhavin, Novikov, and other Russian writers, and were ardent lovers of the theater.

Balls, operas, masquerades, and large dinners were frequent in the larger towns. Some regiments had their own musicians; the governor-general of eastern Siberia, I. V. Iakobi, had a private band. The wealthier merchants of Irkutsk spent much time during the week in visiting each other, by invitation or just paying a friendly call. Card playing and drinking constituted the main pastimes among all classes and often ended in quarrels and fights. The position of women in higher society was ambivalent. As opposed to the traditional withdrawal of merchants' wives and daughters from the public view, the wives of administrative officials, who strove to emulate the fashions and manners of St.

35. Shchapov, *Sochineniia,* 3:712–13.
36. *Ibid.,* p. 678.
37. Sauer, *Account of a Geographical and Astronomical Expedition,* p. 17. Prior to the arrival in Siberia of the exiled Decembrists, members of the Siberian intelligentsia had always striven to go west. After 1825, however, the flower of the nation's youth was deported to Siberia, where they noticeably affected the educational and cultural level of the population.

Petersburg (led by the empress herself), were quite active in social events.

From the time that Russian hegemony first prevailed in Siberia, the main social and economic divisions were between Russians and natives. Yet the Russians in their relations with the natives were not racially minded and showed little discrimination against them. Although natives were often cruelly exploited, the Russians made few strong attempts to change their way of life or religion. If natives became Orthodox Christians, the Russians considered them as equals and would intermarry freely with them. Distinctions were more along religious than racial lines. Nevertheless, the eighteenth century witnessed a gradual but profound transformation in the way of life of the various native peoples and in their relation to the Russian population and authorities. Although by the end of the century the natives had not been fully drawn into the main stream of Russian Siberian life, in all respects they were caught up in its influence.

In general, social and economic conditions among the Siberian natives were steadily deteriorating during the eighteenth century. Ever since the first days of Russian expansion into Siberia, the natives had been forced to pay an annual tribute in furs (*iasak*) to the Russian authorities. As long as fur-bearing animals remained common in an area, a tribe encountered few problems in supplying the tribute. With the disappearance of sable in many places and the decrease of some tribal populations, the iasak became an increasingly greater burden.[38] A second obligation placed upon the natives was labor service, primarily the transport of government officials, supplies, and mail. A third imposition on some natives (such as Tungus and Buryats) was the formation of military regiments to serve as border guards on the Chinese frontier. In addition, natives were subject to encroachments by Russian settlers, in spite of government promises to safeguard their lands. Still another hardship was famine. As tribes grew in numbers or migrated northward to escape registra-

38. By 1728 the authorities allowed the iasak to be paid in cash, but currency was scarce among the remote tribes.

tion and payment of the iasak, and as the richer agricultural areas were taken over by Russian settlers, the possibilities of famine increased.

Furthermore the natives, cut off from China by the Russians in the Baikal and Altai regions, could no longer sell pelts directly to the Chinese as they had done in the past. They became dependent upon Russian merchants for essential articles of exchange, which led to perpetual indebtedness, indentured service, and even slavery. As if all this were not enough, contact with the Russians brought new diseases, especially smallpox and venereal disease, and the mortality rate among many tribes increased by leaps and bounds. Famines and epidemics, however, reduced chiefly the populations of tribes with a primitive hunting economy, who lived either in barren regions of the north or in places where agriculture yielded little return. The natives who lived along the rivers or in regions that favored agriculture, in middle and southern Siberia, increased numerically in spite of famine and disease.

These circumstances gradually brought about a marked disintegration of traditional social systems. The ethnic homogeneity of clan and tribe was breaking up, as members of one tribe mixed with another or with the Russian population. At the same time the Russian administrators, influenced by the political and economic role played by the nobility of European Russia, encouraged the formation of an hereditary nobility among the more advanced peoples, like Buryats, Tungus, and Yakuts. From the early eighteenth century on, clan and tribal chiefs were given Russian titles, ranks (*chin*), privileges, pensions, and, in the 1760's, the right to collect and pay the iasak. This Russification of the upper classes widened the gap between them and the common tribesmen. Moreover, these social changes also occurred among natives who were settling down and taking up agriculture. Instead of the natives profiting from contact with the more advanced Russian culture, their energies and fitness for survival were sapped by the ills attending these new contacts.

The Empress Catherine, disturbed by these problems among

the Siberian peoples, favored recognizing the distinctive characteristics and preserving the moral and social qualities of these "noble savages." Steps were gradually taken by the St. Petersburg government to check the shameless exploitation of the natives by the merchants and to alleviate the burden of services in kind, especially the postal and transportation service. During Catherine's reign the government wholeheartedly encouraged natives to take up agriculture in an effort to keep down the ravages of famine. Yet the natives, and especially the more advanced peoples, acutely felt the absence of rules and laws clearly defining their position with respect to the govenment and to the Russian population. Administrative officials encountered increasing difficulty in handling native affairs as a result of the overall changes in their social, political, and economic conditions. Consequently, the 1790's witnessed an effort to codify the existing administrative rules and customary law of the natives. The situation, in spite of piecemeal efforts toward improvement, drifted until Speransky's administrative reorganization of Siberia in 1822.[39]

Traveling in Siberia in the 1700's meant covering great distances over terrain of varying difficulty in a rigorous and fluctuating climate. The route from St. Petersburg to Irkutsk, for example, was just over 6,000 versts, or about 4,000 miles. By Ledyard's figures, Yakutsk lay more than 2,200 versts beyond Irkutsk, and Okhotsk 900-odd versts farther. Irrespective of the accuracy of these figures, the travel distance from St. Peterburg to the shores of the Pacific was at that time roughly 6,000 miles.[40] Sauer took three and a half months getting from St. Petersburg to Irkutsk in 1785–86; Ledyard covered it in two and a half months.

39. For a good coverage of Siberian natives in the 18th century and before the reforms of Speransky, see Raeff, *Siberia and the Reforms of 1822*, pp. 89–111.

40. On the accuracy of Ledyard's figures, see p. 146, n. 14; for the distance between Irkutsk and Yakutsk his itinerary gives 2,587 versts (p. 135), and his journal 2,266 versts (p. 146); Coxe gives 2,433 versts in *Account of the Russian Discoveries between Asia and America* (1787), p. 350. Many travelers in Siberia during the 1700's recorded distances between towns from the verstmarkers along the highways.

However, de Lesseps, traveling from Irkutsk west in 1788, reached St. Petersburg in a month and a half; in fact he took only three and a half months from Yakutsk to Versailles.[41]

During the period of eastward expansion through the forest zone to the Pacific, water travel along those river networks which ran almost east and west was the most secure means of transport. The Lena River from Kachuga, a point north of Irkutsk, to its mouth continued to be used for transport in the eighteenth century; from October to April, when it was usually entirely frozen, it served as a highway for sledges. Travel between Okhotsk and Kamchatka was undertaken, with few exceptions, by ship. Land travel did not come into its own until the eighteenth century, although before this time a coach service had been organized which by 1650 extended as far east as the Lena. The highways that connected such towns as Omsk, Kolyvan, Krasnoyarsk, and Irkutsk lay somewhat to the south of the river routes. Winter travel on them was undertaken when feasible. Spring was a dangerous time to journey, for the ice on the great rivers thawed, the rivers rose, and lowlands grew increasingly swampy; Jakob Fries, going from Omsk to Tomsk in May 1776, found it "almost impossible to travel onward without the greatest danger to one's life."[42]

The mode of transport along the Siberian highways was the covered, horse-drawn coach called the kibitka. A series of post stations, usually twenty to forty versts apart along the main routes, facilitated the transport of mail and of government officials. The keepers of the stations were required to furnish horses to the next station at a price per verst fixed by the government. On the route between Yakutsk and Okhotsk, for example, the government in 1763 introduced a system of pay transport whereby a fee of 3 rubles 15 kopeks was fixed for each horse (provided by local Yakuts). Often the area around a post station

41. J. B. de Lesseps, *Travels in Kamtschatka,* 2:332–81. Seventy years later the speed of travel had not changed much, for Collins reached Irkutsk from Moscow in 35 days. Collins, *Siberian Journey,* ed. Vevier, p. 84.

42. Letter of 1776 in Kirchner, *Eine Reise durch Sibirien,* p. 74.

constituted the only settlement in the area. There might be thirty to sixty houses—at times fewer, especially in regions north of Irkutsk.

The sparseness of Siberia's population and the vast distances involved led the government to depend upon the local population for transportation (*podvody*) and postal service (*iam*). Highways were kept in repair by road-building crews of peasants, while the transport of government officials and of supplies was attended to by peasants and coachmen. Already by 1725 there were about 7,000 coachmen (*iamshchiki*) along Siberian highways; approximately 100,000 people were employed in some way in the highway transport system, the great majority of them Russian.[43] According to the Siberian Cossack, S. I. Cherepanov, ". . . everybody traveled and made use of the [transportation] service—a distance of 500 versts was of no consequence. . . ."[44] Because this type of employment was a considerable burden upon many natives, during Catherine's reign the government refrained from imposing the iasak upon those natives who took up the postal service on a regular basis. This resulted in the formation of whole villages or settlements of natives whose main occupation was handling the postal service.

It was not difficult for travelers to find lodgings of some sort—though they might often be crude or crawling with vermin. According to the American businessman Perry Collins, who traveled through Siberia in the 1850's: "In many of the interior towns in Siberia, as well as in Russia, there are no hotels. There are seldom any travellers but officers or merchants. Officers apply to the police master of the town, or village, who appoints them quarters in any house in the town that he may choose, while merchants either stop with their friends or hire lodgings the best way they can."[45] This situation had changed little since the late

43. Levin and Potapov, eds., *Narody Sibiri,* p. 140.

44. Cherepanov, "Otryvki iz vospominanii sibirskago kazaka 1810–1848" (Extracts from the Memoirs of a Siberian Cossack 1810–1848), *Drevniaia i novaia Rossiia* (1876), Nos. 6–10; cited in Raeff, *Siberia and the Reforms of 1822,* p. 172.

45. Collins, *Siberian Journey,* ed. Vevier, p. 136.

1700's. In Irkutsk in 1786 Sauer found "neither inns nor coffee-houses; but no stranger, who behaves himself with common civility, will ever be at a loss for a home."[46] Siberians treated "newly arrived strangers as rare guests," Fries noted, "with a kind of politeness and hospitality that is unequaled elsewhere. . . ."[47] "Throughout the whole of Siberia," wrote Sauer, "hospitality prevails in the extreme. A traveller is perfectly secure on the road, and certain of a hearty welcome wherever he puts up, let the cot be ever so homely."[48]

In the course of the eighteenth century, as roads were built and equipped with inns and post stations, travelers became less dependent on the water routes of the Ob, Irtysh, and Yenisei systems to the north. The continually increasing numbers of migrants, officials, and visitors found the land routes more direct and quicker. During the reign of Peter I the highway which since 1598 had crossed the northern Urals through Solikamsk and Verkhotur'e into the interior of Siberia was improved and developed. The route through the central Urals via Ekaterinburg (present-day Sverdlovsk) was not wholly accessible to general travel until 1763, because the government from 1739 on attempted to channel all Siberian exports and imports through Verkhotur'e to prevent smuggling. A third route, also used in the second half of the century, lay south of the Urals, passing through Orenburg on the Ural River and continuing along the southern frontier to Omsk. Below this route lay the territory of the nomadic Kazakh hordes.[49] As the century progressed, the highway between Yakutsk and Okhotsk became of increasing importance for communications and transport to and from Russian America.

Because of the differing capacities in which Ledyard passed

46. Sauer, *Account of a Geographical and Astronomical Expedition,* p. 17.
47. Letter of 1776 in Kirchner, *Eine Reise durch Sibirien,* p. 76.
48. Sauer, *Account of a Geographical and Astronomical Expedition,* p. 18.
49. A line of fortifications extending from Orenburg eastward to the upper Irtysh was set up in 1752 to keep marauding Kazakhs from entering Russian Siberia.

through Siberia—as a foreign visitor with an imperial passport and as an exiled *persona non grata*—his journey offers insight into how both types traveled and were treated in eighteenth-century Siberia. As Ledyard traveled eastward his lodgings were not always the best. At least as far as Barnaul he had to sleep either in his kibitka or in his cloak on the floor of some dwelling. We know, however, that in Tomsk he stayed with a wealthy family and in Yakutsk roomed with two officers, first Lieutenant Laxmann and later Captain Billings. On his forced journey west to Poland he was confined either to his kibitka or to a local jail, and only after crossing the border did he receive a good night's sleep and a hot bath. The quality of his meals varied considerably. At times, as a guest of commandants or wealthy citizens, he was wined and dined without stint. At other times, according to traditional Siberian hospitality, local peasants offered him bread, milk, vegetables, and kvass, asking only a kopek or two in return. After his deportation from Irkutsk, however, he wrote that he had not eaten "anything that may be called food" for more than twenty days. Although Ledyard did not describe the route taken across the Urals, it is certain, since he passed through Kazan and Tobolsk on his way east and through Nizhni Novgorod on his return trip, that he traveled the highway through Ekaterinburg and the central Urals.

4

The History and Editing of the Papers

The chief source of information about Ledyard's journey through Russia and Siberia is the journal he kept from the time of his departure from St. Petersburg on June 1, 1787 (N.S.), to shortly before his arrival in Königsberg in mid-April, 1788 (N.S.). Each entry was written at some point during the journey; entries of 1787 are dated New Style, most of those of 1788 are Old Style. Ledyard had neither time nor inclination to fill in or broaden the journal at some later date. The journal is the only known written material of his own that he was able to salvage and carry with him after his arrest in Irkutsk. Another smaller journal that he kept was left behind somewhere in Siberia. Various other papers he mentions unfortunately remained at Yakutsk; perhaps still more notes were lost elsewhere.

The original journal has been lost, the beginning of it in the United States, the remainder perhaps in England. All that has come down from the original journal is now found in three transcriptions, two of which are far more important than the third.

In London Ledyard left the original manuscript, which covered his journey through Russia, Siberia, and Poland, with Henry

Beaufoy and Sir Joseph Banks, who were sponsoring his trip to Africa. He, of course, was already indebted to Banks for the contribution of a generous sum of money toward financing the Siberian trip. From London Ledyard wrote to his cousin in New York that he would send home a "transcript of the few rude remarks" that he had made while in Siberia. Evidently he never forwarded such a transcript, for after the news of his death in Egypt reached Isaac, the New York doctor sent a letter to Beaufoy requesting that the journal be forwarded to him. A friend of Beaufoy's, the Reverend Richard Price, replied to Isaac as follows: "Mr. Beaufoy . . . tells me that he cannot think himself warranted to give up the Journal in his possession without being assured that he will be subject to no future application for it from the heirs of Mr. Ledyard the traveller.—None of the papers which you wish to obtain can be had without the consent of Sir Joseph Banks and the other gentlemen who have contributed to bear the expenses of Mr. Ledyard's travels."[1]

Isaac had also written to Sir Joseph Banks on January 29, 1790, informing him that Ledyard had wanted him to publish an account of his travels; since the journal was in the hands of Mr. Beaufoy, he desired to have it to complete his compilation. He furthermore requested Banks's patronage of the work. Later that year Sir Joseph replied that Ledyard, upon his departure for Cairo, had deposited the journal in the hands of Beaufoy, to be returned to him if he came back, and in the case of his death to be retained as testimony of gratitude for the favors he had received.[2]

In spite of the confusion over whose permission was needed to forward the journal to Ledyard's cousin, eventually Isaac must have acquired a good share of what Henry Beaufoy held of Ledyard's writings. However, it is not known whether only original manuscripts were forwarded to him or whether transcripts

1. Letter dated June 19, 1790, at Hackney near London (NYHS). Price was a prominent economist and political writer.

2. Banks, *The Banks Letters*, ed. Dawson, p. 525.

were also included. A letter of Isaac's son Daniel throws light on Isaac's motives in collecting Ledyard's writings:

> It was the intention of Dr Ledyard himself to publish the travels of his cousin, a few years after his death, and he had all the letters, from him and all other papers that could throw any light on the subject, prepared for the press, but after the manuscript was finished he concluded, with the advice of his friends, to abandon this intention, the account of his travels being to[o] incomplete to answer the bublic [*sic*] expectation. Since that time the family had given up all idea of making any publication of these travels. . . . [However,] in preference to seeing a very unsatisfactory account of his life before the public, . . . they accordingly sent the manuscript to the Rev Mr Sparks—[3]

In July 1797 Isaac Ledyard gave the original manuscripts to Philip Freneau (1752–1832), the "Poet of the American Revolution." Freneau, related by marriage to Isaac, was entrusted with preparing the papers for the press. On September 1, 1797, Freneau wrote in the literary journal, *The Time Piece,* which he edited: "The subscriber having procured from the hands of his relatives the original MSS. of Mr. Ledyard now offers to the public of the United States an opportunity of gratifying their curiosity and at the same time paying a token of respect to the memory of Ledyard. Ledyard's travels will be compiled by P. Freneau from the original MSS. of the author, consisting of letters, journals, notes, etc., etc., and such documents as have appeared in print, both in America and Europe, particularly a work published by the British African Society. . . ."

Freneau evidently made some progress on the work, for on August 30, 1798, the following notice appeared in *The Time Piece:* "The interesting travels of John Ledyard, with a summary of his life, are now in the hands of the printer. It shall be printed on fine paper with new type ornamented with a full length portrait of the author in the attitude of taking leave on his departure for

3. Letter from Daniel Ledyard to I. S., c/o the Postmaster, Concord, N.H., dated Nov. 21, 1821, at New York; in Jared Sparks MS No. 112, HL.

Africa. Page octavo, handsomely bound and lettered. Calculated to contain between 400 and 500 pages. $2 per volume."[4] Yet the work was never published.

The part of the journal forwarded from England to Isaac Ledyard in New York City and passed on to Freneau encompassed at least the time from Ledyard's departure from St. Petersburg on June 1, 1787, to his arrival in Nizhni Novgorod on March 12, 1788. This portion of the original journal, some of Ledyard's original letters, and other documents were at some later time in Cazenovia, New York, where they were copied by Major Samuel S. Forman (1765–1862), whose sister was married to Benjamin Ledyard, Isaac's brother; Forman had lived in Cazenovia since 1793, the year the village was founded. He probably made his transcription before Isaac Ledyard's death in 1803. According to the Ledyard family, many of the original papers were subsequently lost in the mail when they were returned to New York City, presumably to Isaac Ledyard; Forman's transcripts, entitled "John Ledyard's Papers," are all that remain.[5] They are now in the possession of the Ledyard family of Cazenovia. In 1930 Professor J. D. McCallum of Dartmouth, with the help of Miss Katharine Ledyard Hill, had several photostat sets made of Forman's transcripts; one set is now in the possession of Dartmouth College and another belongs to Professor Vernon Carstensen, whose wife is Miss Hill's niece.

Another problem arises in connection with a second transcription of the journal, which can appropriately be called the Beaufoy transcript. This was made in England from the original manuscript, probably before the first portion of the journal was

4. Both quotations from *The Time Piece* are reprinted in Pattee, ed., *The Poems of Philip Freneau*, 1:lxxiv.

5. John D. Ledyard of Cazenovia, N.Y., wrote to me on July 26, 1964: "John Ledyard's papers were here in Cazenovia at one time but were lost in the mail when they were returned to N.Y. However, they were copied by a Mr. Samuel Forman (1768–1863) who was connected by marriage with the Ledyard family." Jared Sparks (1789–1866) so rearranged and reworded his extracts from Ledyard's writings that it is impossible to determine whether he saw the original manuscripts or Forman transcripts by 1828, the date of the first edition of his *Life of John Ledyard*.

forwarded to America in the early 1790's. Subsequently it became a part of the Beaufoy Library in London. The transcript was later obtained by the Museum Book Store in London and was sold for £85 to Dartmouth College, where it now is. On the spine of this quarto volume runs the inscription: "MSS Ledyard's Travels in Russia." Inside it is entitled somewhat incorrectly: "Original Manuscript Journal of his Journey towards Eastern Siberia and Kamchatka. 1787." The transcript is not, however, in Ledyard's handwriting and in one place contains a note accompanied by the initials JWL.[6] The bearer of these initials was presumably the transcriber.

Pages 1–80 of this transcript overlap the part of Ledyard's Siberian journey described in the Forman transcript that extends from shortly after his arrival in Yakutsk to his short stay in Nizhni Novgorod. The content of both transcripts is much the same, although often arranged and worded differently. The Beaufoy transcript, however, includes a number of observations lacking in the Forman transcript, and often elaborates on certain observations common to both transcripts. Pages 81–161 of the Beaufoy transcript cover the period from just after Ledyard left Moscow on his journey west to just before he reached Königsberg.

The third transcription of the journal is extremely fragmentary in content. Slightly over seven pages containing some observations made at Irkutsk are now in the New-York Historical Society. The origin of this transcript is unknown. We do know, however, that in 1879 it was presented to the New-York Historical Society by Dr. John L. Vandervoort, a distant relative of Ledyard's. The handwriting on these pages is superficially similar to Ledyard's customary style, but the formation of *I*, *T*, *r*, final *s*, and the ampersand betray the hand as that of another. These seven-odd pages overlap with part of the Forman transcript (Journal, pp. 168–70) and vary only slightly in content from that.

The differences in the three transcripts of Ledyard's journal

6. Or perhaps IWL (which incidentally contains two of Isaac Ledyard's initials; his middle initial is unknown). John Ledyard had no middle initial.

indicate that each was transcribed quite freely. In presenting Ledyard's journal here I have used only the Beaufoy and Forman transcripts. Where these two overlap I have followed the Beaufoy transcript because of its fuller detail and closer resemblance to Ledyard's style of composition (as shown in his letters). Thus the Beaufoy transcript has been used here in its entirety. Where the Forman transcript contains more information than the Beaufoy, the lines from the former are presented in a footnote.

Another interesting remnant of Ledyard's Siberian journey is an itinerary of towns and distances along the Lena River from Kachuga to Yakutsk, entitled "Marche route de Katschuga à Jakoutzk." It is not in Ledyard's hand, but the comments on it, some of them in English, are in his writing. It is possible that the fourteen circular signs written on the itinerary indicate the villages or towns at which Ledyard and Laxmann procured supplies, as these marks are often placed beside the names of villages 100 to 150 versts apart.

Of the twenty letters of Ledyard's relating to his journey presented here, nine, written in England, Russia, Siberia, and France, still exist as original manuscripts; of these, seven were donated to the New-York Historical Society by Vandervoort. Forman's transcriptions of the remaining eleven letters are in the John Ledyard Papers at Cazenovia.

In transcribing Ledyard's journal and letters and the other documents, I have tried as faithfully as possible to follow the spelling, punctuation, and capitalization of the sources, with the exceptions noted below. It is at times impossible to tell whether a comma or period was meant or whether an initial *c*, *p*, *w*, or *s* was intended to be capitalized or not. Passages bracketed in the original transcripts, probably by Forman, have been printed in double brackets to distinguish them from my own insertions, which appear in single brackets.

Abbreviations and contractions, commonly used in the eighteenth century, are retained in their original form. But periods which often appeared under the last letter have been omitted for convenience of printing in such words as w^{c} (which), Col^{o} (Colonel), y^{e} (the), y^{o} (you), and others. Words and phrases erroneously or extraneously repeated in the manuscripts and transcripts are omitted and the omission indicated in a footnote. Passages that are crossed out in the sources and are either illegible or insignificant (such as transcribers' errors which were corrected) have been silently omitted; however, a few of interesting and substantial content have been presented in footnotes (for example, # 18, nn. 2 and 6).

Wherever Ledyard entered a new date in his journal, I have begun a new paragraph. I have inserted the page numbers of the Beaufoy transcript in brackets in the appropriate places. The Forman transcript lacks pagination.

For the sake of continuity, twenty-eight related documents are interspersed among Ledyard's twenty letters, in chronological order. This sequence is interrupted only by the journal as a whole, which has been inserted between Pallas's letter to Banks concerning Ledyard in Siberia, dated December 18/29, 1787 (# 33), and Khrapovitskii's comment of December 18 (O.S.) regarding the order to arrest Ledyard (# 34). From this series of texts the reader may see Ledyard's plans and the journey as he saw them and as Thomas Jefferson, the Empress Catherine, and a number of other people saw them.

THE JOURNAL AND THE LETTERS

Letters and Other Documents Written before Ledyard's Departure and during the Journey Eastward February 1786–December 18/29, 1787

1. Marquis de Lafayette to Count de Vergennes

Paris le Mercredi 8. fev[r] 1786

. . . .

il parait qu'on ne se soucie point de faire faire le voyage dont j'avais parlé à Mr le marechal de Castries,[1] et que vous ne desapprouviés pas. le Baron de grimm souhaitte envoier M. ledyard, celui qui propose de traverser le continent Americain, à l'imperatrice de Russie, et si vous n'y trouvés pas d'inconvenient j'arrangerai son marché avec M. de grimm

. . . .

Lafayette

TRANSLATION:

Paris, Wednesday, February 8, 1786

. . . .

it appears that no one has been concerned at all about getting the voyage underway which I had spoken of to the marshal de

Castries,[1] and of which you did not disapprove. Baron von Grimm wishes to send Mr. Ledyard, who proposes to cross the American continent, to the Empress of Russia, and if you find no objection to it, I will arrange his negotiations with Mr. von Grimm.

. . . .

LAFAYETTE

Correspondance politique, États-Unis, Vol. 31, folio 79: AAE (original). Charles Gravier, Count de Vergennes, was Minister of Foreign Affairs at this time.

1. The Marquis de Castries was Minister of the Navy.

2. Thomas Jefferson to Lafayette

Paris Feb. 9. 1786.

Dear Sir

The mr John Ledyard, who proposes to undertake the journey through the Northern parts of Asia & America, is a citizen of Connecticut, one of the united states of America. he accompanied capt Cook in his last voiage to the North-western parts of America, and rendered himself useful to that officer, on some occasions, by a spirit of enterprize which has distinguished his whole life. he has genius, an education better than the common, and a talent for useful & interesting observation. I believe him to be an honest man, and a man of truth. to all this he adds just as much singularity of character, and of that particular kind too, as was necessary to make him undertake the journey he proposes. should he get safe through it, I think he will give an interesting account of what he shall have seen.

I have the honour to be with sentiments of sincere esteem and respect Dear Sir

Your most obedient
and most humble servant
TH: JEFFERSON

Le Marquis de la Fayette:

Thomas Jefferson Papers, Vol. 19, folio 3266: LC (original).

3. Lafayette to Baron von Grimm

[February 1786]

Ce jeudi.

Vous trouverez ici, Monsieur le Baron, la lettre de M. Jefferson, et les propositions de M. Ledyard qui ont été traduites: tout ce que j'ai été à portée de connaitre sur le zélé voyageur me fait croire que Sa Majesté Impériale sera contente de lui. Il n'y a pas un an que je l'ai vu pour la première fois, mais les renseignemens qui j'ai pris sur lui ont tous été favorables. Cet officier est entièrement préoccupé par sa passion dominante, celle des voyages singuliers et avec son caractère je le croirais fait exprès pour ce qu'il propose; il ne m'appartient pas d'apprécier l'importance de cette expédition, mais je pense que le personnel de M. Ledyard doit plutot vous encourager que Vous arrêter dans la communication, de son plan à l'Impératrice de Russie, qui est celle de l'univers dans tout ce qui tient aux sciences, aux découvertes, aux lettres, à la philosophie, et à la gloire.

. . . .

LAFAYETTE.

TRANSLATION:

Thursday

You will find here, your Lordship, Mr. Jefferson's letter and the proposals of Mr. Ledyard, which have been translated: all that I have been inclined to recognize in the ardent traveler makes me believe that Her Imperial Majesty will be satisfied with him. It has not been a year since I saw him for the first time, but the inquiries that I have made about him have all been favorable. This officer is completely preoccupied by his dominant passion, that of remarkable voyages, and with his personality I would believe him to be made expressly for that which he proposes; it is not up to me to determine the importance of this expedition, but I think that Mr. Ledyard's person should rather encourage you than hinder you in communicating his plan to the Empress of Russia, who is Empress of the universe in all that pertains to sciences, discoveries, literature, philosophy, and glory.

. . . .

LAFAYETTE.

"Pis'mo Markiza de Lafaietta k Baronu Grimmu" (A Letter from the Marquis de Lafayette to Baron Grimm), *Sbornik russkago istoricheskago obshchestva,* I (1867):293–94.

4. Ledyard to Isaac Ledyard

[St. Germain-en-Laye] February 1786

TO MONECCA.[1]

My last Letters by the Fitzhughes of Virginia[2] left me in the Metropilis of France, the verry football of chance and I have continued so untill within a verry few days of the date of this Letter. All the distresses that you can imagine incident to such a situation, have most faithfully attatched themselves to me: they are now gone, and once more I greet you with a chearful heart: but so curiously wretched have I been, that without any thing but a clean shirt was I invited from a Gloomy garret to the splendid Tables of the first characters in this Kingdom. The medium of our intercourse will only admit of a summary account of things. In about fourteen days I leave Paris for Brussells, Cologne, Vienne, Dresdon, Berlin, Varsovie, Petersburg, Moscow, Kamchatka Sea of Anadivy,[3] Coast of America, from whence if I find any more cities to New York, when I get there I will name them to you in *propria persona;* and so to save time I make another summary!!!!!!!!!!!!!!! which I think are exactly Nine marks of admiration more than I ever saw before on any occassion: and which perhaps a reader of hieroglyphics would say denoted that after a tour of that kind had been performed, it was subtracted from the twelve and only a Nine days wander remained Take my heart & after sharing it with B.——[4] do what you please with the rest. I will write you from Petersburg after I have seen Kate of the North. I embrace thee;

Farewell
JOSEPHUS

JLP (transcript).

1. Monecca, and Josephus, the first-century Jewish historian, were the pen names Isaac and John Ledyard used in writing each other.

2. The brothers Daniel and Theodorick Fitzhugh had left Paris in mid-October 1785 for the United States.

3. The Gulf of Anadyr is an inlet of the Bering Sea, located across from Alaska.

4. Benjamin Ledyard, Isaac's brother.

5. Ledyard to Isaac Ledyard

St. Germains near Paris April 8th 86

TO MONECCA.

If congress are at New York, this will be delivered by my freind, almost every bodies freind and almost always his own freind—Col Humphreys whom you & my dear B.—— knew in days of yore.[1] He is Secretary to our Legation at the Court of France: a voluptuos animal, has a good heart and good head. and is devoutly fond of women, wine, & religion; provided they are each of good quality: but the creatures hobby is poetry: and as the English Reviewers allow him merit therein I may venture verry safely to do it. He is a friendly good soul, a sincere Yanky and so affectionately fond of his country, that to be in his Society here is at least as good to me, as a dream of being at home. I imagine he brings dispatches, but as we are Republicans a little more polished than on your side the Water, we never presume to ask impertinent Questions. I imagine you have by this time received my Letters by Mr Barrett of Boston.[2] Your hearing from me so often by those who intimately know my Situation, and are so much my freinds is a most happy circumstance: but I would freely have relinquished the pleasure, I have in writing this Letter to have been where I supposed I should have been when I wrote you last: but soon after the Departure of Barrett, our minister, the Russian Minister and the American Broker (I mean the marquiss La Fayette) took it into their heads that I should not go directly to St Petersburgh, but wait untill I was sent for which is the occassion of my being here to write you at this time. You see I have so many freinds that I cannot do just as I please. I am verry well in health; a Gracious Providence, & the Indian corn I fed upon in my Infancy, added to the robust Scenes I have since passed thro', have left me at the same age at which my Father died "healthy, active, vigourous & strong."*[3] I am a few weeks at the little Town where my Letter is dated, and as I live upon the Skirt of a Royal forest: I am every day in it: and it is usual for me to run Two Miles an End & return: I am like one of Swift's Hughhainums.[4] Ask Humphreys If I did not walk into Paris last Week and return to dine with Mad[m] Barclay at S[t] Germains the same morning which is at least twenty four of our miles: But this is not the work of Nature: She made me a voluptuous, pensive animal and intended me for the tranquil scenes of domestic life; for ease and contemplation; and a thous[d] other fine soft matters that I have thought nothing about since I was in Love with R—— . . . E—— . . of Stonington.[5] What Fate intends further I leave to Fate But it is verry certain that there has ever been a great difference, between the manner of life I have actually led and that which I should have chosen: and this I do not attribute more to the irregular incidents that have alternately caressed and insulted me on my Journey, than to the irregularity of my genius. Tom Barclay our consul who knows mankind & me verry well, tells me that he never saw such a medley as in me. The Virgi[ni]an Gentlemen here call me Oliver Cromwell, and say, that like him I shall be damned to Fame; but however have never dared to prophecy that it would be by a Virginian Poet.—You see what a Budget[6] I have sent you again: you will not receive such another verry soon.—I every hour expect my Summons from the Russian Minister to the Court of his Mistress, where you shall hear from me.[7] I have a delightful Season to pass through Germany, tho it does not suit my tour well I shall loose a Season by it. I am not certain about the result of this Business, and shall not be perfectly at ease, untill I have been introduced to the Empress. Col Humphries is going over with dispatches relative to us and Great Britain. I meant to have said relative to our commercial concerns, but the Ham & mustard in my mouth relish better than my subject. I am hungry, having just been two hours upon the Banks of the River Seine to see the new invented method of walking upon the Water: but the trial failed: The man walked not half over the river before the things on which he floated turned him heels over head & he was taken up by the Boat.[8] It is sillily imagined and worse executed: and will not admit of improvement. Your Letter must be in Paris tomorrow mor[n]ing, I go 12 miles on foot to carry it: It is now Nine O'Clock in the Evening and I have other Letters to write. Receive my Embrace: keep me in your mind—Adieu! Adieu my dear B.—— also Adieu best of cousins best of friends

JOSEPHUS.—

JLP (transcript).

1. David Humphreys (1752–1818) of Connecticut was a soldier, statesman, and poet. He became a lieutenant colonel at the end of the Revolutionary War and was now in Paris, after having accepted the "Secretaryship to the Commission for Negotiating Treaties with Foreign Powers."

2. Nathaniel Barrett in February had taken various items of mail to America by packet boat, after having concluded in Paris a six-year contract for whale oil.

3. The asterisk indicates the following footnote in the transcript: "*A line from his Fathers Tomb Stone: at this time 35 years old".

4. Houyhnhms: horses in *Gulliver's Travels.*

5. According to Munford, her name was Rose, but he gives no documentation (*John Ledyard, an American Marco Polo,* pp. 43–45). Augur states that "We know only the initials of this lost love . . ." (*Passage to Glory,* p. 51). Ledyard fell in love with R.E. sometime after his return home from Gibraltar in 1774. Stonington is about nine miles east of Groton.

6. Bundle of news.

7. The Russian Minister to France at that time was Ivan Matveevich Simolin.

8. I was unable to discover further information on this "new invented method of walking upon the Water."

6. Empress Catherine II to Grimm

A Pella, ce 17 juin 1786, à quatre heures après-dîner.

. . . .

M. Ledyar fera bien de prendre un autre chemin que celui du Kamtchatka, parce que, pour cette expédition,[1] il n'y a plus le moyen de l'atteindre. Au reste, tout ce qu'on a publié de cette expédition est parfaitement faux et un rêve creux:[2] jamais il n'y a eu de compagnie ambulante, et tout se réduit à l'expédition du capitaine Billing et d'un équipage choisi par lui et Pallas. Laissez à l'Américain l'argent que vous lui avez donné ou promis; mais ne jetez pas à l'avenir mon argent par les fenêtres: je ne connais point ces gens-là et n'ai aucune affaire jusqu'ici avec eux.[3]

. . . .

"Pis'ma Imperatritsy Ekateriny II k Grimmu (1774–1796)" (Letters of Empress Catherine II to Grimm), *Sbornik imperatorskago russkago istoricheskago obshchestva,* 23 (1878):378. Pella, where this letter was written, was an imperial palace about twenty miles southeast of St. Petersburg. For an English translation, see p. 39–40.

1. This was Capt. Joseph Billings' expedition to explore the Kolyma River basin and the northwest coast of America. On Billings, see p. 23.
2. This probably refers to documents ## 1 and 2, copies of which had been forwarded to Catherine, and to Grimm's apparent suggestion that Ledyard catch up with Billings' expedition.
3. A reference to Americans.

7. Catherine II to Grimm

Ce 23 juillet [1786].

. . . .

. . . Je vous ai dit tout ce que j'avais à dire sur le Sr Ledyar . . .

. . . .

"Pis'ma Imperatritsy," *Sbornik imperatorskago russkago istoricheskago obshchestva,* 23 (1878):381. An English translation is on p. 40.

8. Jefferson to Ledyard

Paris July 27 1786.

Sir

The Baron de Grimm spoke to me on Sunday last on the subject of your affairs. he said you had desired him to transact with you thro' me, to which he should have had no objection, but that he had informed the Empress from the beginning that it was with the M. de la fayette he was negotiating the matter & that therefore he should not be justified in treating it with any other person. on the receipt of your letter this morning, knowing that the Marquis would leave town tomorrow for two months, I instantly wrote to him to let him know nothing would be done with any other person during his absence, & prayed him to see Baron Grimm before he left town as well to get for you a present supply as to know explicitly whether you are to look for a continuance of it.[1] as soon as I receive his reply I will send it to you. I am sorry it is not in my power to send you your book.[2] very soon after I received it from you I lent it to Madame de la fayette, who has been obliged to lend it from hand to hand & has never returned it. I am Sir

Your very humble serv[t]
TH: JEFFERSON

Mr Lediard

Thomas Jefferson Papers, Vol. 23, folio 3907: LC (original). Ledyard at this time was still in Paris.

1. For the results of Lafayette's talk with Grimm see doc. # 9.
2. A copy of Ledyard's *Journal of Captain Cook's Last Voyage.*

9. Lafayette to Jefferson

MalesHerbes August the 2d [1786]

My Dear Sir

I Have spoken with Baron de Grimm who, it Seems, Has No Notion to Continue the Monthly 25 guineas, and says He Has taken no other Engagement But to advance that sum once[1]—for you must know, *Between You and me* that the 25 guineas exceeding this Sum Have Been delivered under his Name on my Account, which of course the Empress will Reimburse if She Accepts of the proposal. In the mean while Baron de Grimm advises our friend Ledyard not to Throw a way Any other opportunity that might offer.

. . . .

LAFAYETTE

PTJ, 10:188. Recipient copy is in LC.

1. It appears that Lafayette and Jefferson had urged Grimm to continue his support of Ledyard and on a monthly basis. However, Grimm had only once donated 25 guineas (600 livres)—in February 1786; see p. 38, n. 7.

10. Ledyard to Isaac Ledyard

St. Germains Aug 8th, 1786

TO MONECCA.

Next to my friendship for you which is very naturally extended to a Degree even romantic by my long separation and misfortunes, I would willingly inform you of the situation of my affairs as the next most important Subject between us, but at this whimsical and uninteresting instant I have not a syllable of the kind for thee. I give you my word that the Strumpet has kissed me as often as she [h]as kick'd me and why she should not smash or kick you all as well as me I know not. Why should I be thus painfully distinguished or by kicks or kisses. If it be for my own sins or the sins of the family. I have been must have been a Devil of a Rake—and rakes capital must you have all been and deeply in debt if it be for you all that I enjoy the painful preeminence.—You will be right to suppose me in a kind of foolish good-natured delirium to write thus and what does it signify how one is if one be happy or even endeavouring to make oneself so: To be foolishly happy is still happiness and to be wiseley so is no more.

For my part I am sick of the little particoloured patches of science I have so long played the harlequin in and of that something that I once was taught to call Philosophy. Those appendages of an illiberal education have sharpened every misfortune, that has attended me since I have been in France. Like Macbeth's Physician not one of them all has been able to administer to a mind diseased. One single thought that has been the offspring of nature only has gone beyond them all: and If I enjoy any happiness this moment I owe it to the exertion of a native sentiment. How often my good departed Ancestors have I had just occasion to damn the Stupidity of the Life they taught me and to damn myself for compleating the deformed thing by my subsequent conduct. but Peace to your faults, and to my own, and peace to my present feelings, for I have unlearnt what you learned me.

I have begun the Letter without knowing I shall ever send it you will therefore treat it as you would a friend who pops in with an undress to take Coffee with you, no Ceremony I beseech you. Having begun to stain a new sheet of paper let me sacrafice the virgin part of it to our friendships. How do you all do? behold me on my knee before ye in all the ardour of esteem when I ask the question: Ye who know me can bear a part with me in these my feelings but none of you all have suffered like me in long and distant separations from those ye loved: so that ye happily have not to sympathise with me in this part of my sensations: in every thing else ye have, and thank Heaven it is not in my power to go beyond you in thinking of friendship or performing its duties; This is one of the few happy circumstance that the malice of fortune will lastly deprive me of if ever, and however foiled by the maloccurrences of Fate while I have the friendship of you and your Brother believe me my dear Monecca I shall always think worth while to live—

It is twelve months since I have heard from you a thousand things contrary to my wishes for your happiness may have happened, or on the contrary a thousand things may have occurred to render you happier than I may reasonably imagine: in either case our friendship is unmoved and beg you will accomodate all my greetings to the Statu quo of things when you read this. Does the dance inspire you or the jocund song "none more blithe than I"—? Is Love the favourite God—the God I love and am his constant votary. Is grief the[1] theme—I know it well. Ah too well! and can follow you to the very cave of moping melancholy—the bursting of the heart strings—the dark abyss of despair itself—does Ambition fire your Souls?—"Why I'd pluck it from the moon"—The only circumstance wherein I cannot give entire response to your enjoyments and sufferings is your hymenials:[2] there I cry ye mercy. The last letter I wrote you was by Colonel Humphries whom I hope you have seen: I have been at St Germains ever since waiting for the issue of my affairs at St Petersburg. You wonder by what means I exist having brought with me to Paris this time only three Louis d'ors. Ask vice consuls, consuls, plenipotentiaries, ministers and whores of fortune all of whom have had the honor to be tributary to me. At present I have tributized the minister Plenipotentiary of the Duke of Saxe Gotha[3] and have laid plans to subjugate the Chancellor of the British Exchequer. You think I joke—no upon my honor; and however irreconcileable to my temper, genius, disposition or education, it is nevertheless strictly true: Nay more I have even proposed the subsidy to the King of France, he read my *Bull* after he had eat a *large Poulard* which he does at every meal or something equivalent to it and it is thought would have swallowed my Bull with as much unconcern as he did the *poulard* but for the wary Vergennes,[4] and so it was not swallowed and the Devil take their Genius for Intrigue—It is as universal a talent among the French as Basketmaking is among our American Indians and much resembles it—Every day of my life my dear Cousin is a day of Expectation and consequently a day of disappointment. Whether I shall have a morsel of bread to eat at the end of two months is as much an uncertainty as it was 14 months ago and not more so—If I had been raised to happiness or plunged in distress twelve months ago I should not have been surprized: it is the near approach I have so often made to each extreme without absolutely entering into either, that astonishes, and has eventually rendered me so hardy as to meet either without an extra palpitation. Altho' extraordinary situations naturally imply some extraordinary occurrence as necessarily incidental to them, Permit me to relate one which I do not think necessarily incidental to my situation. About a fortnight passed Sir James Hall an English gentlemen on his [way] from Paris to Cherbourg stopped his Coach at our door and came up to my Chamber to see me—I was in bed at 6 OClock in the morning & having flung on my Robe de Chambre and met him at the door of the anti-chamber, I was glad to see him but surprized—he observed he had to make up his opinion of me with as much exactness as possible and concluded that no kind of visit whatever would surprise me: I could do no other than observe his Opinion surprised me at least; and the Conversation took another turn In walking across the Chamber he laughingly put his hand on a Six Livre piece and a Louis d'or that lay on my toilet & with a half stifled blush asked me "how I was in the money way" blushes commonly beget blushes and I blushed partly because he did, and partly on other accounts: If fifteen Guineas interrupting the answer he had demanded will be of any service to you, there they are and put them on the Table—. I am a traveller myself and tho' I have some fortune myself to support my travels. yet I have been so situated as to want money which you ought not to do.—You have my address in London &c&c and wished me a good morning and left me This Gentleman was a total stranger to the situation of my finances and that I had by mere accident met at an ordinary in Paris. we had conversed together several times, and he once sent his Carriage for me to dine with him I found him handsomely lodged in the best fauxbourg in the City, two Members of the English house of Commons, two Lords Beaumarchais,[5] and several Members of the Royal Academy at Paris at his Table. He two or three times after that had seen me and expressed the highest Opinion of the Tour I had determined to make and said he would as a Citizen of the world, do any thing in his power to promote it. But I had no more Idea of receiving money from him than I have this moment of receiving it from Tippoo Saib.[6] However I took it without any hesitation and told him that I would be as complaisant to him if occasion ever offered. You see what a medley of a life I lead by my Letter.[7] If the Heart by debauch is rendered callous to the severe feelings such reflections would otherwise give, the man who has it should visit those hospitals in large Capitals that are receptacles of Infants thus produced and Women thus neglected. I have once seen them both in Paris, twice I believe I never shall—Not all the morality from Confucius to Addison could give me such feelings. Eighteen Foundlings were brought the day I visited. One was brought in while I was there, and there were about three hundred in all. Dear little Innocents! but ye are happily insensible of your situations—Where are your unfortunate mothers?—perhaps in the adjoining hospital—She has to feel for you and herself too—but where is the wretch—the villain—the monster—I was not six minutes in the House It is customary to leave a few pence—I flung down six Livres and retired. Determined to persevere I continued my visit over the way to the Hospital De Dieu I entered first the apartments of the women, very few of them are here for any other than the vener[e]al disease—What havoc does Lust make among mankind Well may there be eighty thousand registered prostitutes in Paris. The number here accounts for it—or that accounts for this.—Why will you my dear Sisters I was going to say as I passed along thro' beds in ranks—why will ye be—But I was interrupted by a melancholy figure, that appeared at its last gasp or already dead. She's dead said I to a German gentleman who was with me—and nobody knows or cares any thing about it—. We approached the Bed-side. I observed a slight undulating motion in one of the jugular arteries. She is not dead said I, and siezed her hand to search her pulse. I hoped to find Life but it was gone: the word dead being again pronounced bro't the Nuns to the Bed. My God! exclaimed the head Nun "she is dead." Jesus Maria exclaimed the other Nuns in their defence she's dead: The head nun scolded the others for their malattendance—"My God" continued she "She's dead without the form! Dieu! said the others she died so silently. "Silence said the elder—perhaps she is not dead—say the form;

the form was said and the Sheet flung over her face. I know not how I happened to turn my eye round but while the Benediction was repeated, it struck those of a most beautiful young Nun that was among the rest, and who was as debonair, gay and even lascivious as if She had been in the Palais Royale, and seemed as ready to become a sacrafice to pleasure as the unfortunate victim she had been dismissing with her Benediction had been—. And if she had, said the Gentleman to whom I made the observation—she would not have been the *first* who had, from this very place—I took a walk to Paris this morning, The Marquiss La Fayette has three of the finest Asses I ever saw which he means to send to General Washington. He sent to the Isle of Malta for them, he is a good fellow this same Marquiss: I esteem him and even love him, and so we all do except some few who worship him. I make these Trips to Paris often sometimes to dine with this aimiable Frenchman, sometimes with our minister who is a Brother to me, & sometimes I go buy a fine pair of pumps to walk in. I am too much alive to care and Ambitiou[s] to sit still.

The villanous, unprofitable life I have led goads me I would willingly crowd as much merit as possible into the Autumn & Winter of it. Like Milton's hero in Paradise lost (who happens to be the Devil himself) it behoves me now to use both Oar, & Sail to gain my Port—While in Normandy I was at the seat of Conflans the successor of him that was so unfortunate in a Naval affair with Hawke of England—[8]It is the Lordship of the Manory. The peasants live or die at the smiles or frowns of their Lord, and avaricious of the former they fly to communicate to him any uncommon occurrence in the Village and such they thought our arrival—The place to be sure is very remote and the Gentleman I accompanied an Englishman rode in a superb manner. His Coach, his Servants were in a most elegant Stile, Mr Conflans was informed of it It was my turn that day to cater and the little country taverns in France are such as to oblige [one] to cook for himself if he would eat. I was consequently busy in the Kitchen. The Otaheite marks on my hands were discovered.[9] The

Mistress and the maids asked our Servants the History of so strange a sight. they were answered that I was a Gentleman who had been round the *world*

It was enough—. Conflans knew of it and sent a Billet written in good English to know if he could have the honor of seeing us at his Mansion & if he could be thus distinguished, he would come & wait on us there himself.—It was too late; the Englishman & I had begun pell mell upon a joint of roast. If Jove himself had sent a Card by Blanchard inviting us it would have been the same.—We would honor our selves to wait on the Marquis de Conflans in the Evening.—We did so—We could not but be honored with the reception we met. It did honor to a French Nobleman.—Our Minister informs us that New York has at length acceded to the five Per Cent impost—by your Leave, Mr Yorker I think ye have been a little Coquetish in this matter.[10] and—I was going to say something very wise—but your Committee meetings and Oyster Clubs render you so redoubtable in sentimental Politics that I beg to withdraw my motion. The Paris Papers of To-day announces the discovery of some valuable Gold mines in Montgomery County—Virginia which I rejoice to hear but hope they will not yeild too much of it, for as Poor Richard says "Too much of one thing is good for nothing" All that I can say is, that if it is as bad as *too little* of it the Lord help ye when it happens to be the case with ye as he has me, who in spite of my Poverty am plump & hearty, and as merry as a fool as appeareth by my Letter. I die with anxiety to be on the back of the American States, after having either come from or penetrated to the Pacific Ocean.[11] There is an extensive field for the acquirement of honest fame. A blush of generous regret sits on my Cheek to hear of any discovery there that I have not part in, & particularly at this auspicious period: The American Revolution invites to a thourough discovery of the Continent and the honor of doing it would become a foreigner. But a Native only could feel the pleasure of the Atchievement. It was necessary that an European should discover the Existance of that Continent, but in the name of Amor Patria. Let a Native of it Explore its Boundary. It is my wish to be the Man I will not yet resign that wish nor my pretension to that distinction.

Thus far my new Ass whom I beg leave to introduce to you as an Ass that sprung from the Ashes of my Ass Commerce whom I entered Last January in Paris. Etatis suae thirty months—[12] Peace to its manes.—I shall neither forget the pleasures or the pains it gave me they form too interesting a part of my Existence —But farewell old Ass & welcome new Ass—and farewell to you too for I have just received news which hurries me to London[13]— What fate intends is always a secret—fortitude is the word. I leave this Letter with my Brother & my father our Minister—he will send it the first private conveyance—— Adieu!

JOSEPHUS

JLP (transcript).

1. "the" is repeated in the transcript.

2. Isaac Ledyard married in March 1785.

3. Baron von Grimm, confidential agent of Empress Catherine in Paris.

4. Count de Vergennes (1717–February 1787), French foreign minister. *Poulard:* a pullet.

5. Pierre Augustin Caron de Beaumarchais (1732–99), French dramatist. The "two Lords" do not refer to Beaumarchais.

6. Tippoo Sahib (1753–99), Sultan of Mysore since 1784.

7. At this point the transcriber has enclosed in parentheses the following words: "after some Reflections on unprincipled Libertinism the Letter proceeds."

8. The Conflans Ledyard met was the son of Marshal de Conflans (1690–1777), admiral of the French fleet, who was defeated by the English admiral, Edward Hawke (1705–81), in a naval battle at Quiberon in 1759.

9. Ledyard had had his hands tattooed while in Tahiti.

10. In order to pay the public debt, Congress in 1783 had asked the states to grant it the power to impose a duty on imports not exceeding 5 percent ad valorem. Because of growing Antifederalist sentiment in New York, that state repeatedly refused to allow Congress to collect the impost; Isaac Ledyard, however, was prominent in the opposition to this sentiment. Finally, by the Act of May 4, 1786, the New York legislature agreed to the impost, but substituted state collectors for federal ones, thus rendering the act useless for the purposes of Congress. By July 9 Jefferson learned that New York had "ceded the impost in the form desired by Congress," and, unaware of the stipulations attached, had communicated the news to Ledyard. Only in late August did Jefferson learn the full story. *PTJ,* 10: 106, 288.

11. This indicates his willingness to cross the continent in either direction.

12. Ledyard had often written to Isaac of his "Hobby" or his "Ass," referring to his pursuit of reaching the northwest coast by ship. In September 1785 he wrote, "I may venture to say that my Enterprize with Paul

Jones is no more: that I shall inter this Hobby at Paris. . . ." Before January 1786 Ledyard had spent over thirty months ("etatis suae thirty months"), since May 1783, on this undertaking, and now he was again to attempt the voyage.

13. The following news, which on August 1, 1786, appeared in the London *Universal Daily Register,* had probably reached Ledyard: "A large ship is fitting out, at Deptford, with all possible expedition, for a voyage round the world, on particular discoveries: The officers and seamen are picked persons, and the most expert and best navigators that can be got. . . ."

11. Jefferson to Ledyard

Paris Aug. 16. 1786.

Sir

I saw Baron de Grimm yesterday at Versailles, and he told me he had received an answer from the Empress, who declines the proposition made on your account. she thinks it chimaerical. I am in hopes your execution of it from our side of the continent will prove the contrary. I thought it necessary to give you this information that you might suffer no suspence from expectations from that quarter. I wish you success in whatever enterprize you adopt and am Sir

Your most obed^t humble serv^t
TH: JEFFERSON

Mr Ledyard.

Thomas Jefferson Papers, Vol. 23, folio 4016:LC (original). Ledyard was at this time in London.

12. Ledyard to Jefferson

London August 16th 1786—

TO THOMAS JEFFERSON ESQ^r

Sir

Whenever I have occasion to write to you I shall not want to say so much on the score of Gratitude, that if I do not tire you with the Repetition of my thanks I shall at least do injustice to the other parts of my Letters unless you will be so good as to accept of a single honest heartfelt *Thank You* for the whole in that case I shall always proceed to plain narration

The same Sir James Hall that made me the remarkable visit at St Germains is my friend here. I have arrived most opportunely indeed. An English Ship sails in three days for *Nootka Sound:* I am introduced by Sir James Hall to the Merchants who welcome me to a passage[1] there and as one of them goes himself thank me for my comp[any.] I shall go on board to morrow: An Officer of Capt Cooks goes also. He is hig[h]ly pleased at my accompaning them. Sir J Hall presented me with twenty Guineas Pro Bono Publico—I bought two great Dogs, an Indian pipe and a hatchet My want of time as well as more money, will prevent my going otherwise than indifferently equipped for such an Enterprise: but it is certain I shall be more in want before I see Virginia: why should I repine? You know how much I owe the aimiable La Fayette, will you do me the honor to present my most grateful thanks to him?—If I find in my Travels a mountain as much above the Mountains as he is above ordinary men I will name it La Fayette—I beg the honor also of my compliments to Mr Short who has also been my friend and like the good Widow in S[c]ripture cast in—not only his mite but more than he was able, to my assisstance.[2] Adieu

I have the honor to be
Sir your most grateful
and most Obed[t] hum[l] Serv[t]
JOHN LEDYARD

JLP (transcript). According to Jefferson's "Summary Journal of Letters," located in LC, this letter was received on October 3, 1786 (*PTJ*, 10:259).

1. The phrase "to a passage" is repeated in the transcript.

2. William Short (1759–1849), American diplomat, acted as Jefferson's private secretary and later became secretary of the American Legation in France. The widow: Mark 12:42–44, and Luke 21:2–4.

13. Ledyard to Isaac Ledyard

London August 18th 1786

TO MONECCA—

Coll Smith secretary to the embassy here[1] will send you this and my other written in France by the first private conveyance. I leave them in his hands Adieu to Europe! I have but a moment to write you though the last moment I may ever employ in the tender task. I embark this day on board an English Merchant Ship that sails by Cape Horne into the Pacific Ocean and to the N.W. coast of[2] America on a Trading voyage. I land at Nootka Sound which you will find on the charts & Prints I sent you in Lat. 49° N.—from thence I mean to make an attempt to cross the continent to Virginia. I go alone except my two Dogs. If I live to see you it will be in two or three years. Think a little of me and remember me to all my friends—but I would not wish that all of them or people in general should know my pursuits. I send you some little matters within that I ask you to keep for me; it is like parting with life to leave them but I cannot carry them where I shall go: receive my embrace. Adieu

JOSEPHUS

I am received with the greatest politeness in London particularly by the Gentlemen who go the voyage among whom are some of science and one of Capt Cook's Officers.

The Sir James Hall mentioned in my other Letter has been the means of this. Sir Joseph Banks also is my friend, yet I am a deserter in London.[3] What a world is this ha! ha! ha!

Adieu—

JLP (transcript).

1. Col. William Stephens Smith (1755–1816) had been appointed secretary of the American Legation in London in 1785.

2. "of" is repeated in the transcript.

3. A reference to his escape from a British warship off Long Island in 1782.

14. Jefferson to Ezra Stiles

Paris Sep. 1. 1786.

. . . —A countryman of yours, a Mr. Lediard who was with Capt. Cook on his last voiage, proposes either to go to Kamschatka, cross from thence to the Western side of America, and penetrate through the Continent to our side of it, or to go to Kentucke, and thence penetrate Westwardly to the South sea. He went from hence lately to London, where if he found a passage to Kamschatka or the Western coast of America he would avail himself of it; otherwise he proposed to return to our side of

America to attempt that route. I think him well calculated for such an enterprize, and wish he may undertake it. . . .

TH: JEFFERSON

PTJ, 10:316–17. Press copy is in LC. Ezra Stiles (1727–95), a Connecticut clergyman, was president of Yale College from 1778 to 1795. Ledyard had visited Stiles in New Haven on February 3, 1784; Jefferson may not have been aware of their acquaintance.

15. William S. Smith to John Jay

London September 1st 1786—

Sir—

. . . During my tour on the Continent the last season, I formed an acquaintance with a Mr Ledyard, a Gentleman from Connecticut, who accompanied Capt Cook on his last Voyage to Kamtsckatka; he was about offering his services to the Empress of Russia, for exploring the western Coast of America, which it is the received opinion is not very distant from the back parts of Siberia and the place abovemention'd—he has been disappointed in his pursuits, notwithstanding in Paris, he was much countenanced and protected by Mr Jefferson and the Marquis de Lafayette, in his negotiations with the Russian Ambassador &c &c—after meeting with various impediments he gave up all thoughts of bringing the subject to that benificial point of operation, which he at first expected, and in consequence of some allurements from an English nobleman at Paris,[1] he came here with an intention of entering into the service of this Country for the purpose of visiting & exploring that Coast and Country—

Upon being acquainted with his pursuits, I endeavour'd to convince him, that it was his duty as an American Citizen, to exercise his talents and Industry for the immediate service of his own Country—and if the Project he was upon, could be benificial to any, his Country upon every Principle was entitled to those services—

After a few conversations on the subject, he consented to move independent of this Court—and a vessel being on the point of sailing for that Coast, after supplying himself with a few necessary articles for his Voyage, and march, he procured a Passage, with a promise from the Captain to land him on the Western Coast, from which he means to attempt a march thro' the Indian nations, to the back parts of the Atlantic States, for the purpose of examining the Country and its Inhabitants, and expects he will be able to make his way thro', possessed of such information of that Country and its produce, as will be of great advantage to ours—this is to be proved—It is a daring, wild attempt—and I have my doubts of his success—but finding him determined to pursue the subject, I thought he had better do it in the way he now is, than bind himself in any manner to this people[2]—he embarked the last week *free and independant of the World,* pursuing his plan unimbarassed by Contract or obligation—if he succeeds, and in the Course of 2 or 3 years, should visit our Country by this amaizing Circuit, he may bring with him some interesting information,—if he fails, and is never heard of—which I think most probable, there is no harm done—he dies in an unknown Country, and if he composes himself in his last moments with this reflection, that his project was great, and the undertaking, what few men are capable of—it will, to his mind, smooth the passage—he is perfectly calculated for the attempt—he is robust and healthy—& has an immense passion to make some discoveries which will benifit society and insure him, agreable to his own expression, "a small degree of honest fame" —The vessel sails round Cape Horn, bound to Nootka sound in the Pacific ocean, situated on the north west Coast of America in Lat. 40° N° [3] at this place he intends to land, and begin his march nearly a south East course—It may not be improper for your Excellency to be acquainted with these Circumstances, & you are the best judge of the propriety of extending them further —I am with the greatest respect—Your Excellency's

Most obed[t]
Humble Serv[t]
W.. S.. SMITH

His Excellency John Jay *&c: &c: &c.*

Papers of the Continental Congress, No. 92, pp. 136–39: NA (original). John Jay was at this time secretary of foreign affairs for the Continental Congress.

1. Sir James Hall.
2. The English.
3. Nootka Sound is actually at lat. 49° 40′ N.

16. William S. Smith, Letter of Introduction for John Ledyard

By Wm. S Smith late Colonel in the Service of the United States of America Secretary of Legation and (in the absence of his Excellency John Adams Esquire Minister Plenipotentiary) charged with the affairs of the said United States at the court of Great Britain—

An Introduction is given to the Bearer Mr John Ledyard a Citizen of the United States of America, at present on his Travels to Hamburg in Germany to Petersburgh the Capital of Russia to Moscow a western Province in said Empire and from thence through Siberia to Kamschatka and from thence over the Northern Pacific Ocean to any part of the N.W. Coast of America for the purpose of acquiring a Knowledge of the last mentioned Country and passing through the same to that district known by the name of the United States of North America,[1] in addition to which Mr Ledyard's object is to enquire into the natural History of the Countrys through which he may pass for the Extension of Science and the Benefit of Mankind. All Persons whom it may concern are requested to give him every necessary passport and Protection to enable him to compleat his Tour with despatch, and that he may be protected from every delay or detention, not Justified by the Laws of the place where he may be— M Ledyard's good character & Conduct, it is expected will ensure him civility & respect and the great Object he has in view be a particular reason why the friends of Merit and of Science should aid him with their countenance and protection: he having also spent several years past in pursuit of objects which contribute largely to render him fit, for this Enterprize and particularly having accompanied the late celebrated Capt Ja[s] Cook on his last voyage are points, which exclusively of Mr Ledyard's personal merit it is hoped will ensure him the passports & protection requested

Given at Westminster in the Kingdom of Great
Britain this 4th day of September, 1786
W. S SMITH

To Those whom it may
concern . . . — —

JLP (transcript).

1. The phrase "for the purpose of acquiring a Knowledge . . . of North America" is repeated almost verbatim in the transcript.

17. Ledyard to Smith

Deptford 18th Sept. 1786

To COL. W. S SMITH ESQR.

Sir. The situation of my affairs until yesterday were so uncertain that I omitted writing to you: they appear now to be settled & I expect to sail the day after tomorrow on board the Harriet[1] Ship. We go to Ireland & from thence to the Canarys.

Wherever I am you shall hear of me. Had you not requested your generous friendship for me, and your personal Merit would have prompted me to do it—farewell

I have the honor to be
with sincere regard & most perfect esteem
Sir your most humble
& most obed^t Servt
JOHN LEDYARD

JLP (transcript).

1. The handwriting is unclear; this could also be read "Hamet" or "Harnet."

18. Ledyard to Jefferson

London Novr 25th 1786

My friend, my brother, my Father,—I know not by what title to address you—you are very dear to me. embrace the dear Mar-

Conjectured Portrait of John Ledyard Made for Judge John Aiken of Greenfield, Massachusetts, Sometime before 1927 by an Unknown Artist. From a Copy in the Baker Library of Dartmouth College.

Милостивый государь мой Григорий Алексеевич!

С сим явится к вам американской Георгии уроженец Ледиард, следующий из С.-П.-бурга через здешния места в Америку для приобретения себе в натуральной истории вящих опытов знания и открытия. Он человек довольно изрядной и намерение его клонится натуральною к тому, чтобы совокупиться ему с известною морскою северною Экспедициею; а посему я и прошу вас по-прежнему его г-на Ледиарда принять столько можно благосклоннее, и во всех его желаниях оказывать возможным образом должные вспоможения ваши равномерно и доставить его в помянутую Экспедицию без малейшего промедления. За сим имею быть с истинным моим почтением.

Вашего милостивого государя моего

покорный слуга

Иван Якобий

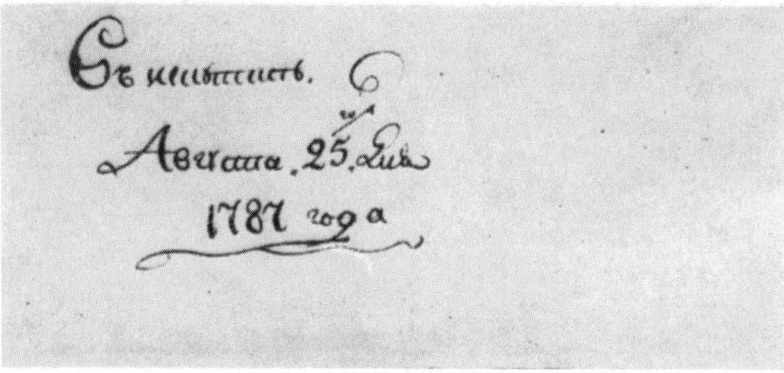

Governor-General Iakobi's Letter of Introduction for Ledyard to the Commandant at Yakutsk. From a Manuscript, Dated August 25, 1787, at Irkutsk, in the Sparks Collection No. 112, Houghton Library, Harvard University.

Ledyard's Signature. From a Letter to Thomas Jefferson Dated November 25, 1786, at London.

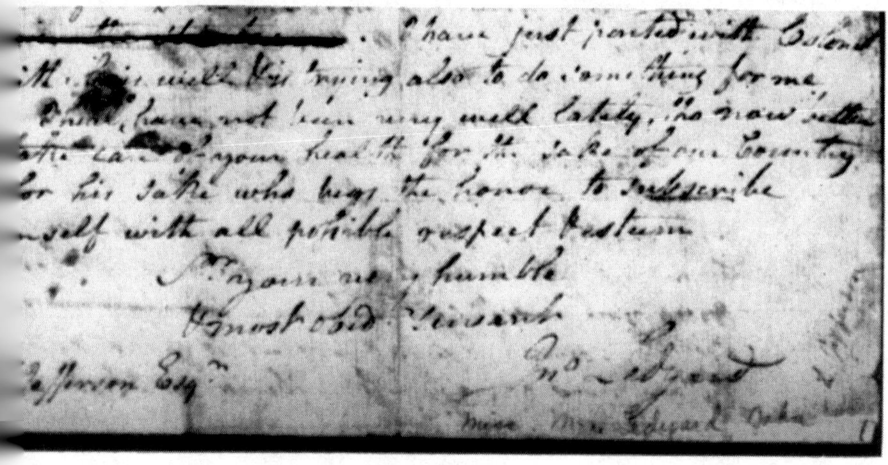

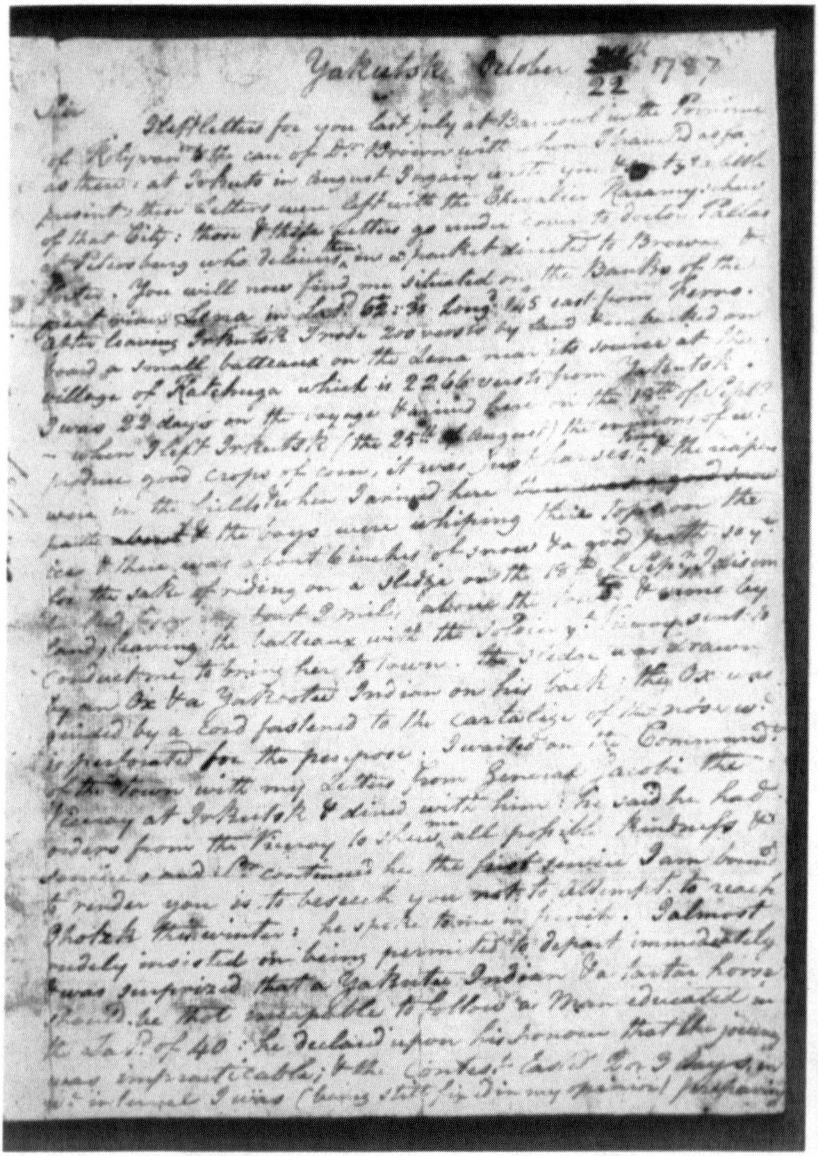

Ledyard's Letter to William Smith, from Yakutsk Dated October 22, 1787, first page.

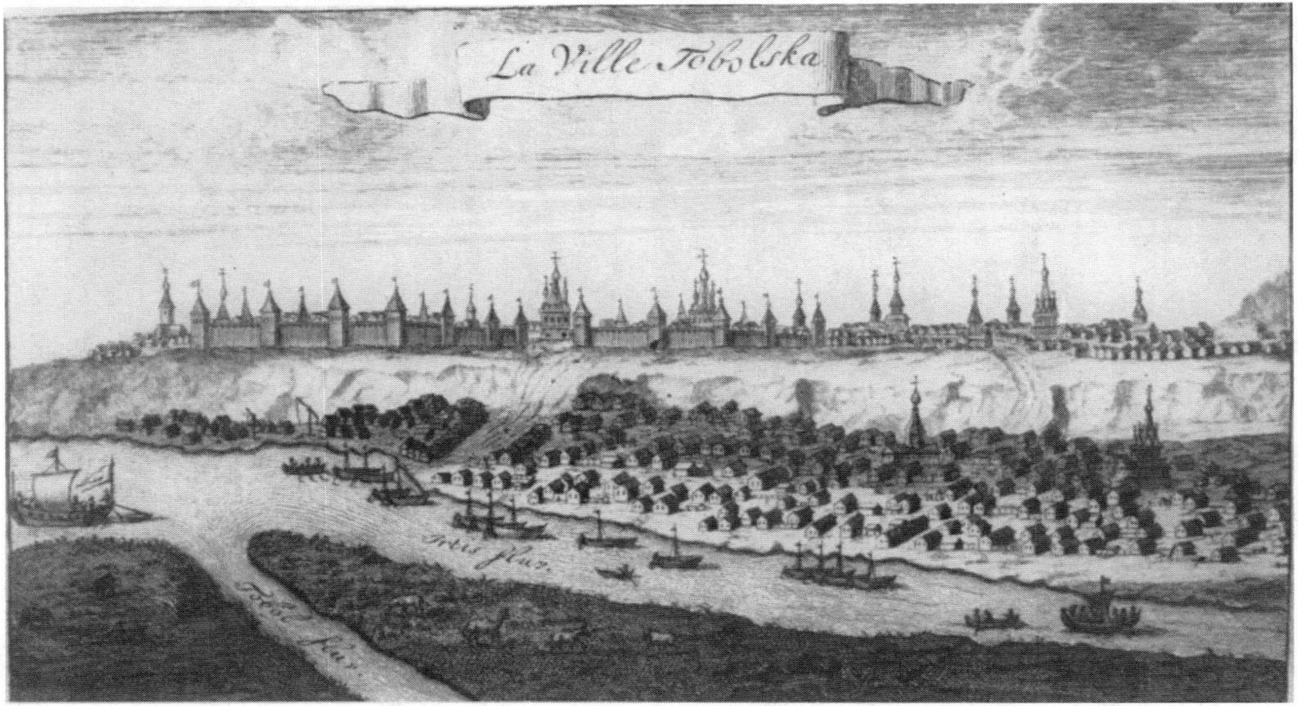

View of Tobolsk, Early Eighteenth Century. From Cornelius de Bruyn, *Voyages de Corneille le Brun*, Amsterdam, 1718.

Siberian Natives Hunting Reindeer. From Cornelius de Bruyn, *Voyages de Corneille le Brun,* Amsterdam, 1718.

Tungus Encampment near Okhotsk. From Martin Sauer, *An Account of a Geographical and Astronomical Expedition,* London, 1802.

View of Yakutsk, Early Eighteenth Century. From Nicholaas Witsen, *Noord en Oost Tartaryen*, Vol. 2, Amsterdam, 1785.

Tungus Man and Woman in their Summer Dress. From G. A. Sarytschew, *Account of a Voyage*, London,

Tattooed Chukchi Woman. From Martin Sauer, *An Account of a Geographical and Astronomical Expedi-*

quis la Fayette for me: he has all the virtues of his country without any of its little foibles. I am indeed a very plain Man, but do not think that mountains or oceans shall oppose my passage to[1] glory while I have such friends in remembrance—I have pledged myself—difficulties have intervened—my heart is on fire—ye stimulate, & I shall gain the victory. Thus I think of you—thus I have thought of you daily—& thus I shall think of you.[2] After all the fair prospects that attended me when I last wrote—I still am persecuted—still the slave of accident & the son of care. The Ship I embarked in was seized by the Custom house & is this day exchequered. If a small subscription now begun in London by Sr Joseph Banks & Doct^r^ Hunter[3] will enable me to proceed you will probably hear from me at Hamburgh: if I arive at Petersbourg you most certainly will. You see the course I was purs[u]ing to fame reverted & I am now going across Siberia as I had once before intended from Paris this time twelve month—what a twelve months! I do defy fortune to be more malicious during another. I fear my subscription will be small: it adds to my anxiety to reach those dominions where I shall not want money—I do not mean the dominions that may be beyond death: I shall never wish to die while you the Marquis & Mr Barclay are alive:—pray S^r^ if that dear & genuine friend of mine is any where near you do me the honour to present me sur mes genoux devant lui—j'adore son coeur genereux. May I beg to be[4] presented to Mr Short, to Commodore Jones & to Col^o^ Franks[5] if with you:[6] I have just parted with Colonel Smith: he is well & is trying also to do something for me.

I hear y^o^ have not been very well lately, tho now better—take care of your health for the sake of our Country & for his sake who begs the honor to subscribe himself with all possible respect & esteem

S^r^ your very humble
& most obed^t^ servant
Jno Ledyard

Thos Jefferson Esqr

NYHS (original). Recorded in Jefferson's Summary Journal of Letters as received December 20, 1786.

1. "to" is repeated in the MS.

2. A passage which begins here has been crossed out: "untill it ceases to be a virtue to think—with regard to myself this cannot be the case while either of you exist."

3. Dr. John Hunter (1728–93), well-known English anatomist and surgeon. The subscription is printed here as # 20.

4. "be" is repeated in the MS.

5. Lt. Col. David S. Franks had been sent by the United States government to negotiate with the sultan of Morocco; en route he stayed in Paris from October 1785 to mid-January 1786. Thomas Barclay, the American consul general in Paris, accompanied him to Morocco.

6. A passage which follows here has been crossed out in the MS: "a present je pense comme lui de la gouvernement de cet pays ici—tout est un cabal meme dans leur rues—heureusment pour moi j'entend bien a don[ner] des coups du poins, & have litteraly been obliged to thrash 5 or 6 of those haughty turbulent & very insolent people: one of them at the theatre where I assure you one is still more liable to insult than in the streets even."

19. Ledyard to Isaac Ledyard

London Nov 1786

To Monecca

I am still the Slave of Fortune and the son of care: you will be surprized that I am yet in London unless you conclude with me that after what has happened nothing can be surprizing. I think my last Letter informed you that I was absolutely embarked on board a Ship in the Thames bound to the N.W. Coast of America from whence I intended to cross that Continent to New York: this will inform you that I have disembarked from said Ship on account of her having been unfortunately siezed by the Customhouse & eventually exchequered and that I am obliged in consequence to alter my route & in short, every thing—all my little Baggage shield Buckler lance Dogs—Squire & all gone—. I only left—left to what—to some damned riddle I'll warrant you—or at all events will not warrant any thing else—My heart is rather too much troubled at this moment to write you as I ought to do

I am going in a few days to make the Tour of the Globe on foot from London east. am here without funds or friends sufficient for the purpose—may in a few days want Bread—or may lie on the road to Fame or may be d——d to Fame—am thinking of myself at times—of you am writing my friends in France brush my own Coat clean my own Boots. am a Deserter in this Country. dine with Sir this & Sir that on board a Ship one moment in a proud insolent stiff English Tavern the next—Boxing some Puppy at the Theatre a la mode d'anglais—in the museum and the Lord knows where. Excuse therefore the manner in which I write—if you cannot call me mad—say I am thus—but that I love thee do this—& doing it say we love him also. and then what ever may betide Josephus he will pass it by as the necessary alloy to perfect happiness, that the Good must meet—but not regard—.

London Decr 1786

I shall Embark in two or three days for Hamburg—have just receved my passport as an American Citizen to the courts of Petersburg Moscow Tobolskoi, Jenenskoi Obriskoi Bolcheretskoi, Kamschatka, Nootka Origon Naudowessie Chippeway[1] &c—farewell.—I shall make Colonel Smith, Secretary to an Embassy here, the medium of information between us—he desires it. and to be presented to you & your Brother as good old friends I dare not write you any more: to introduce you to the real State of my affairs would confound you. farewell fortitude—Adieu.

JOSEPHUS

JLP (transcript).

1. "Naudowessie" refers to the Nadowessioux Indians of the Dakota plains, popularly called the Sioux; "Chippeway" probably refers to the Chippewa Indians or River, then called the Chipoway, or possibly to the Chipewyan Indians of the Athabasca region of northern Canada.

20. Subscription for Ledyard's Journey to North America

done at London
Novem^r^ 1786.

We the subscribers have given the several sums annexed to our names as testimonies of our approbation of the Enterprize they are given to promote & the character of Mr Ledyard who undertakes it. The Enterprize is to cross the continent of north America from Nootka to New York, to be done either by sailing from

London to Nootka or by passing east from London to Petersbourg Moscow Kamchatka & thence across the northern pacific ocean to Nootka from New York to London.[1] One of the two tours by the blessing of providence Mr Ledyard will commence as soon as the subscription will enable him & if in his power will most certainly perform. Mr Ledyard engages to preserve this writing as a public testimony of the assistance he received in London & by whom he was assisted, & he hopes that his own conduct & still much more that the discoveries he may make will reflect some honour on those who may please to Assist him.

Mr Ledyard has public & private Letters as Vouchers for his character which he will with pleasure exhibit to those gentlemen who may think themselves sufficiently interested to require it.

Jos: Banks	£5 - 5 - 0
Jno Walsh Esqr	1 - 1 - 0
Mr Seward	1 - 1 - 0

W.. S.. *Smith* wishing Mr Ledyard not to confine himself to the particular views of any Gentlemen in England and that he should not be under the necessity of reporting to them the discoveries he may make in America will make such advances of Cash as will enable him to move upon principles of economy free from those shackles which they appear disposed to confine him with—
£ .. - .. - .. -

Copy to one of the same tenor in the hands of S^{r} J Banks & another in the hands of Mr John Hunter

Novr 1786. London
Mr Ledyard's
Subscription

NYHS (original).

1. Ledyard's English patrons apparently expected him to return to England and give them an account of his travels. On this see Smith's addendum to the subscription, a paragraph in different handwriting and blacker ink.

21. Ledyard to Smith

Hamburg Decr 20th 1786

To W. S. Smith Esqr

Sir

I am here with ten guineas exactly I am in perfect health, one of my Dogs is no more. I lost him on my passage up the River Elbe in a Snow storm I was out in it forty hours in an open Boat. My other faithful companion is under the Table I write upon. I dined to day (having just come to town) with Madam Parish Lady to the Gentleman I mentioned to you:[1] it is a Scotch house of the first commercial distinction here. The Scotch are very capable of a Refinement in manners, and have by Nature a Majesty of person and dignity of Sentiment that renders them very accomplished. I could go to Heaven with Madam Parish but she had some Englishmen at her Table that I could not go to Heaven with—I cannot submit to a haughty eccentricity of manners so prevalent among the English. They have millions of Virtues but damn their vices, they are enormous. My fate has sent me to the Tavern where Major Langburne was three weeks: [2] he is now at Copenhagen, left his Baggage here to be sent on to him.—by some Mistake he has not Received it and has written the master of the Hotel on the Subject. I shall see his Letter as soon as the Master comes in. I shall write him and give him my address at Petersburgh. I should wish to see him at all events, but to have him accompany me in my voyage would be a Pleasure indeed. I happened to be speaking of going to Petersburg and the Landlord told me "a Gentleman—a very good kind of man and an odd kind of man who had travelled much had lately left him for that Place, took only a Shirt in his Pocket and always went on foot, had been in America in Paris in London &c &c" It immediately struck me it must be Major Langburne; and upon enquiry I am sure it is he. He came here from New Castle but the Landlord says he spells his name Laburne—I have not yet seen his Letter—it is Langburne! I read his Letter this evening in three days from Copenhagen has not I am afraid nor ever will see his Baggage again took only one Shirt with him complains exceedingly of the awkwardness of his situation: he says it makes People suspicious of him. Whether he left money in his trunk or Papers necessary to negociate Bills I cannot say. but he intimates a want of money from the want of his Trunk. I will fly to him with my little all and some clothes and lay them at his feet at the moment I may be useful to him: he is my Countryman, a Gentleman a Traveller he may go with me on my voyage. if he does I am blessed if not I merit his attention and am not much out of my way to Petersburg I dined to day with the ingenious Doct Ross, Physician to the English Hamburg Company and a Stiff rumped Calvanistical Chaplain and his mummy of a Wife a pair of very Self Sufficient Stiff Scotch-Germans—but I have happily been compensated by an hour with Madam Parish. You See I take a Sup from the cup of pleasure on the Road. I wish I had established a little Fame and Fortune that I might take some larger draught and even be intoxicated without Danger—to be as happy as Nature intended I should be—I go to deserve it—Adieu. My compliments to your happy Lady[3] I have the honor to be—

LEDYARD—

JLP (transcript).

1. Mr. Parish, of the mercantile house of Parish and Thomson.

2. Maj. William Langborn, Virginian traveler, in July had been in London, where he had dined as a guest of the American Minister, John Adams. Smith had later spoken of him to Ledyard.

3. Smith had married Abigail Amelia Adams, daughter of the United States Minister to England, John Adams, in June 1786.

22. Ledyard to Smith

Copenh[a]gen Janu'y 5th 1787

To WILLIAM S. SMITH ESQR

Sir I hope this will reach you soon and be some apology for my drawing on you so soon in favour of Messrs Parrish & Thompson and for adding one Guinea to the Sum: Charge it to Heaven for by ——— it was an act of Necessity in me and one of Charity in you to accept of it that on your part perhaps can never happen & on mine never shall happen again. Never more will I trouble you. —if I write you after this it will be to compensate you for your friendship to me by something in the History of my Travels worthy of your attention. I shall be at Petersburg before you read this. Thomson's Goodness to me in accepting the Bill on you relying wholly on my honor has saved me from Perdition and will enable me to reach Petersburg comfortably tho' a march of a thousand miles and upwards. I must go higher up the Gulf of Bothnia than Stockholm in order to cross the ice into the Gulf of Finland. I must inform you that Major Langburne is here and that the Embarrassments I have laboured under proceeded from my coming here to meet him and from supposing that he would from what you said to me of him undertake the Tour with me. He will not. We have lived together here with the Strictest friendship—he was here two Months without his Trunk and consequently embarrassed for the time in his finances—We talked of you and I told him of my Draught on you but he would not permit me to say any thing of him to you then and does not know that I do so now—he will write you when it suits his humor which tho good and like other peoples when applied to others yet left to himself is very Singular. I see in him the Soldier (which predominates). the Countryman and the generous friend but he would hang me if he knew I had written a word to you about him and so I will say no more than just inform you that he means to wander this Winter through Norway Swedish Lapland and Sweden and in the Spring to visit Petersburg. I asked to attend him through his Route to Petersburgh—no—I esteem you but I can travel in the manner I do with no man on Earth—

Adieu! I have the honor
to be most faithfully your
humble & obed[t] Servt
JNO LEDYARD

JLP (transcript).

23. Ledyard to Jefferson

St Petersbourg March 19th 1787

Sir

It will be one of the remaining pleasures of my life to thank you for the many instances of your friendship to me & wherever I am to pursue you incessantly with the tale of my gratitude

If Mr Barclay should be at Paris let him rank with you as my next friend: I hardly know how to estimate the goodness of the Marquis la Fayette to me—but I think a french nobleman of the first character in his country never did more to serve an obscure citizen of another than the Marquis has done for me: & I am as sure that it is impossible (without some kind of soul made express for the purpose) that an obscure citizen in such a situation can be more gratefull than I am: may he be told so & with my Compliments to his Lady: my Compliments wait on Mr Short, Commodore Jones & Col° Franks if at Paris—with thanks for their favours also. If I was sure Mr Barclay was at Paris I would write him, for no man less acquainted with him esteems him more than I do, believing verily that of such as him consisteth the Kingdom of heaven. I cannot tell you by what means I came to Petersbourg, & hardly know by what means I shall quit it in the further prossecution of my tour round the world by Land: if I have any merit in the affair it is perseverence, for most severely have I been buffeted—& yet still am I even more obstinate than before—& fate as obstinate continues her assaults how the matter will terminate I know not: the most probable Conjecture is that I shall succeed, & be kicked round the world as I have hitherto been from England thro Denmark, thro Sweeden, thro Sweedish lapland, Sweedish finland & the most unfrequented parts of Russian finland to this Aurora Borealis of a City. I cannot give you a history of myself since I saw you, or since I wrote you last: however abridged, it would be too long: upon the whole, mankind have used me well, & tho I have as yet reached only the first stage of my journey I feel myself much indebted to that urbanity which I always thought more general than many think it to be, & was it not for the villianous laws &

bad examples of some Governments I have passed thro I am persuaded that I should have been able to have given y^o still better accounts of our fellow creatures.

But I am hastning to those countries where goodness if natural to the human heart will appear independant of example & furnish an Annecdote of the character of man not unworthy the attention of him who wrote the declaration of American Independence.

I did not hear of the death of Monsieur de Vergenes untill I arived here—permit me to express my regret at the loss of so great a man & of so good a Man. Permit me also to congratulate you as the Minister of my Country on account of the additional commercial privileges granted by france to America & to send you my ardent wishes that the friendly spirit which dictated them may last forever: I was extremely pleased at reading this account, & to heighten the satisfaction I felt I found the name of la Fayette there.[1] There was a report a few days ago of which I have heard nothing since, that the french ships under the Command [of] Capt Lapereux had arived at Kamchatka.[2] There is an equipment now on foot here for that ocean & it is first to *visit* the NW Coast of America: it is to consist of four ships.[3] This & the equipment that went from here 12 months since by land to Kamchatka[4] are to cooperate in a design of some sort in the northern pacific Ocean—the lord knows what—nor does it matter what with me—nor need it with you, or any other Minister or any Potentate southward of 50° of Latitude. I can only say that you are in no danger of having the luxurious repose of your charming climates disturbed by a second incursion of either Goth Vandal Hun or Scythian. I dined to day with Doct^r Pallas Professor of Natural history &c &c—an accomplished Sweed: my friend: has been all thro European & Asiatic Russia:[5] I find the little french I have of infinite service to me: I could not do without it: it is a most extraordinary language: I believe that wolves rocks, woods & snow understand it, for I have addressed them in it & they have all been very complaisant to me: but I dined in a shirt that I had worn *four* days—I have but *two:* & I suppose when I write you next I shall have none.

We had a Scythian at table that belongs to the royal society of Physicians here: the moment the savage knew me & my designs he became my friend & it will be by his generous assistance joined with that of Doct^r Pallas that I shall be able to procure a *royal passport* without which I cannot stir: but this must be done th[r]o the application of the *french* Minister (there being no American one here) & to whose secretary I shall apply with Dr Pallas to morrow: & beg liberty to make use of your name & the Marquis la fayettes as to my character. As all my Letters of recommendation have been English & as I have been hitherto used[6] by them with the greatest kindness & respect I first applied to the English Embassy: but with^t success: the ostensible apology was that the present political moment between England & Russia would make it disagreeable for the English minister to ask any favour:[7] but I saw the reason—the true reason in the specula of the secretarys eye—& so damn his eyes—which in this case particularly I concieve to be polite language: I hate ill nature & pity a fool.

Sir I have waited on the Secretary of the french embassy who will dispatch my Letter with one of his accompanying it to the Count Segur to morrow morning. I will endeavour to write you again before I leave Petersbourg & give you some further accounts of myself—In the meantime I wish you health. I have wrote a very short Letter to the Marquis. Adieu!

I have the honor to be with respect & friendship
Sr Your much obliged
& most ob^t
& most hbl Servt
LEDYARD

His Excellency
Thomas Jefferson Esqr

NYHS (original). Addressed: To his Excellency/ Thomas Jefferson Esquire/ Minister Plenipotentiary from the/ United States of America to the Court/ of Versailles—/ Paris. Recorded in Jefferson's Summary Journal of Letters (*PTJ*, 11:218) as received on May 25, 1787, at Bordeaux.

1. Regulation of American trade with France was concluded on October 22, 1786, by Jefferson and Calonne, the comptroller-general of finance;

Lafayette was instrumental in bringing about French approval of the conditions proposed by Jefferson.

2. The naval expedition of Jean-François de Galaup, Count de la Pérouse (1741–88), actually did not stop at Petropavlovsk until September 1787. See de Lesseps, *Travels in Kamtschatka,* 1:5.

3. According to Bezborodko's and Vorontsov's plan of December 1786 (see above, p. 52), the squadron of naval vessels under Captain Mulovskii, to be sent from the Baltic to the Pacific Ocean, was to be divided there, two of the vessels proceeding to the American coast, the other two to the Kuriles. The outbreak of war with Turkey, and later with Sweden, compelled Catherine to cancel this military expedition.

4. Billings' expedition, which had left St. Petersburg in October 1785.

5. Ledyard is referring to the travels of the German-born Pallas through Russia and Siberia in 1767–74. "Sweed" is an error.

6. "used" is repeated in the MS.

7. The British envoy extraordinary at this time was Alleyne Fitzherbert (1753–1839), who was then with the court in the Crimea. Anglo-Russian relations at this time were beginning to deteriorate; Catherine was annoyed at Britain's support of the Fürstenbund, which was directed against her ally, Joseph II of Austria.

24. Ledyard to Smith

Petersburg May 15—1787.

Sir

You & I had both concieved wrong notions about traveling in this Country, & there is only a possibility of doing it as either of us supposed: there is no country in Europe or Asia (leaving out of consideration the extent of a tour) so difficult to pass through as this & the difficulty arises from the manners & dispositions of the inhabitants: excuse me if I explain myself to you only by saying that if the inhabitants were all Sweeds (for instance) I could eat drink sleep & travel at my *ease,* or if you please in the manner we each concieved of when I saw you in London—.

—but they are not Sweeds. I shall *ride* full 4000 english miles in company with a young Scotch physician, & after I leave him 7 or 800 miles on the river Lena & then the lord knows how for about 300 miles more to Ohotsk in Kamchatka—I write you this because it goes by water to London & because I am determined you shall hear from me *to the last.* I would be circumstantial in this Letter, but my spirits are bad: my heart is ill:—it is oppressed: I think too severely: my designs are generous—why is my fate otherwise: the Comte de Segur has not yet sent my passport: but this shall not stop me. I shall surmount all things, & at least deserve success. There are 4 American Ships here & 4 more expected: you see by this that I am not the only American of enterprize[1]

There is no particular news here & I am too angry with the Country to write any thing of its political affairs I had however a visit this afternoon from a Russian officer a great favourite in the family of the Grand Duke: a friend of mine/ & will tell you a little of our chat—that is exactly 10 words "Sir we pay no attention to any thing but *eclat.*" He was in the Country with the Grand Duke when he rec^{d} a billet of mine—about 25 miles from town[2] & came on purpose to see me—this was polite & friendly—he is more, he is a *thinking* Russian.

The best of all is that I am likely to obtain a passport by his means of the Chancellor:[3] if so I set out immediately.

I know not what kind of a winter I shall have of it in Kamchatka—but if able shall write you. My Compliments to your Lady—

farewell Yours always

J. LEDYARD

NYHS (original). Addressed: His Exc^{y} Mr Adams's/ Grosvenor Square/ W. S. Smith Esquire/ Secretary to the American Embassy/ London. Sender: Petersburg May 15th 1787. Ledyard—

1. Four ships from Salem alone visited St. Petersburg in 1787; American ships usually brought tea, coffee, and sugar, and carried back such Russian exports as hemp, shipcloth, and iron.

2. This was Grand Duke Paul's palace at Gatchina, 28 miles southwest of St. Petersburg. The fact that Ledyard ultimately gained his passport through a member of Grand Duke Paul's entourage may have been more than accidental. Paul and his party were always bitterly opposed to Empress Catherine and all her policies. Catherine's decision to arrest Ledyard may even have been influenced by this connection with the Gatchina group.

3. Probably Count Ivan Osterman.

25. Jefferson to John Banister, Jr.

Paris June 19. 1787.

. . . I had a letter from Lediard lately dated at St. Petersburg. He had but two shirts, and yet more shirts than shillings. Still he was determined to obtain the palm of being the first circumambulator of the earth. He sais that having no money they kick him from place to place and thus he expects to be kicked round the globe. . . .

. . . .

TH: JEFFERSON

PTJ, 11:476–77. Press copy in LC. John Banister (1734–88) was a Virginia landowner and grandson of the eminent botanist of the same name. He had been in Paris when Ledyard was there.

26. Ledyard to Jefferson

Town of Barnowl[1] in Siberia July 29th 1787

Sir you will find this town by the Russian charts situated in about the Lat[d] 52°: & Long[d] 100: it is near the town of Kolyvan & in the province of Kolyvan: the residence of the Governor of the province: it is near the silver mines & has a foundery in it w[e] produces anualy 650 poods of silver bullion besides some gold—a pood is 36 pounds english: it is also situated near the salt lakes w[e] produces more to the revenue than the mines: I am 4539 versts from petersburg & have 4950 versts to go before I arive at Ohotsk, & if I go to Peter & Paul[2] in Kamchatka I have 1065 versts more to go before I see that Ocean which I hope will bear me on its boosom to the coast of America; how I have come thus far & how I am still to go farther is an enigma that I must disclose to you on some happier occasion. I shall never be able without seeing you in person & perhaps not even then to inform you how universaly & circumstantialy the Tartars resemble the aborigines of America: they are the same people—the most antient, & most numerous of any other, & had not a small sea divided them, they would all have still been known by the *same name*. The cloak of civilization sits as ill upon them as our American tartars—they have been a long time Tartars & it will be a long time before they are any other kind of people. I shall send this Letter to Petersburg to the care of Doctor Pallas Professor, of the royal Academy president, & historyographer to the Admiralty: I hope he will transmit it to you together with one to the Marquis in the Mail of the count de Segur. I hope y° & your friends & mine enjoy as much good health as I do which is of the purest kind—but notwithstanding all the vigour of my body—my mind keeps the start of me & anticipates my future fate with the most sublimated ardour [[It is certainly Pity it is that in such a career one should be subjected like a horse to the beggarly impediments of sleep & hunger]]—

The Banks of the large Rivers in this country every where abound with some thing curious in the fossil world. I have found the leg-bone of a very large animal on the banks of the Oby & have sent it to Dr Pallas & told him to render me an acct of it hereafter—it is either the Elephant or Rinoceros bone, for the latter Animal has also been in this Country: there is a compleat head of one in a high state of preservation at Petersburg.[3] I am a curiosity myself in this country: those who have heard of America flock round me to see me: unfortunately the marks on my hands procures me & my Countrymen the appelation of wild men. Among the better sort we are somewhat more known: the Governor & his family get a peep at the history of our existance thro the medium of a Septennial pamphlet of some kind.[4] We have however two Stars that shine even in the Galaxy of Barnowl, & the healths of Dr Franklin & of Genl Washington have been drank in compliment to me at the Governors table: I am treated with great hospitality here—hitherto I have fared comfortably when I could make a port any where—but when totaly in the Country I have been a little incommoded: hospitality however I have found as universal as the face of Man

When you read this—perhaps 2 mo[n]ths before you do If I do well I shall be at Ohotsk where I will do myself the honour to trouble you again & if possible will write more at large

If Mr Barclay should be with you I pray you present me to him —my compliments wait on all my Parisian friends—remember that I am & always shall be with the highest esteem & gratitude

Sr yr much obliged
most obt hbl Servt
LEDYARD

NYHS (original).

1. Barnaul.

2. Petropavlosk, originally named after Bering's two ships, *Peter* and *Paul.*

3. According to Pennant, "An entire Rhinoceros was found buried in a bank of a Siberian river, in the antient frozen soil, with the skin, tendons, and some of the flesh in the highest preservation. . . . as an evidence, the complete head is now preserved in the Museum at Petersburg: the body was discovered in 1772, in the sandy banks of the Vitim, a river falling into the Lena below Jakutsk . . ." (*A History of Quadrupeds,* 1:141).

4. In his letter to Smith of Aug. 20, 1787 (# 27), Ledyard describes this pamphlet as an English gazette. It could have been *The British Gazette, The English Review,* or the *Sunday London Gazette,* all published during the 1780's. A weekly publication may have been misinterpreted as "septennial."

27. Ledyard to Smith

Irkutsk August 20th 1787

To William S Smith Esqr

Sir. Pray receive my compliments of friendship & present them to your Lady also. I am on the wings and can only say how d'ye to any of my friends at present, the principal reason of this extreme haste is that I fear being overtaken by the winter before my arrival on the Borders of the Pacific Ocean, for I have 1000 versts to go where there is no road at the best season of the year, but in Autumn impassible, unless on foot, and without a guide which is an inconvenience too great not to be avoided when in my power. You and I were extremely uninformed, in Our conversation together at London of this Country. With my finances I never should have been able to have passed through it on foot. Yet as I have travelled it I am here and shall arrive at Kamskatka comfortably situated in that respect. At this place I am in a circle as gay, rich, polite, and as scientific, as if at Petersburg I drink my French and Spanish wines: and have Majors Colonels, and Brigadiers, by Brigades, to wait on me in the town, and disciples of Linnaeus to accompany me in my philosophic walks.[1] In Rusia I am treated as an American with politeness & respect and on my account the healths of Dr Franklin and General Washington have been drunk at the tables of two Governors: and at Irkutsk the name of Adams has found its Way. Among the middling Class of People, I am a kind of Phenomenon, among the peasantry a right down wizard. The first characters know very little of our History, except the military part of it and that they have had thro' the medium of some Septennial English Gazette

I am now about two-thirds of my Asiatic voyage; 6271 versts from Petersburgh or 4704½ miles English. You will find the City I write from near the South part of the great Lake Baikal on the banks of the great River Angam[2] which has its Source from the Baikal. From here I shall go 200 Versts by land and then embark in a Batteau on the River Lena—the largest in this vast Empire

I continue my voyage on the Lena 2266 versts to the City of Yakutsk which you will find situated on its banks to the northward: from thence if I am not too late, I shall ride "a la mode des Tatars["] thro' a wilderness of about 1000 versts to Ohotsk, which is the end of my journey here: If I am too late I know not how I Shall go—as no post goes after Snow falls—at least very seldom: I suppose either on a Sledge drawn by dogs or rein-deer I am told so; here As for going on foot, it is ridiculous in this Country. It has been to this moment a source of misfortunes to me that I did not begin to ride post from Hamburg. I have footed it at a great expence besides the Loss of my Baggage, which I severely feel this instant Never did I adopt an Idea so fatal to my happiness, it is I hope nearly past however.

If you have opportunity remember me to Dr Ledyard at New York, and he will inform my other friends where I am—Farewell

I am with esteem & friendship. Your much Obliged,
and most Obed^t humble Servt

LEDYARD—

Col Smith

JLP (transcript).

1. Ledyard is speaking of Aleksandr Matveevich Karamyshev (d. 1791), subsequently referred to in the Forman transcript as "Karamyscherff." Karamyshev wrote a dissertation on Siberian plants in 1766 under the guidance of Linnaeus at the University of Uppsala. He taught chemistry and metallurgy at the St. Petersburg Mining Institute from 1773 to 1779, and in 1779 he became a correspondent of the St. Petersburg Academy of

Sciences. That same year he became director of the bank in Irkutsk and held that position until 1789. Karamyshev was active in the local literary and intellectual circles of Irkutsk during his residence there.

2. The Angara River.

28. Ivan Vartholomeevich Iakobi to Grigorii Alekseevich Marklovskii

Milostivyi gosudar' moi Grigoreiu Aleksieevich!

S *sim* iavitsia u vas amerikanskoi "dvorianin" dzhon lediard slieduvshchii iz S:P:burga chrez zdieshniia miesta k Ameriku dlia priobrieteniia sebie s naturalnoi istorii vovsiekh *onykh* znaniia i sviedeniia. On cheloviek dopol'no izriadnoi i namierenie ego *klonitsia* na takoi konets chtoby sovokupit'sia emu s izviestnoiu morskoiu sekretnoiu ekspeditsiiu;[1] a po semu ia i proshu vas pokorno ego G^na^ Lediarda priniat' koliko mozhno *blagosklonnee,* i vovsiekh ego *zhelaniakh okazyvat'* vozhmozhnym obrazom nuzhnye *vspomozheniia* kak ravnomierno i dostavit' ego v pomianutuiu Ekspeditsiiu bez malieishago promiedleniia. Za tiem chest' imieiu byt' s istinnym moim k vam pochteniem.

Vash milostivago Gosudaria moego
Pokornyi Sluga
IVAN IAKOBI

S irkutskie
Avgusta "25" dnia
1787 goda

TRANSLATION:

My dear Grigorii Alekseevich!

With this letter the American "gentleman" John Ledyard comes to you traveling from St. Petersburg through this country to America for the acquisition of knowledge and information about natural history in all its departments. He is a pretty good man and his intention inclines toward joining up with a certain secret naval expedition;[1] and for this reason I request you humbly to receive Mr. Ledyard with as much favor as possible, and in all his desires uniformly to render him assistance in every possible way and to deliver him to the above-mentioned Expedition without the slightest delay. For this favor I am genuinely indebted to you.

My dear Sir I am
Your humble servant
IVAN IAKOBI

From Irkutsk
August 25
1787

Transliteration from the original MS in Cyrillic script, in Jared Sparks MS No. 112, HL (original). The manuscript was given to Sparks in 1822 by P. I. Poletika, Russian Minister to the United States from 1817 to 1822. Poletika wrote to Sparks that this was a letter of introduction given to the American citizen, John Ledyard, by the governor-general of Siberia, John Jacobi, dated Irkutsk, August 25, 1787. The person to whom the letter was directed is indicated only by the first two names; Sarychev and de Lesseps give the last name of the Yakutsk commandant as Marklovskii. *Puteshestvie po severo-vostochnoi chasti Sibiri*, p. 92, and *Travels in Kamtschatka*, 2:318, respectively.

1. Although by this Iakobi meant Billings' expedition, Marklovskii may have interpreted it as a secret foreign expedition in the North Pacific.

29. Itinerary from Kachuga to Yakutsk

Marche route de Katschuga à Jakoutzk.

		Werst
1.	Katschuga. [Kachuga][1]	
2.	Werkolensk. [Verkholensk]	x 29.
3.	Tumenskoi. [Tiumentseva]	x 24.
4.	Korkin. [Korkino]	x 16.
5.	Pirogowa.	x 20.
6.	Davydowska.	x 26.
7.	Toutourskoi. [Tutura]	x 14.
8.	Sschigalowskoi. [Zhigalovo]	x 10.
9.	Oust Uga. [Ust' Ilga]	x 30.
10.	Grousnowskaja. [Gruznovka]	x 24.

			Werst
11.	Botowskoi.		x 24.
12.	Golaja. [Golovskoe]		x 26.
13.	Diadino.		x 31.
14.	Basowa. [Basova]	o[2]	x 20.
15.	Orlenga.		21.
16.	Tarasowskaia. [Tarasova]		14.
17.	Skobnina. [Skoknina]		22.
18.	Boiarskaia. [Boiarsk]		20.
19.	Amalaëwskaia.		23.
20.	Riga.	o	17.
21.	Touroutzkoi. [Turuka]		34.
22.	Ouskut. [Ust' Kut]		15.
23.	Jakourim.		18.
24.	Podymakino.	o	28.
25.	Taura.		30.
26.	Nasorowskoi. [Nazarovo]		40.
27.	Kira.	o	34.
28.	Oulkan. [Ul' Kan]		8.
29.	Potapowsko.		32.
30.	Panskaia.		20.
31.	Zaborie.		20.
32.	Polorotow.		24.
33.	La ville *Kirenga.* [Kirensk]	o	7.
34.	Alexeewskaia. [Alekseevsk]		24.
35.	Podkamennoë. [Podkamenka]		15.
36.	Tschetschoui. [Chechuisk]		20.
37.	Weschniakowa.		15.
38.	Sposchnaia. [Sposhino]		20.
39.	Ilinskoi. [Il'inskaia]	o	25.
40.	Dariinskaia.		20.
41.	Itschora. [Ichëra]		30.
42.	Dawydowskaia.		16.
43.	Korschounowa. [Korshunovo]		15.
44.	Tschastinskoi.	o	41.
45.	Doubrowa. [Dubrovskoe]		37.

			Werst
46.	Kourilskoi. [Kureiskaia]		29.
47.	Parschino. [Parshino]		40.
48.	Tschui. [Chuia]	o	47.
49.	Witim new horizon appears. [Vitim]		21.
50.	Peledoui. [Peledui]		27.
51.	Kritow.[3]		27.
52.	Jalowskoi.		27.
53.	Kamrinskoi. [Khamra]	o	50.
54.	Konkinskoi.	o	27.
55.	*Mochtouinskoi.[4] [Mukhtuia]		48.
56.	Mougourii.	o	25.
57.	Soldicoulia.		40.
58.	Nuiskoi. [Niuia]		30.
59.	Cherba.		30.
60.	Ouschakan, ou Kamennoi ostrow.	o	35.
61.	Sschadaï. [Zhedai]		25.
62.	Matsche. [Macha]		30.
63.	Karabtschibi.		50.
64.	Delguei.	o	33.
65.	Nelena.		33.
66.	Tscherendoui. [Cherendei]		25.
67.	Bersinka. [Biriuk]		38.
68.	La ville *Olekma.* [Olekminsk]	o	32.
69.	Zalenka. [Solianka]		25.
70.	Namana.		44.
71.	Karabalyk.		44.
72.	Katyn-Toumoul.		44.
73.	Marka. [Markha]		22.
74.	Zanaëktak. [Sangyiakhtakh]		42.
75.	Malikan.		37.
76.	Isik. [Isit']		35.
77.	Sschoura. [Krytyl-Zhura]		34.
78.	Onmouran.		25.
79.	Tschinewo.		30.
80.	Batamaï		27.
81.	Kitora.		22.

	Werst
82. Toën-naryn.	42.
83. Bestatskaia. [Bestiakh]	27.
84. Oulakanskoi $_x$. [Ulakhan]	34.
85. Tabaguinskoi. [Shabaga]	33.
86. La ville Jakoutzk.	22.
de Katschuga jusq'Jakoutzk	2357
By land to the river[5]	230
total dist. from Irkutsk by water to Yakutsk	2587

NYHS (original).

1. The modern equivalents are in brackets.
2. "o" may indicate where Ledyard stopped to procure supplies. It does not indicate overnight stops, for at Kirensk, according to the journal, the stop was in the daytime. "x" may represent Ledyard's marking of places passed at the beginning of the trip.
3. Here the words "half way" are written in with pencil.
4. Mochtouinskoi is the last entry on the first page of the MS. Underneath it in Ledyard's hand are the interesting words: at y[r] last stage y[e] Mon ran away/—inform y[e] Gov[r].
5. The English is in Ledyard's handwriting.

30. Jefferson to Charles Thomson

Paris Sep. 20. 1787.

. . . There is an American of the name of Ledyard, he who was with Capt. Cook on his last voiage and wrote an account of that voiage, who is gone to Petersburg, from thence he was to go to Kamschatka, to cross over thence to the Northwest coast of America, and to penetrate through the main continent to our side of it. He is a person of ingenuity and information. Unfortunately he has too much imagination. However, if he escapes safely, he will give us new, various, and useful information. I had a letter from him dated last March, when he was about to leave St. Petersburgh on his way to Kamschatka.

. . . .

Th: Jefferson

PTJ, 12:159–60. Press copy and recipient copy are in LC. Charles Thomson (1729–1824) was secretary of the Continental Congress.

31. Ledyard to Smith

Yakutsk October 22 1787

Sir

I left letters for you last july at Barnowl in the Province of Kolyvan in the care of Dr Brown with whom I traveled as far as there: at Irkuts[k] in August I again wrote you & sent y° a little present; these Letters were left with the Chevalier Karamyschew of that City: those & these Letters go under cover to doctor Pallas at Petersburg who delivers them in a packet directed to Browne & Porter. You will now find me situated on the Banks of the great river Lena in Lat^{d} 62°: 30″ Long^{d} 145° east from Ferro.[1] After leaving Irkutsk I rode 200 versts by land & embarked on board a small batteaux on the Lena near its source at the village of Katchuga which is 2266 versts from Yakutsk.[2] I was 22 days on the voyage & arived here on the 18th of Sept^{r}—when I left Irkutsk (the 25th of August) the environs of w^{c} produce good crops of corn, it was just harvest time & the reapers were in the fields & when I arived here the boys were whip[p]ing their tops on the ice & there was about 6 inches of snow & a good path so y^{t} for the sake of riding on a sledge on the 18th of Sept^{r}, I disembarked from my boat 2 miles above the town & came by land, leaving the batteaux with the Soldier ye Viceroy sent to conduct me to bring here to town. the sledge was drawn by an Ox & a Yakootee Indian on his back: the Ox was guided by a cord fastened to the cartalige of the nose w^{c} is perforated for the purpose. I waited on the Command^{t} of the town[3] with my Letters from General Jacobi the Viceroy at Irkutsk[4] & dined with him: he said he had orders from the Viceroy to shew me all possible kindness & service; and S^{r} continued he the first service I am bound to render you is to beseech you not to attempt to reach Ohotzk this winter: he spoke to me in french. I almost rudely insisted on being permited to depart immediately & was surprized that a Yakutee Indian & a tartar horse should be thot incapable to follow a Man educated in the Lat[d] of 40: he declared upon his honour that the journey was impracticable; & the contest lasted 2 or 3 days, in w[c] interval I was (being still fixed in my opinion) preparing for the journey by taking some rest after a *very* fatiging passage on the Lena in w[c] I took the severest cold I ever had. The Commandant at length waited on me & brot with him a Trader (a very good respectable looking Man of 50) who had for 9 or 12 years uniformly passed from & to Ohotzk here as a witness of the truth & propriety of his advice to me: I was obliged however severely I lamented the misfortune to surrender to two such advocates for my happiness: the Trader held out to me all the horrors of the winter here & of the severity of y[e] journey in the best season, & y[e] Command[t] the goodness of his house & the society here all of which would be at my service.

The difficulty of y[e] journey I was aware of: when I consented to the impracticability of it, it was a compliment for I do not believe it so to a European & hardly any thing else—it is certainly bad in theory to suppose that the seasons can triumph over the efforts of an honest man.

The proffered hospitality of the Commandant I had a good opinion of because in Russia in general & particularly in Siberia it is the fashion to be hospitable: it is brobable [*sic*] also that it is a natural principle. I should however have said less to them about the matter if I had not been naked for want of cloaths & with only a guinea & ¼ in my purse—& in a place where every necessary of life is dearer than in Europe & clothing of any kind still dearer by the same comparison: and besides the people here of all descriptions as far as they are able live in all the excess of asiatic luxury joined also with such european excesses as have migrated hither: add to all this that they are universaly & extremely ignorant & averse to every species of sentimental enjoyment, & I will declare that I never was so totaly at loss how to accommodate myself to my situation. The only consolation I have of the argumentative kind is to reflect that him who travels for information must be supposed to want it, & tho a little enigmatical it is I think equaly true that to be traveling is to be in error: that this must more or less necessarily anticede the other, and that an error in judgement only, is always to be forgiven. I shall be able by being here 8 months to make my observations much more extensive with respect to the Country & its inhabitants than if I had passed immediately thro it & that also is a satisfaction. I have already made myself tolerably acquainted with that of the Buretti, Bratskoi, Calmuc or Mongul tartars[5] who are & have been since the time of Zingis-Chan[6] the most warlike & most numerous of any no[r]thern tartars: those in the province of Irkutsk that pay tribute (Men only) am^{t} to 49764 & 5000 horsemen who pay no tax. I am now among the Yakutee & Tonguse nations, the next most considerable Tribes: the Yakutee am^{t} to 42956, & the Tonguse to 13264:[7] these were driven hither from the fronteirs of China by the Calmucs & have more of the Chinese manners, particularly the Yakutee than any other tribe. The tout en semble is a feast to me at all times. I cannot say that my voyage on the Lena has furnished me with any thing new—& yet no traveller ever passed by scenes that more constantly engage the heart & the imagination & yet I suppose y^{t} no two disinterested philosophers would think alike about them: two painters & two poets would be much more likely to act in unison. There are however some circumstances that are not unworthy of philosophical enquiry & when I am by the side of a philosopher I will talk with him about it: the River Lena at Katchuga is forty yards wide: here it is 5 english miles over but not so wide by 2 miles above & I believe not below Yakutsk: it is but very ind[i]fferent for navigation from here towards Irkutsk. There is in some mountains near the Lena large salt mines that constantly afford a supply to all the adjacent country: it is a pure solid transparent mineral salt found in veins: the peicies that I have seen here with the Commandant are 6 & 9 inches square: when pulverized for the table it is much the most delicate salt I ever saw: of a perfict white: & an agreeable taste: but I imagine not so strong by ⅓ as our West Indian salt. there are also upon the banks of this river & indeed all over this country great quantities of elephants bones:[8]

there are here with the Commandant some teeth of y[t] animal larger than any that I saw in the royal Museum at Petersburg & are as sound as they ever were—The Com[dt] has the hafts of knives, spoons & a variety of other things made from them & they equal any ivory I ever saw from Africa: if I can I will send you a spemicen[9] of this fine bone, & the salt also. Indeed I want to send you many things: but it is an embarrassing circumstance when one has correspondents among the antipodes, & tho no man could shew more kindness or render more service to a traveller than doctor Pallas has to me yet I am reserved in asking them upon all occasions. poor Brown & Porter too: I wonder their patience is not exhausted: it has been as thoroughly tryed as yours was while I was at Petersbourg. The fact is I am a bankrupt to the world but I hope it will consider well the occasion of my being such: I believe it will: my English creditors are the most numerous & I have great consolation on that account because they think & act with such heavenly propriety: in most parts of the world & as much in Russia as any where, & in Siberia more so it is the Custom not to think at all: in this case it is difficult to liquidate rationaly a reciept & expenditure of three dinners & a bow—for the same reason when I left france my accounts were not closed & from y[t] day to this I know not whether I owe france or france me, but here at Yakutsk it will be infinitely worse; & without any violence to the metaphor, or pedantic affectation, I declare to you that to leave Yakutsk with respectability & to reach Ohotsk alive will be to pass a Scilly & Charibdis that I have never yet encountered. both you & I my friends had formed at London very wrong opinions of the equipment necessary to pass thro this country & particularly of the manner of traveling: it has been the source of *all* my troubles: they have been many; & I have done wrong to feel them so severely: I owe the world some services which I shall make great efforts to perform—any efforts that do not render me realy miserable— —& they shall be my judges; & you my dear S[r] shall be president. farewell! Make my best compliments to my friends &

tell them I have a heart as big as S[t] Pauls church in such service as theirs.—I have the honor to be—

LEDYARD

NYHS (original).

1. Ferro: westernmost island in the Canary group.

2. According to Sauer's reckoning, the distance from Kachuga to Yakutsk was 2,390 versts, and from Irkutsk to Kachuga, 230 versts. See *Account of a Geographical and Astronomical Expedition,* Appendix III.

3. Grigorii Alekseevich Marklovskii.

4. Ivan Vartholomeevich Iakobi (1726–1803) was then governor-general of Irkutsk and Kolyvan provinces (i.e. Eastern Siberia). The one of these letters known to have survived is printed here as doc. # 28.

5. In other words, the Buryat (Latin: Buretti; 18th-century Russian: Bratskoi), Kalmyk, and Mongol Tartars.

6. Genghis Khan (1162?–1227).

7. For comparison with the 1783 population figures see p. 56n.

8. Bones of the mammoth.

9. "specimen."

32. Catherine II to Grimm

Ce 26 novembre 1787.

. . . .

. . . Vous avez eu tort, ne vous en déplaise, de rayer de mes comptes la très petite dépense de l'Américain le Dijar;[1] au reste, il est très juste que vous ayez votre pension au même taux que tous ceux qui sont hors du pays. Pour ce qui regarde le Dijar, ce qui fait trouvaille pour les autres, ne le fait pas toujours pour nous, vu la différence des langues, des moeurs et des usages; j'ai vu de ces trouvailles que personne ne comprenait et qui nous devenaient inutiles. . . .

. . . .

"Pis'ma Imperatritsy," *Sbornik imperatorskago russkago istoricheskago obshchestva,* 23 (1878):424. For a partial translation and explication see p. 45.

1. "Le Dijar": Ledyard.

33. Professor P. S. Pallas to Sir Joseph Banks

Dear Sir,

I have the pleasure to send you hereinclosed some Letters from M[r] Ledyard, the American traveller, received last week from

Sibiria. I am very glad the recommendations I gave him for Irkutsk have been so essentially useful to him, as to procure him a free & speedy passage to Ochotsk, which, I was very much in doubt, would not be allowed. He left Irkutsk in August, being sent from the Governor as Messenger, to make him pass without expence, all the way from Irkutsk to the Ocean, in the same manner as we dispatched him from hence with one Dr. Browne, to Kolyvan. I wish he may farther succeed & give good accounts of the unknown parts of the American Continent.

. . . .

Your
most obed[t] & much
obliged humble Serv[t]
P. S. PALLAS

S. Petersburgh
18/29 Dec. 1787
[postscript omitted]

Additional Manuscripts Collection, 8097, folios 106, 106b: BM (original).

The Siberian Journal
June 1787–April 1788

BEGINNING OF THE JOURNAL FROM THE FORMAN TRANSCRIPT

1788.—

Journal of his Travels thro' Siberia, to the Pacific Ocean, in his attempt to circumnambulate the Globe—

June 1st 1787} After having been three months in Petersburg, I left it in company with Mr William Brown physician, who was going as far as the Province of Kolyvan to reside.—From Petersburgh to Moscow, we rode post, and arrived there the 6th. The last day's ride, overtook the Grand Duke & his Retinue: who were going to Moscow to meet the Empress, on her arrival from Cherson.[1]

Habitka travelling is the remains of the Caravan travelling—it is your only home—it is like a Ship at Sea. On the 8th we left

1. Catherine reached Moscow on June 27 from her Crimean trip. She was not to arrive in St. Petersburg until July 22.

Moscow with hired horses and a driver, who is to carry us to Kazan and drive three horses for 34 Roubles—The distance from Moscow to Kazan is 735 versts about 550 English miles. We arrived all well at Kazan—began here first to feel the want of houses of entertainment.

Description of Kazan[2]

The interior parts of Continents, as well as of Islands, are the highest. Their *Lakes* give rise, & their height, force to Rivers. Having staid about a week at Kazan, we set off for Tobolsk.

On the 11th of July arrived at Tobolsk.[3] The country between this and Tobolsk, about 50 versts and which formerly belonged to the Poles,[4] must be poor indeed, if judged of by the wretched appearance of its inhabitants: this, in a greater or less degree, is observable generally of those places which are so unhappy as to be the frontiers between nations.—

Like step-children are they. The practice of burying among trees is hitherto uniform through the Country I have passed. Having staid at Tobolsk three days we set off for the town of Barnowl, the capital of Kolyvan, where we arrived the 23[d] of July.

General Observations, and most remarkable Occurrences, before arriving at *Barnowl.*

The face of the Country from Petersburgh to Kolivan, is one continued plain. The country before arriving at Kazan, is very well cultivated, afterwards cultivation gradually decreases. Before arriving at Kazan in many places, and particularly near a

2. The transcriber made the following insertion at this point: "{Blanks were left here as in many other places in these Journals to be filled up when conveniency and leisure would permit: but as this did not happen to be the case, we are left only to lament such probably important deficiencies]."

3. Tobolsk, which contained 2,300 houses in 1786, was reduced to ashes the next year. See Sauer, *Account of a Geographical and Astronomical Expedition*, p. 7.

4. If we assume that Ledyard is speaking of the land between Kazan and Tobolsk, it is obviously incorrect that this land formerly belonged to the Poles. Until the mid-16th century this territory, from Kazan eastward, remained in the hands of the Kazan Tartars; then it became Muscovite.

town called Waldivia,[5] we saw large mounds of earth of 10, 20, 30, 40 feet elevation: which I conjectured, and on enquiry found to be ancient Sepulchres.[6] There is Analogy between those, our own graves, and egyptian pyramids; but an exact similarity with those piles, supposed to be of monumental earth, found among some of the Tribes of North America.*[7]

The first Tartars we saw was before our arrival at Kazan.[8] Their dress, the large cap &c—

See little Journal,[9] Saw a woman with her nails painted, like the Co[c]hin Chinese, red. Notwithstanding the modern introduction of Linen into Russia, the garments of the peasantry still retain not only the form, but manner of ornamenting them when they wore skins. This resembles the Ornamenting of the Tartars: & this is but a modification of the *Wampum* ornamenting, that is still discernable westward from Russia to Denmark thro' the Finlands, Laplands, and Swedes. The nice Gradation by which I pass from Civilization to Incivilization appears in every thing: their manners, their dress, their Language, and particularly that remarkable & important circumstance of *Colour* which I am now fully convinced originates from natural Causes; and is the effect of external and local circumstances. I think the same of *Feature*. I see here the large mouth, the thick lip, and broad flat nose as well as in Africa—and the same village of Tartars. I see also in the same village as great a difference of Complexion—from the

5. Possibly the town then called Vasiliursk, situated on the Volga between Nizhni Novgorod and Kazan. It might also have been Vladimir.

6. These are the remarkable burial mounds or barrows (Russian: *kurgany*) built by nomads, at times reaching 45–60 feet in height. This form of burial among the nomads extended from the Copper and Bronze ages up to the 18th century. The rich grave goods these barrows often contained made them especially subject to plunder; Ledyard mentions an example under the date August 3, below.

7. Here the asterisk in the transcript refers to a footnote: "*See Jefferson's Notes on Virginia" (Thomas Jefferson, *Notes on the State of Virginia*, New York, 1964, pp. 93–96).

8. These Volga Tartars, inhabiting the region around Kazan, were among the few native peoples he observed who actually went by the name of Tartar.

9. "(This is lost)" has been inserted here.

fair hair, fair skin, and white eyes, to the olive, the black jetty hair and eyes: and these all of the same Language, same dress, and I suppose same tribe. I have frequently observed in Russian villages—obscured, and dirty, mean and poor, that the women of the peasantry paint their faces profusely both red and white. I have had occasion from this, and many other circumstances I shall mention to suppose that the Russians are a People, who have been very early attached to *Luxury*. They are every where fond of *Eclat*. The Contour of their manners is Asiatic and not European I ascribe also their disposition to thieving to the Same cause. The Tartars universally neater than the Russians, particularly in their houses.

The Tartar however situated is a voluptuary: and it is an Original and striking trait in their Character from the Grand Signor to him who pitches his tent, on the wild frontiers of Russia & China, that they deviate less from the pursuit & enjoyment of real sensual pleasure, than any other people. The Emperor of Germany—the Kings of England and of France have pursuits that give an entire different turn to their enjoyments—& so have their respective Subjects—Would a Tartar live on *Vive le Roi?* would he spend ten years in constructing a Watch? or twenty in forming a Telescope? In the United States of America as in Russia we have made our efforts to convert our Tartars to think and act like us, but to what effect? Among us Sampson Occum*[10] was pushed the farthest within the pales: but just as the Sanguine Divine who brot. him there was about to canonize him—he fled and sought his own heaven in the Bosom of his native forests: In Russia they have had none so distinguished. They[11] are generally footmen or lacquies of some other kind.

The Marquis de la Fayette had a young American Tartar of

10. The asterisk in the text refers to the following footnote: "*This Indian visited England sometime before the Revolutionary War in America where he preached to numerous & once or twice to royal hearers." Samson Occom (1723–92) was trained by Eleazar Wheelock, "the Sanguine Divine," at Dartmouth College.

11. "They" is repeated in the transcript.

the Onandaga Tribe who came to see him, and the Marquis at great expence equipped him in rich Indian dresses—After staying some time he did as Occum did.[12] When I was at School at Mount Ida†[13] there were many Indians there: most of whom gave some hopes of Civilizing: and some were sent forth to preach, but as far as I observed myself and have been since informed they all, like the ungained Sow returned to the mire

Diary from Barnowl, and from thence towards Ohotsk. Arrived at Barnowl on Friday the 23rd of July and billetted at the House of the Treasurer—Treated with great Hospitality: but obliged to sleep in my Cloak on the Floor, as I have done ever since I left Petersburgh. On Saturday dined with the Governor (See the other Journal) On Monday Tuseday and Wednesday dined with two old discharged officers (Colonels) who at their own request have quitted the Service, and constituted Judges and Justices of the *Law*. On Tuseday evening we quitted the house where we billeted and went to hired rooms—miserable they are: But it was fortunate for us: for the same night the house we left, with twenty four others, in the same Street were burnt to the ground. Our Host was a good hospitable creature; and sent word to us next morning of the disaster. Doct^r B went—found him very merry—Three hours after I met him in the Street bawling out Ivan! Ivan! without a hat & very drunk—I had no body to give consolation to

—Distances according to the Russian Almanac,

from Petersburg to Barnowl — Versts	4539
Barnowl to Irkutsk - - - - - - - do	1732
Irkutsk to Yakutsk - - - - - - - do	2266
Yakutsk to Ohotsk - - - - - - - do	952
Total distance from Petersburg to Ohotsk - -	9489

12. This was a twelve-year-old Onandaga boy named Kayenlaha, whom Lafayette brought with him when he returned to France from America in January 1785.

13. The dagger in the transcript refers to the footnote: "†Dartmouth College."

From Ohotsk to the Bay Awatka in Kamschatka[14]

1065 + 9489 = 10554—

Distance come - -	4539	10,554 Versts equal
Do - to - go - - -	4950	7916 miles English

Thursday 29th. dined with the Governor. Saw the Armorial Bearings of forty two Provinces in this Empire—informed that the Salt produced by the Salt Lakes in this province affords some what more to the Revenue than the mines: the Governor says also that this province sends more to the Revenue than any other: estimate the value of 650 poods (36 English pounds to each pood) of Silver Bullion.

Suppose the produce of the Salt-works equal to that sum: tho' the Governor says more—then allow for the Gold extracted from the Bullion about ——— poods and you have pretty nearly the Sum total of the Revenue of this province. This without filling up the Blank for the gold extracted in the process of fining the Silver would be a[15] very large Sum even for so vast a province as Kolivan: The Governor must therefore mean it for the whole product of the province. With respect to Longitudinal distance I want only 100 English Miles easting to be in the Centre of this part of the Continent reckoning from Petersburg to Ohotsk. And if I count from the Western Coast of Norway to the Eastern Coast of Kamschatka somewhat more In this Central situation between the Atlantic and Pacific Oceans. I find the Climate is very hot. and must at times be subject to furious gales of wind: which in many places (some I have passed) tears up by the roots, or breaks down the trees for nine or ten miles in extent I am told here that if a fall of Snow is accompanied by one of those Gales of Wind nothing can oppose its fury—And that it often buries the Traveller in drifts of Snow: and where often he is lost. This town is situated on the Banks of the Oby: and by the Russian Charts in Lat 52 and odd Long 100 east from the Russ

14. Avacha Bay. By Ledyard's calculations a verst equaled three-quarters of an English mile, instead of two-thirds.
15. "a" is repeated in the transcript.

Meridian (which is the Island of Ferro).[16] The mornings here are exceedingly hot: a serene cloudless sky—and a dead Calm.—After the Meridian,[17] have a little air which increases by gentle degrees, towards evening, and continues thro' the night until Sunrise the next morning—I am told that it seldom rains here—

30th July dined with the Governors son in Law—saw his little Cabinet—a piece of curiously petrified wood and a great variety of minerals. Doct^r^ Pallas says this piece of petrified wood is a Tropical production.—[18]

31st At home preparing to recommence my journey this evening. At nine OClock waited on the Governor with my passport. —He was well pleased with it, gave me a Co[r]poral to conduct the affairs of the Mail; told me I had nothing to do but sit in my Kabitka; and mustered up French enough to say "Monsieur, Je vous souhaite un bon voyage" I took an affectionate farewell of the worthy Dr Brown, and left Barnowl.

On Tuseday the 3^d^ of August, I arrived at the town of Tomsk. at 6 in the morning, 407 versts from Barnowl: this is upwards of 300 English miles, & was travelled in two days, and three nights. Tomsk, stands near the banks of a good river, to which it gives name: This river is about the size of the Irtis where I crossed it; and is the first river I have met with since leaving Petersburg which had a gravelly bottom or shore.[19] Its appearance in other respects is like the other large rivers in this Country: It has many times changed its bed—formed Islands and left them. and formed banks and left them. I find near its banks those little mounds of earth, which I at first supposed, but now know to have been the dwelling places of those who inhabited it before the time of the Russians: these were the Bratskoi or the Calmucs. Some of these hillocks have been dug into and laid open—I

16. Barnaul is situated at lat. 53° N. and long. 84° E. from Greenwich. Ferro lies at long. 18° W.

17. By "Meridian" here Ledyard of course meant mid-day.

18. Presumably Pallas had informed the governor's son-in-law of this fact while on his Siberian expedition.

19. This is the Tom River. The Irtysh River, situated to the west of Tomsk on the other side of the Baraba steppe, flows through the town of Omsk, through which Ledyard must have passed on his way to Barnaul.

suppose by some former traveller. I find the nights very cold: I have not felt the like in any Country I have yet seen where it was as hot by day. From Barnowl here those hard winds I have before mentioned have done still greater damage—and must have blown with greater violence: since they have not only blown down trees but have broken down & destroyed whole fields of Corn also—Since leaving—*Barnowl* a sudden alteration has taken place in the manners of the peasantry—They are like the people at Barnowl very hospitable; and it is very rare that I can prevail on them to take any thing for what I eat and drink, and when they do it is inconceivably trifling. I had yesterday as much good barley soup, onions, quass,[20] bread & milk, as served me and the co[r]poral for *one Kopeek* and the woman would not take more. Elephants Teeth do not seem very rare here or regarded much as curiosities. I saw two to-day lying in the Streets—

Wednesday 4th of August } Went last evening to see the Commandant of the Town who kept me to sup with him, and kept me drinking strong Liquors until 1. OClock and departed quite fuddled: but did not think myself so much so as I really was. I never was so ill after a debauch as I have been to-day. The Commandant is 73 years; add to this that he is a Frenchman, and I never saw any of that nation drink like him. He has been 25 years in Siberia 30 odd in Russia: and from France—and is now a healthy man. He has forgotten a great deal of his native language, speaks it very imperfectly, and writes it still worse. Saw the Shoulder Blade of an Elephant at his house—. His name is Tomas, born in the Rue de Grennel in Paris[21]—spoke much of his birth and family.—I asked him if the town or its environs afforded any thing curious in natural History: his answer was that there were in it,—thieves, liars, rascals, whores, rogues, and villains of every discription. W[h]ether he meant these as natural curiosities I did not ask him—I was convinced however that he

20. Kvass: common Russian beverage prepared from rye bread and malt.

21. Both Fries, in 1776, and de Lesseps, in 1788, testified that the name of this governor was Villeneuve. Fries stated that he was born in Montpellier. Thomas was perhaps his first name. See Kirchner, *Eine Reise durch Sibirien*, p. 75; de Lesseps, *Travels in Kamtschatka*, 2:367.

was one himself. He lives expensively and has a considerable fortune. Took a walk towards evening and bathed in the fine river Tomsk,—feel better after it—.

Thursday, 5th of August. It seems that I am detain[ed] for the arrival of the *mail* from Tobolsk. I find the Russians very charitable to their poor.

In the house where I lodge, who are pretty wealthy people: their is every morning 10, or 12 farthing pieces of money laid in the window for the charitable purposes of the day. Early in the morning the Beggars begin their rounds and go formally from house to house, and very rarely go away without something. Those who do not give money give bread. First come the Slaves in Irons, and then others: if the money first deposited in the window is gone they put more there. They never ask any questions of the Beggars but give indiscriminately and without grudging. The demand is uniformly made "pour L'amour de Dieu"—for which one may have more in this Country than any I have seen.

Irkutsk August 15th 1786[22]—I arrived here Sunday the 15th and presented myself and the Corporal at the Levee of the Govr &c &c.

Observations on the road from Tomsk—

General face of the Country. open and pretty well cultivated. Approaching the river Yennessee at the town of Krastnyack, and on the banks of the Yinnessee I first find the real craggy peaked high hill or mountain.[23] Krastnyack is beautifully situated on the Banks of the Yennessy, is about the size of Tomsk Tobolsk and Barnowl.[24] The Commandant is a Prussian. I eat and drank with him, he was drunk. By information here the Yennessy is 260 feet deep, and 3000 and some perches wide.[25]

22. The transcript shows 1787 changed to 1786.

23. This is the town of Krasnoyarsk on the Yenisei River. The craggy peaks are of the Eastern Sayan Range.

24. Krasnoyarsk at the end of the 18th century had a population of about 2,000 inhabitants.

25. A perch is 5½ yards, or one rod. Thus by Ledyard's calculations the Yenisei would be about ten miles wide. It is this large only at its mouth.

It is a fine stream runs opposite the town 5 knots—gravelly bottom. From this river all the rest to Irkutsk run swifter by 2, 3, and 4 knots than the western ones. From Barnowl here I have ferried over 10 good navigable rivers, and some smaller ones From Petersburgh here 25 rivers all running north

I am now just about two-thirds of my distance from Petersburgh to Ohotsk. I shall have [crossed] 37 large navigable rivers, every one of which except the Wolga discharge themselves in the northern Ocean—Allowing the rivers between here and Ohotsk to be as wide as those I have passed: and those average half a mile in breadth, and eight fathoms in depth: and there will be a column of Water 18½ miles breadth, and 296 fathoms deep, constantly flowing into the Northern Ocean—Allow that where those rivers disembogue themselves into the Ocean they are only as wide, and as deep again: then I have a column of Water 37 miles in breadth, and 592 fathoms in depth. But considering the difference of distance from the Sea, where these rivers were crossed; all of them[26] a great way from it, and some of them near their sources:—this ground of calculation is too vague to be much relied on. Taking the account of the Officer at Krastniack as a leading data of computation, it would very much enlarge the idea of these rivers: tho he could not make me understand him, what part of the Yennessy he meant, as being 3000 Archuns (about 3 miles english) wide and above 80 fathoms deep: but even suppose he meant at its arrival at Ocean (which is not [at] all probable) yet considering that many other rivers, as the Oby, Kolyma, Tobolsk, Kama, &c are nearly of the same size; and the Lena and some others larger than the Yennessy: and the unusual depth of their beds generally here: and then allowing 37 [miles of column] in all, supposes a vast quantity of water indeed moving in this direction: and must be the cause of the great quantity of Ice about the Pole. An estimate on this data, reducing the whole to one body as above would make it about a hundred miles broad and about 3000 fathoms deep. Tho' this ground for calculation must be allowed to be as vague as the other: yet both

26. "all of them" is repeated in the transcript.

together, enable the reader to conceive of a very great flux to the Ocean, and the ingenious *observer* to form his opinion on the above hypothesis.—Passing on east from the Yennessy to Irkutsk the Country is thinly peopled. A very few and those, miserable houses are to be seen on the road, and none at all from it. The Country is hilly, rough, and mountainious and covered with thick forests, and that which I have passed on the road now disappears.

Yennessy is the first stony road I have met with. The rivers here also have rocky beds and are rapid in a degree from 3 to 5 miles per hour.

The autumnal rains are now begun, and they set in severely. I have passed some of the Calmucs, who are married with the Russians—I staid at quarters all day, and took some rest after a very fatiguing route—rendered so by several very disagreeable circumstances—going with the Courier, and driving with wild tartar horses at a most rapid rate over a wild and ragged Country.—breaking and upsetting Kabitkas—beswarmed by Musquetoes—all the way hard rains and when I arrived at Irkutsk I was, and had been the last 48 hours wet thro' and thro'—and one complete mass of mud—delivered my letter to Mr Directeur of the Barque,[27] who waits on me to morrow.—

Monday 16th August. I have not been out this morning, but I shrewdly suspect by what I see from my poor little talc window that I shall *even here* find all the fashionable follies—the cruel ridiculous extravagance, and ruinous *eclat* of Petersburg.—

I have been out, and find my suspicions well founded—Dined with a Brigadier, Colonel, and Major, a little out of town—Germans—had at the table a French Exile who had been an Adjutant. Not a day passes scarcely but an exile of some sort arrives here There are in this town at present 150. The most of the Inhabitants, and particularly of this remote part of Siberia, are

27. A mistake in the transcript for Banque. Ledyard must have had a letter of introduction to Karamyshev (director of the bank) written by Pallas (see #33). This would account for Karamyshev's hospitality to Ledyard so soon after his arrival in Irkutsk.

convicts. I find that the worst idea I had formed of the Country, and its Inhabitants does not require correction. This Country originally inhabited by the great Mongul or Calmuc Tartars who are I conclude the same people. No fruit will grow here any more than at Tobolsk—Cold by Reaumers Ther' sometimes at 30 degrees[28]—Find no account about the Calumet. The French Exile had been at Quebec and thinks the Tartars here much inferior to the American Indians both in their understandings and persons. I find the Tonguse to be the Tribe who have not the Mongul and Calmuc faces: but moderately long, and considerably like the European face. These form the second class of Tartars; so apparently distinguished by their feautures from other Tartars and from Europeans What I call the third class, are the lighteyed and fair complexioned Tartars which I believe include the Cossacs

The Ischutskoi are the only northern Tartars that remain unsubjugated to the Government.[29] The Lake Baikal 60 versts from here is 800 versts long and 400 wide surrounded by high cragged mountains: has a ragged bottom: and among its few fish, is the Chien de la Mer.[30] Town of Irkutsk is the residence of a Viceroy (Jacobi) a General, and has in it two Battalions of infantry—has 2000 poor Log houses and 10 Churches.[31]—to think of the rascality of this place.—10 kopeeks for shaving me. Jacobi commands from here to the Pacific Ocean—an immense Country. There are no volcanoes in this Country. Waited this morning on the Director of the Bank Mr: Karamyscherff—find he was a pupil of Linnæus—He is very assiduous to oblige me in everything: Sent for three Calmucs in the dress of their Country—nothing particu-

28. By the thermometer scale invented around 1730 by the French scientist Réaumur, −30° would equal −35° Fahrenheit; water boils at 80° R.

29. The Chukchi, who live in the extreme northeastern corner of Siberia, during the 18th century resisted the Russian tribute system. They maintained their independence in many respects until well into the 20th century.

30. The "chien de la mer" or "sea dog," as Steller called it, was actually the seal. Among the few fish found in Lake Baikal are sturgeon; various kinds of salmon; the *omuly*, which are not unlike herring; and the unique *golomianki*, which somewhat resemble northern pike and are found only here.

31. For Sauer's description of Irkutsk see p. 72 above.

larly curious about them: but their pipes which are coarsely made of copper, by themselves *the form altogether Chinese.* Information from Karamyscherff, the Mongul and Calmuc Tartars the *same people* From his house I went with the Consillier d'etat,[32] who introduced me to Monsieur Jacobi the Viceroy; he is an old venerable man; and tho I believe like Pallas he is "an homme de Bois,"[33] yet he received me standing and uncovered. Our conversation was merely respecting my going with the Post, which he granted me and besides that told me I should [be] particularly well accomodated—wished me a good and successful voyage,—and that my travels might be productive of information to mankind. Spoke to him in french thro the interpretation of the Consellor who informed [me] as follows "The white Tartars you saw about Kazan are natives of that country, and we call them Kazan Tartars. Kazan was once a kingdom of theirs. From here to Yakutsk you pass among the Calmucs At Yakutsk you see the Yakutsk[34] and also the Tonguse who are more personable than the Calmucs or Monguls and more sensible: but the Yakutsk are more sensible than either They are indeed a people of good natural parts and genius: and by experience are found capable of any kind of learning. From Yakutsk to Ohotsk you pass through the Tonguse all the way to Ohotsk. In the time of Zinghis Khan the Tergiss and Thibet Tartars[35]—viz—Calmucs or Moguls made incursions into this Country—We have 200:000 Russians: and as near as we can estimate, half the number of Indians of all discriptions in this Province. Marriages, in and near the villages take place between the Russians and the Tartars—but they are not frequent I believe the extreme cold and want of snow here[36] during winter, and the sudden change of weather in the summer season to be the reason, why we cant have any fruit here. We

32. "Conseiller d'état" (*statskii sovietnik*): a civil servant in the fifth class of the Table of Ranks.

33. Ledyard perhaps meant a man unaffected by social etiquette, i.e. "a man of the woods."

34. "Yakuts."

35. Kirgiz and Tibetans.

36. "and want of snow here" is repeated in the transcript.

have often here in the months of May and June ice, three and four inches thick: Besides this Country as you have observed is subject to terrible gales of wind, which blows away both bud & blossom. We have nevertheless a few little Apples about the size of a Buck-shot, which we eat at our tables, and they are not without flavour"—thus much the Counseller. Trees of all kinds in this Country are generally rotten in the heart: they are almost altogether Birch.—No Lava about the Baikal—But some of it scattered about in different parts of the Country. Mr Karamyscherff tells me there are many Bones of the Rhinoceros in this Country: and also the same large bones that are found on the banks of the Ohio in America.[37] It seems that the places to find those and other curious fossils is at the mouths of the great rivers yennesy Lena &c among Islands that are formed in their different mouths. Here they all are lodged that are washed from underground thro' the different Countries which those Rivers traverse. Irkutsk situated on the River Angam[38] which is a Mongul Word. 16th—To day it seems the Jubilee (on account of the Empress having reigned 25 years) is observed.[39]—In coming from Karamyscherff's I met the Governor and his suit of Officers.

The Brigadier I dined with yesterday &c to the amount of 200 Officers all going to dine with the Viceroy who on the Occasion *keeps open house.* The Governor and all saluted me as they [passed]: those who did not know me wondering what could procure me such attention to one so poorly and oddly attired. I was pressed by some of the company to go and dine. If I had good clothes I would have gone—but I will dine with Karamyscherff—Dined with Mr Karamyscherff, it is a Tartar name and he is of tartarian extraction: Saw in his Garden an Apple tree, and he gave me specimens of the fruit, and the size is that

37. Ledyard must have read the following observation of Pennant concerning the rhinoceros: "An animal only known in a fossil state, and that but partially; from the teeth, some of the jaw-bones, the thigh-bones, and *vertebrae,* found with many others five or six feet beneath the surface, on the banks of the *Ohio,* not remote from the river Miame . . ." (*History of Quadrupeds,* 1:160).

38. The Angara.

39. Empress Catherine II was crowned on June 28, 1762.

of a full sized pea in France and England. It is the true and real apple and their Naturalists distinguish it by the name of Pyrus Ranata. These are the only apples in Siberia those are found only in the environs of Irkutsk. Karamyscherff says that the Yakutsky tartars are the *veritables tartars*, by which I understand a people less mixed with other tartars than any other—their language he says is the *oldest langu[a]ge* and that all the other Tartars understand it.[40] They in this respect resemble the Cherokees in America.[41] The Yakutsky formerly possessed this Country but were dispossessed by the Calmucs, who attacked them by *surprise* and by a succession of surprises drove them to the Lena on which they fled and settled at Yakutsk.[42] After rising from table the Russians first cross themselves and bow to their images and then to each other. Karamyscherff has in his house four children descended of a Calmuc man and a Russian woman: The first resembled its father, and is entirely Calmuc; the other its mother with fair hair and eyes and &c and is entire Russian and the other two alternately Calmuc and Russian: they are all likely healthy Children and I saw three of them myself with him. I find that Karamyscheff knows not among what nation to rank the Khamchadales. He acknowledges with me that their faces are entirely Calmuc: but says they come from America, which controverts the natural opinion that America was peopled after Asia. He is bedevil'd with the wild system of the french naturalist Buffon.[43] I find universally that the Tartars have their beards. The ears of Calmuc and Mongul Tartars, project uniformly and universally farther from their heads than those of the Europeans. I measured

40. The Yakuts in their language have preserved one of the oldest Turkic dialects, containing many archaic features. However, many Mongol and Tungusic elements have crept into their grammar.

41. The Cherokees of the southern Appalachians belong to the Iroquoian linguistic family, which in the 18th century included many northern Indian groups; their language was comprehensible to many Indians of the east coast.

42. On these migrations north from the region of Lake Baikal, which probably lasted into the 1500's, the Yakuts brought with them their horses and cattle. They thus became the only stock-breeding people of the Siberian north.

43. Regarding Buffon and this controversy, see pp. 33–34, 34n.

those of three Calmucs at Karamyscheff's to-day and on a medium they projected 1½ inches and they were by no means extraordinary examples.—the ears of the Chinese are the same.—Informed that Ischutskoi are tatowed. People here are subject to frequent disease: especially a very active and putrid fever, which often proves suddenly fatal. Many die here also of apoplectic disorders. The fevers by what I could learn are not of the intermitting kind. I find French & Spanish wines here: but so mutilated that I was told of it before I knew it to be wine Karamyscherff is fully sensible of the Luxury & vanity I complain of in this Country, that is but[44] *begining to begin,* as I told him to day—and laments it, and declared to me frankly that Patriotism and the true solid virtues of a Citizen were hardly known. The Geographical termination of Russia and commencement of Siberia is at the city of Perm: The natural boundary is the river Yennessy.[45] I observe that the face of the country is very different, and Karamyscherff being a Botanist observes that the vegetable produc[ts] are as different. Archangel Dress the true Russian Dress and is derived from Greece and Egypt.[46] Mongul and Calmuc are Thibet Indians—Counted Sixty Streams that empty themselves into the Baikal (there are more see fo[r]ward).[47]

Tuseday 17 August. Went this morning to see Some Curiosities from different parts of Siberia. Saw some Sandwich Island Cloth at the same place. This was obtained from Capt Cook's Ship at Kamschatka when he was there.[48] Saw the Skin of a Chinese Goat. the hair of which was the whitest, longest and most deli-

44. "but" is repeated in the transcript.

45. At this time Perm province, to the west of the Urals, was administratively part of Siberia by virtue of its incorporation into the governor-generalship of Western Siberia. The Yenisei River was a rough dividing line between the eastern and western parts of Siberia; the Siberian highland begins immediately east of the river.

46. This strange statement may bear some relation to the sketches drawn by Le Brun (de Bruyn) during his stay at Archangel in 1701 of a Samoyed man and woman, both fully attired. These were reproduced in *Voyages de Corneille le Brun par la Moscovie* (plates 7–8), which Ledyard had read.

47. See Journal; p. 160. This is possibly the transcriber's insertion.

48. This "cloth" was acquired in Hawaii in 1779; it was actually *tapa* (bark cloth).

cate I ever saw. I also saw some excellent Sea Otter Skins: the best valued at 200 Roubles. Saw likewise the Bow, quiver, and all the military apparatus of a Calmuc, which was very heavy. The Calmuc and Mongul are here called the Burett or in Latin Buretti.[49] Went to the Archbishop's[50] to see a young Savage of the Ischutskoi: The good Bishop to whom I related the story, like Dr Wheelock with Sampson Occum, had taken great pains to humanize him—but informed me he had lately taken to drink and *died drunk:* or in the Conclusion of the Bishops own words "Somebody had given him a present of ½ a Rouble and he went out with it but never returned, and was found dead by the Side of a Kabai"[51] Dined with my friend K—— who presented me in lieu of a domestic, a young Lieutenant to go with me to buy a few things, "but" says he "don't put any money in his hands, he will not return it." We had at the table the wife of a Clerk to Mr Karamyscherff whose mother was a Savage near Ischutskoi and her father a Russian. She is a fine Creature and her Complexion of a good middling colour: It strengtheneth my opinion that the difference of Colour in Man is not the effect of any design in the Creator; but of causes simple in themselves, and will perhaps soon be well ascertained—It is an extraordinary circumstance but I think I ought not on that account to conclude that it is not a Work of Nature—

Wednesday August 18th—For the second time I have observed that in the Wells about 12 feet down there is a great deal of Ice adhering to the Sides. I am told that in [latitudes] 58 and 60, it never thaws above two or three feet down. Went this morning to see a Merchant owner of a Vessel that had passed from Kamschatka to different parts of the Coast of America.[52]

49. In English, Buryats.

50. The Bishop of Irkutsk at this time was Mikhail Mitkevich (since 1782).

51. *Kabak:* public house.

52. This was probably Grigorii Shelikhov, who in 1783 had left Okhotsk for the shores of America and had established a colony on Kodiak Island. Here he collected a rich supply of furs and made rough maps of the area. On April 6, 1787, he returned to Irkutsk. He left for St. Petersburg the following December.

Shewed some Charts rudely discriptive of his voyages. He says there are on different parts of the Coast of America 2000 Russians: and that as near as he can judge the number of skins produced by them in that Country amount to 12.000: has a Vessel of his own at Ohotsk. which leaves that Country for America next Summer, and offers me a passage in her.[53] Dined with a German Colonel, and after dinner went to the Lake—Baikal which in the Calmuc Language (the original inhabitants of its environs to the Thibet)[54] signifies the *North Sea.*[55] After a good and friendly dinner with the Colonel. the Chevalier and I mounted his drosky, with post horses and set out for the Lake—.[56] After 7 hours ride over a miserable road. we arrived at the little hamlet of Nicolskoi where formerly the Russian Embassadors resided before they embarked to cross the Lake to China—After crossing the Lake they go south about 300 versts to the town of Kiatka, which is now the frontier town, and where they meet the Ambassadors from Pekin. This village has a Church in it dedicated to the Russian Neptune St Nicholas[57] & all the Sailors on the Lake resort to it. We lodged here during the night, and next morning early renewed our Journey and reached the little village. Here is a Galliot that plies as packet in the Summer across the Lake and 6 or 7 houses among which the largest is a house ordered to be built by the Empress for the accomodation of all Strangers that should pass this way. We hailed the Galliot which was at anchor in the Lake the Capt. came to see us, and we went off with him in a small Boat with a line and Lead to take

53. In spite of good relations between Ledyard and this merchant (presumably Shelikhov), it is possible that the latter, like Karamyshev apparently, changed his mind about Ledyard and later urged his arrest. Perhaps Shelikhov had been drinking when Ledyard met him. Regarding the vessel at Okhotsk, see p. 45, n. 19.

54. The Kalmyks, a western branch of the Mongols, originally inhabited western China before many of them migrated to the north or west into Russia during the 17th century.

55. In Tartar, Baikal means "rich lake" (Bai-Kul); in Mongol, "holy sea" (Dalai-Nor).

56. The Chevalier was Karamyshev. A drosky, or droshky (Russian: *drozhki*) is a low, four-wheeled open carriage.

57. St. Nicholas, Bishop of Myra (d. *ca.* 345), besides being the patron saint of Russia, is also that of sailors and merchants.

soundings, but having only 50 fathoms line, and it raining very hard we could not make much progress; 100 feet from the shore took all my line viz 50 fathoms: we retired to the house, breakfasted and waited an hour for the rain to abate, but finding it to continue, we requested of the Captain to send us in his boat to Irkutsk, he complied with our request and made us a canopy of hides to defend us from the rain, we sent our d[r]ochky back by the Post-Boy and embarked with two Sailors to row us.—we passed from there along the shore to the mouth or[58] outlet and down the river to Irkutsk. This Lake is 769 versts in its longest and 60 versts in its broadest part, its depth said to be unfathomable:[59] it has an annual ebb and flux: The one is caused by the autumnal rains, and the other by the dry Springs It has emptying into it 169 small streams from 20 to 80 yards wide and 3 larger ones from ¼ to ½ mile It is supplied with but one outlet by which to dispose of this redundancy from all these influxes. The one mentioned, called by the Calmucs or Monguls—Angara and this which is but ¼ of a mile is very shallow at its Offset from the Lake and far from being rapid*[60] Dined with a Gentleman at his Glass manufactory[61] and returned in the evening to Irkutsk—

58. "or" is repeated in the transcript.

59. Lake Baikal is 390 miles long, 20–50 miles wide, and its greatest depth is 5,660 feet. It is the deepest lake in the world. Under the date August 16 Ledyard had written that it "is 800 versts long and 400 wide."

60. The asterisk refers to the following passage inserted in the text of the transcript: "*Calculating the number and sizes of the streams as here stated, upon a reasonable average the Column of water which is continually supplying this vast Lake in length nearly 600 English miles destroys all idea of the little Angara as its *outlet*. The Baikal then, if no subterraneous communication is supposed must be a real Ocean: but in so high a latitude it would seem difficult to account for the dissipation of its water by evaporation, and in that Case it would be expected that the water should be Salt or at least brackish for the same reason that all Oceans are but of this the Journal makes no mention. Among its fish which are but few there is the real '*chien de la mer.*' The Angara after winding a great extent of Country loses its name in the Yennessy, Jennessy as some pronounce it—"

61. This gentleman was quite likely Erik Laxmann (1737–96), who, besides his many scientific investigations in Siberia, established a glass works near Lake Baikal. Sauer too mentions this factory (*Account of a Geographical and Astronomical Expedition*, p. 15). Laxmann's second son, Adam Erikovich Laxmann, was probably Ledyard's traveling companion to Yakutsk.

Saturday 20th August[62] } The Government of Irkutsk has four Districts, three north and one South of it viz. Its own Province Irkutsk, 2d Yakutsk 3d Ohotsk and 4th Narchintsk.[63] Each of those provinces are sub-divided into smaller districts. Irkutsk has 4 viz. Irkutsk, Verchna Oodintsk, Kerensk, and Noshnayoodintsk.[64] In these Districts, the Inhabitants are Russ Burett (or Calmuc) Tonguse, Yakoot, Lamootkee, and Ukagee.[65] Province of Ohotsk has 4 Districts viz Gesheginsk Aklansk and Nashknay. Kamschatsk—(called by us Kamchatka)[66] the inhabitants are Russ. Tonguse Yakoot. Koriakhee Kamchadales. Alutore,[67] Kuriles Ischutskoi and other Indians yet unsubjugated. Province of Narchintsk has 4 districts: viz Narchintsk, Barguzin, Straytinsk[68] and Doroninsk, The inhabitants are Russ. Burett and Tonguse. Mr Karamyscherff says that they suppose here that those extraordinary large bones were the Behemoth Houses here guarded by great Dogs—every yard full of them. The Russ proper are descended of the Polanders, Sclavonians, Bohemians, and Hungarians, those of the Greeks and they of the Egyptians, and they of the Chaldeans.[69] The present Russ Dress is Egyptian

Monday 22d August—Informed by the Viceroy that the post

62. This and the subsequent dates for a week are behind by one day, as the preceding Wednesday was August 18.

63. Nerchinsk.

64. The Irkutsk region (*oblast'*) as of 1783 consisted of the districts (*uezdy*) of Kirensk, Nizhne Udinsk, Verkhne Udinsk (present-day Ulan Ude), and Irkutsk (*Polnoe sobranie zakonov rossiiskago imperii s 1649 goda* [Complete Collection of the Laws of the Russian Empire since 1649], 21:15.675, March 2, 1783, St. Petersburg, 1830).

65. Ledyard is referring to the districts of Irkutsk region. Lamootkee (Lamuts) were a people closely related to the Tungus; however the Ukagee (Yukagirs) then inhabited the region extending from the lower Lena basin to the Pacific Ocean north of Kamchatka, far to the north of these districts.

66. In Okhotsk "province" (*oblast'*), Gesheginsk (present-day Gizhiga) is located on Shelikhov Bay; "Nashknay. Kamschatsk" is Nizhne Kamchatsk; Aklansk is at the end of Penzhina Bay, northeast of Gizhiga. The fourth district was Okhotsk itself.

67. The Alyutary are a branch of the Maritime Koryak, living in northeastern Kamchatka.

68. Barguzinsk and Sretensk.

69. This idea of ancestry may be connected with the legend that the Russians were descendants of the mythical Russ, fourth son of Japheth; see Abulgazi, *A General History of the Turks, Moguls, and Tatars,* 2:668.

will not be ready until Wedenesday He sent a Surveyor with the latest Chart of the Province to give me the dimensions of the province or Government of Irkutsk as I had requested and by exact measurement I found its Latitudinal extent from its Southern extremity in the Lat. 49° 10′ N to the Icy Ocean N. to be 2700 versts: and its Longitudinal extent from the Longitude 113° 30′ to the Iskutskoi Nos its eastern extremity[70] on the Strait that divides the Continent from America opposite the Cape Prince of Wales of the Coast—to be 3.900 versts. I find that I have lost some of my linen between a servant and the washerwoman: the universal propensity to thieving in this Country from people of some condition to the lowest orders is a severe tax on the budget of so poor a traveller as I am

Tuseday 23[d] August I find that the commerce of Irkutsk is very little with Europe and consequently at present is at a very low ebb, since there is no open trade with the Chinese who are their nearest neighbours of a commercial Character.[71] The frontiers between this Country and that are principally defended by an army of the Burett or Calmuc Tartars. They are mostly horsemen like the Cossacs in the western dominions and amount to 5273 men, there are two Convents near the town, one of men and one of women separated by a river—I observe in Siberia that in all their Cities their is one great burying place and that wherever that is (and it is commonly out of town) there is a Church and the best Church of the place—this is but another kind of *Pyramid,* a *large mound* or a mound modified. The averaged population of the Russian Empire is 274 men to each square-german-mile total amount twenty millions and a half—the same estimate has not yet been made of Siberia: Of this province it may be

70. "Iskutskoi Nos" (Chukotski Peninsula) is present-day Cape Dezhnev, the easternmost tip of Siberia.

71. According to Coxe, writing in 1787: "Since the year 1755 no caravans have been sent to Pekin. The first discontinuance was occasioned by a misunderstanding between the two courts of Petersburg and Pekin . . ." (*Account of the Russian Discoveries,* 1787, p. 310). Although state commercial relations were not resumed until 1792, private trade with China continued during this period.

made easily by the table I have of it. England Ireland & Scotland is said to have to each German-square mile 2942 total twelve millions & a half—

Wednesday 25th August. This morning leave town: find the Country well cultivated between here and the river and a good Country Among the Burett or Calmucs find the American mockasin—the common mockasin like the finland mockasin.[72] The houses have octagonal sides covered with turf, fire-place in the centre; an aperture above for the Smoke. The true American Wigwam and like the first calmuc tartar house I saw in this Country which was near Kazan. Mr Karamyscherff says they have the wild horse on their Chinese frontiers. The people here (the Burett) ride and work the horned cattle; they pe[r]forate the cartilage and put a cord thro' it to guide them by. This is to be wondered at as this Country is so level and they have such vast droves of horses.

Thursday 26th. Had last night a hard white frost and it was very cold: my feet suffered. run away with by these cursed unbroke tartar horses and saved myself each time by jumping out of the Kabitka—Thank heaven! 90 versts more will probably put an end to my Kabitka Journeying for ever.

Friday 27th August Arrived 10 OClock at the Lena[73] Autumn must have made its appearance 10 or 14 days ago, the trees have most of them dropt their foliage. The river here twenty yards wide surrounded by high steep mountains. a number of little falls—river in general 234 feet water—

Saturday Aug. 28th The prevailing wood on the borders of the Lena is small pines. The environs of Irkutsk well cultivated: there are fine fields of wheat, rye and barley a good breed of cattle: and the mutton particularly is of a good size: and have the fat tail like the sheep at the Cape of Good-Hope.[74] it however not particularly well flavoured

72. The mukluk.
73. This was at Kachuga, located on the Lena, 150 miles north of Irkutsk.
74. Ledyard had stopped at the Cape of Good Hope in November 1776.

Monday 30 August Mountains decrease, and the country opens with the increase of the river which is yet small. Very cold with fogs all night until 11 OClock in the morning.

Tuseday 31st August. River widens. but does not alter its depth much. Mountains are come to hills and horizon enlarges: my ink frose in the Boat last night tho' we were covered overhead: we stopped at the Stage an hour this morning to get a little stores: They killed us a sheep gave us three quarts of milk, two loaves of Bread and some cakes with carrots and radishes baked in them Onions 1 doz fresh and 2 doz salt fish, Straw also and bark to mend the covering of our Boat for only 40 kopeeks about 14 pence sterling![75] They complained (so Lieut Laxman a young Swedish Officer who travels with me said)[76] of a scarcity of bread, and the poor creatures brot us their straw to shew us their grain blasted by the frost: and it had been reaped 10 days past which makes it the 21st of August. The borders of this river have a few poor houses as Stages for Boats, for those who go by water: and horses for those who go by land. The peasants say those mountains are full of bears and wolves Plenty of wild fowl which we shoot as we please. I have seen no fish but ca[r]p and salmon —trout.—they fish with Seins and also with spears and a torch: this last custom is a very universal one for they fish with the torch in Otaheite.[77] The Burett inhabit all the borders of the Lake Bailkal: they have tents or wigwams covered with matting bark or Skins, and are the genuine American wigwam form thus.

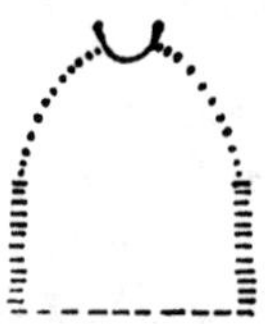

I find we go about 110 or 20 versts a day. The double headed paddle or Esquimaux is here.—[78]

September 1st Wednesday. Yakootsk is the last place where you will be able to make any *enquiries*. therefore let them be extensive. If Mercury was the

75. A ruble was then worth about four shillings, and a kopek less than a half-penny.

76. This was probably Adam Laxmann (1766–after 1796), an army lieutenant; he had been district police officer in Gizhiginsk since 1786. In 1792 he was sent to Japan, where he acquired the right for Russian ships to visit Nagasaki harbor.

77. Tahiti.

78. This is the kayak paddle.

God of theft among the Ancients the Russians ought to enroll him in their mythology I find the Chinese Pipe universally among the Siberian Tartars and think it therefore probable that the custom of Smoking migrated with them to America and thence by Sir Walter Raleigh made its way east to England—if so customs travel in a singular manner for why did it not come W. to England.—One English book in the Library of Chevalier Karamyscherff printed London 1621 Sir John Denham's works.[79]

Thursday Sept 2d Stopped this morning at a Little village to complete the hospitable invitation of a Merchant and a priest with them: My rascal of a Soldier stole our brandy got drunk and impertinent. I was obliged to handle him roughly to preserve order fixed a little sail to our boat. Mr Karamyscherff and I were both of opinion that *wampum* is of Grecian origin 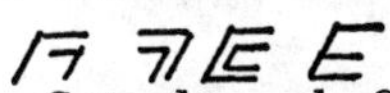 some how like that.

Saturday 4th September arrived at the village or town of Keringa[80] at day-light and staid with the Commandant until noon and was treated very hospitably by him and some Merchants sent us some stores. It is the custom here if they hear of the arrival of a foreignor to load him with their little services. It is almost impossible to pass a town of any kind without being arrested by them, and their hospitality is of the natural kind, or that which has not Civilization for its cause. They have the earnestness of hospitality They fill their tables with *every thing* they have to eat and drink, and not content with that they fill their wallet. I wish I could think them as honest as they are hospitable. Keringa situated between the rivers Lena and Keringa has 700 inhabitants, of those 300 are women, 6 merchants 15 Officers, a few soldiers 12 superranuated among which there are those of 70, 80, and 92 years, 5 privates and 50 men in a *Convent*. The reason why this Commandant at Keringa did not shew his wife, was because he was jealous of her. I have observed this to

79. Sir John Denham (1615–61), an English poet. Ledyard's date is incorrect by at least four decades, for the first collected edition of Denham's poems appeared in 1668.

80. Kirensk, 520 miles downstream from Kachuga, at that time had 80 houses, three churches, and one monastery.

be a prevailing passion here. NB. The word Chamant signifies Priest—[81]

Monday 6th September. At Keringa	R[ubles]	K[opeks]
beef p Pood		90
Sugar	15	0
Tea	10	0
poor Bread		60
best do		90

The stones I send to Irkutsk were taken at the foot of the highest cliff of rocky mountains between Ischastinskoi and Doubroua.[82] They are the highest mass of rocks I ever saw I suppose that among the Stones there is part of the leg of an Elephant—The river here bounded on each side by those vast stony cliffs. Birch and pine share pretty equally the soil.

Tuseday 7th September. For the first time I have had any horizon at all. I have one appearing a head 30 english miles, we are within a few versts [of] half our distance to Yakootskoi.[83]

September 13th Monday. Have had for several days hard head winds and rain—went ashore to day to dress our provisions. saw the hide of a bullock fixed on the top of a tree; supposed to be put there by the Shamant as a sacrifice.

Wednesday 15th Sept. Snow squalls with fresh gales, up all night at the helm myself

Friday 17th Sept Had squally weather till now—am 90 versts from Yakootsk. Passed yesterday a very odd arrangement of rocks which form the margin of the river for about 60 versts—they are of *Talc* and appear to have formerly been covered with earth but are now entirely naked. they are all of a pyramidyical form, extending to about 150 feet height—detached from their

81. Among Siberian natives a *shaman* is a medicine man, magician, and a specialist in evoking and controlling trances.

82. These two villages, located between Kirensk and Vitim, are spelled as "Tschastinskoi" and "Doubrowa" on Ledyard's itinerary.

83. Ledyard's itinerary gives the distance from Irkutsk to Yakutsk as roughly 1,700 miles (2,587 versts).

bases & disposed with extraordinary regularity. Those rocky banks at present appear to terminate the long mountainous South and east bank of the Lena that have uniformly continued from Katchuga here. I am now in upwards of 60° N.L. and which as it applies here might be called the Latitude of Low-land: 90 versts from hence (viz) at Yakutsk it takes it[s] long northern and north-western direction.

Saturday Sept 18th Arrived at Yakutsk after a very fatiguing voyage on the Lena of 22 days—delivered my letters to the Commandant of the town,[84] who very politely procured me quarters and waited on me there: but in our first conversation received the dejecting intelligence that it is impossible to proceed to Ohotsk this winter. What alas! shall I do for I am miserably provided for this unlooked for delay. By tarrying the winter I cannot expect to resume my march until May, which is 8 months. My funds! I have but two long frozen Stages more[85] and I shall be beyond the want or aid of money, until emerging from her deep deserts I gain the American Atlantic States and then thy glow[i]ng Climates. Africa explored, I lay me down and claim a little portion of the Globe I've viewed—may it not be before. How many of the noble minded have been subsidiary to me or to my enterprizes: and yet that meagre devil POVERTY who hand in hand has travelled with me o'r half the globe—and witnessed what Oh ye feeling Souls!—the tale I'll not unfold—'twould break the fibrils of your gentle hearts. Ye Sons of ener[v]ating Luxury ye Children of wealth and idleness! what profitable Commerce might be made between us, had you the will, and I the power to enter on the trade. A little of my toil might better brace your nerves. give spring to mind, and zest to your enjoyments and a very little of that wealth you scatter round you, would [put it] beyond the powers of any thing but death to

84. Presumably Grigorii Alekseevich Marklovskii. From the accounts of Sarychev and de Lesseps we know the commandant's last name; and from doc. # 28 we know his Christian name and patronymic.

85. Ledyard probably meant those stages to Okhotsk and across the Pacific to America.

oppose my kindred greetings with all on earth that bear the stamp of man. This is the third time I have been overtaken and arrested by winter and in both the others by giving time for my *evil genius* to rally her hosts about me have defeated the Enterprize. Fortune thou hast humbled me at length, for I am at this moment the slave of cowardly solicitude, least in the womb of this dread winter, there lurks the seeds of disappointment to my ardent desire of gaining the opposite Continent. I submit and proceed with my remarks. At Kazan there is abundance of snow, at Irkutsk which is in about the same latitude there is very little Kazan situated low, the air is more temperate and admits the snow to fall. Irkutsk is in a higher situation[86] is much colder and the snow cannot so readily descend—Here at Yakutsk the Atmosphere is constantly charged with Snow: it sometimes falls but very sparingly and that in the day rarely if ever at night. The air is much like that we experienced with Capt Cook in *Mare Glaciale* in Lat. 70° to 72° seldom a serene sky or detached Clouds, the upper region is a dark still expanded vapour with few openings in it, in the lower Atmosphere there is a constant succession of Snow. Clouds floating over head resembling Fog-Banks. In general the motion of every thing above and below is languid. The Summers are dry days very hot, the nights cold. The weather exceedingly changeble, subject to high winds, generally from the North, and sometimes heavy Snows in August. I have seen but one Aurora Borealis, and that not an extraordinary one. The first settlers in the time of Ivan Ivanitch, which was about 250 years ago came round by the North Sea[87] The present Viceroy has per annum 6000 Roubles and is allowed 6000 more for his Table. As nearly as I can estimate the whole Amount of

86. Irkutsk is about 1,500 feet above sea level, Kazan about 150 feet.

87. Around 250 years before this time Tsars Vasilii Ivanovich (1505–33) and Ivan Vasilievich, the Terrible (1533–84), ruled Muscovy. According to various legends, the Ust' Russians, one of the most ancient Russian groups in Siberia, who lived at the mouth of the Indigirka, "sailed there in boats and settled here during the reign of Ivan the Terrible. The legends mention Russian noblemen among these early settlers." Levin and Potapov, eds., *Narody Sibiri*, p. 116.

Government expenditure is about 156000 Roubles. There is a large mine of pure transparent salt formed into large crystals in a mountain near the Lena It runs in veins like other mines it affects meat like Saltpetre There is also a blue and red sort. Here are many instances of Longevity [there is a man][88] of 110 years in perfect health and labours daily. The images in the Russian houses, which I should take for a kind of Household Gods: are very expensive: the principal ones have a great deal of silver lavished on them.

To furnish out a house properly with these *Dii Minores* would cost 8 or 1000 Roubles: when burnt out which I have witnessed several times, they have appeared more anxious for these than any thing else. The warm bath is used here by the peasantry early in life from which it is common to plunge themselves into the river: and if there happens to be a new-fallen snow, they come naked reeking from the bath and wallow therein. Their Dance is accompanied or rather performed by the same odd twisting and wreathing of the hips as at Otaheite. In their marriages among the Kamchdales the woman draws on several pairs of breeches the man is naked, of all the other grades or divisions of man the Savage is the most formal and ceremonious and these among a people whose wants and occupations are but few whose minds necessity has [not][89] tortured almost to disstraction for the means of preservation on account of difficulties which the Luxury of Civilization hath created even for its ordinary members, he who with a happy indifference can endure a State of privation whose apprehensions are not racked with the Legends of future purgations, and whose heaven is peace and leisure, these are ceremonials with him like the uninterrupted tenor of his mind may be supposed to be transmitted unchanged thro' many generations: hence many things which marked the earliest period of history & which have left no vestige among civilized men show themselves at this day among Savages and

88. Bracketed words are taken from the fragmentary transcript in NYHS.
89. Bracketed word is taken from the fragmentary transcript in NYHS.

testify for record, Their Luxury if such it may be called is of that kind which nature intimates. Dress which in hot climates is an inconvenience further than for the concealment of modesty does not become so much the object of delight. here therefore the Savage is more nice and scrupulous in the indulgence of his appetites. On the other hand in cold climates bodily covering being of all importance, ingenuity is directed to that point: a feeble kind of infant fancy grows out of the efforts of necessity, and displays its little arts about the persons of such regions in awkward and fantastic decorations. But here the appetites are less lively and distinguished with respect to food the vilest and that totally unprepared does not come amiss, and the most delicate is not siezed with ardour. Voracity does not exist near the 60th Degree of Lat not even with the animals. Give a cake to a Swedish Finlander or northern Tartar and he eats it leisurely: do the same to an Otaheitan, and Italian peasant or a Spanish fisherman and he will put the whole Cake into his mouth if he can. The Empress has caused houses to be built at the expence of the Government in the Russian manner and ordered them to be offered to Yakuttee upon the single condition of their dwelling in them, but they have universally refused: prefering their apparently more uncomfortable Yoorts or Wigwaums. Dogs are esteemed there nearly in the same degree that horses are in England for besides answering the same purpose in their way [of] travelling. they aid them in the Chace and after toiling for them the whole day become their safe-guard at night. They therefore command their greatest attention. They have *Dog-Farriers* to attend them in sickness, who are no despicable rivals in art, at least in pretension to the Horse-Doctors of civilized Europe. They command also a high price. What they called a leading dog of prime character will sell for 3 or 400 Roubles. It is true that Volcanoes are almost universally where there is water—but it is salt water for I know of none near the largest Lakes or rivers. The compact part of a Continent approaches the Ocean by a regular descent from the highland in the centre. To be travelling into the interior parts of a continent you will pass first an extent of low-land proportioned to the extent of the Continent in the direction in which you travel. if contrary wise you first encounter ragged mountains; you may generally conclude that your march will be intercepted by Gulfs &c. when this is not the Case you will perhaps find those mountains to be, or you may conclude they have been volcanoes—Tonguse tatowed—Samoiede have the doubl-headed paddle Manner of fishing with nets under the ice. Buretti have the Mahometan lock of hair, The Russians half (22 in all) of the Islands[90] under their Government. Kuriles are tatwood[91] A Journal from a Russ Officer says that the Kuriles are very hairy: Mostly where we have it. but the arms, legs and thighs are altogether covered with hair.[92] Their traffic with the Japanese. Feathers and fish. The Islands have little vegetation. Kuriles reserved and sentimental in conversation: They are a comely people: have their[93] materials for boat or house building from the Continent or Japanese They are very wild and receive all strangers with the most threatening and formidable appearances—but afterwards they are kind and hospitable. The Coast of the frozen Ocean[94] full of trees and drift wood for 5 versts out. It is remarked by the Russians that since their knowledge of that Country the land has increased towards the Sea and drove it northward: 100 versts. a circumstance perhaps attributable to the large Rivers that empty themselves there. The Yakuttee is the mother language of all the Tartars and they all know something of it tho' they do not speak it From the following short specimen the reader may form some little idea of this (no doubt) very antient language—To a girl to go with me) Will you go and live with me at Kamschatka? Nay eezwalishlay yayhut somenoyoo e jeet ev Kamschatkay[95]—I want a woman to go and live with me

90. The Kurile Islands.
91. In other words, the Kurilians are tattooed.
92. The Kurilians are a branch of the "hairy" Ainu.
93. "their" is repeated in the transcript.
94. The Arctic Ocean.
95. Ledyard has mistaken Russian for the Yakut language. The modern Russian would be something like this: "Ne izvolish' li ekhat' so mnoiu i zhit' v Kamchatke." This clearly indicates that Ledyard's knowledge of Russian was poor.

at Kamschatka—Ya hoctchoo eemayt de efkoo ektobooy soglasshalass jeet somenoyoo ev Kamchatka.[96]

CONTINUATION OF THE JOURNAL FROM THE BEAUFOY TRANSCRIPT

People at Yakutsk have no wells, they have tried them 50 & 60 feet deep; but they freeze: the consequence is that they have all their water from the River Lena. This in Summer is very well but in Winter they cannot bring Water from thence, it freezes in the Cisterns in which they bring it, so that in the Winter they bring large Cakes of Ice to their Houses & pile them up in their yards & as they want them bring them into their warm rooms where they thaw & become fit for use

The Yakutee bring milk to market in Winter in frozen Cakes. a Yakut came into our house to day with a Bag full of Ice—What the Devil said I to Laxman has the Man brought [p. 2] Ice to sell —it was Milk.[97]

Tonguse are a wandering People, who solely live by the Chase. They have Tents or Yoorts made of Bark which they leave on the spot where they have encamped: They never stay above 2 or 3 days in a place, & the day they march they tell their Women that they go to such a Mountain, River, Lake, Plain, or Forest, & leave them to bring the Baggage.—They are extremely active in the Chace—They have no Letters, & do not write their Language. The Tents or Yoorts are universally of the same form & that is

96. The Russian equivalent of this is: "Ia khochu imet' devku chtoby soglashalas' zhit' so mnoiu v Kamchatke." In the transcript, underneath the word "de efkoo" are inserted in small letters the words "a girl."

97. Cow's milk is used by the Yakuts to make a great variety of products. Among them is *sourat*, a kind of thick sour milk to which cream is added if desired. They prepare sourat for winter supply by keeping it in large birchbark vats and adding berries, roots, bones, and leftover milk products. The mixture is frozen and used to make a drink called *buturgas*.

that of the American Wigwaum. Tonguse are often found dead, having [p. 3] pursued the Chace down some precipice.

The *Calmuc* or *Buretti* write their Language in Columns like the Chinese.[98]

The *Cossacs* or *Kazan Tartars* like the Hebrews from the right to left.[99]

The Calmucs live mostly by their Flocks & Herds which consist of Horses, sheep, Goats & Cows. In the Summer they dwell in the plains—In the Winter they retreat to the Mountains for Shelter & where their Flocks feed on Buds Moss &c—They have much Milk which they eat, & of which they also make Brandy—They hunt also. If they have any of their Flock Sick or lame they eat them.

I observe that there is one continued [p. 4] flow of Good nature & Chearfulness among the Tartars—They never call names & abuse each other by words, but when angry look for revenge either secret or open.

The Tonguse fight Duels with their Bows or Knives. They & the other roving Tartars have their hunting grounds marked, ascertained, & limited like the Americans. A Sentiment I observe that those Nations who like the Tartars & Negroes from time immemorial have not commixed,* and &c[100] and intermarried with other Nations are not so handsome (admitting our Ideas of Beauty) so strong, nor have so much Genius as us.

The Reason why the Buretti write is that they are last migrated from Thibet.

There is not another Asiatic Tribe in all Siberia that write their Language [p. 5] or have any remains of writing or orthography

98. The spread of Buddhism in the 17th century from Tibet and Mongolia to the region of the Buryats brought this vertical form of writing, the only well-developed non-Russian alphabet in all Siberia. In the 18th century native lamas, who played the role of intellectual and professional leaders, used the Tibetan form of writing.

99. The Arabic script, predominant among Moslems of Russia and Central Asia.

100. In the transcript the remainder of this sentence is found at the bottom of p. 5 and top of p. 6, and at this point there appears a parenthetical note, probably the transcriber's: "(vid: next page near the bottom)."

among them. a Proof, if there were no other, of their latest migration—perhaps of something else.

It is almost an universal Custom among the Russian Women to make their Teeth black, it is consequently considered as a great Ornament. This Custom prevails now in Persia, India, & I think in China.

The *Sound* of the Yakutee language is exactly like the Chinese, & so indeed are the languages of all the Asiatic Tartars.

[p. 6] People in this Country that are born half Russ, half Tartar are very different & much superior in their Persons to either the Tartars or Russ.—The European Nations that commix and intermarry most with other nations are the handsomest.—How far might this Cause be supposed to have made the Negro & Tartar so different from the European—or might not this commixing have originally made the European different from the Tartar or the Negro—might not this circumstance have been the greatest Cause of that difference among Mankind which exists.

A Gentleman showed me to day a copy of a Marriage [contract][101] done at Moscow [p. 7] 205 years ago. It is a folio page in length; & there are only 16 words intelligible to an ordinary reader or that correspond with the orthography of the present day:[102] This rapid alteration in the Russ language bears a proportion to the alteration in their manners since that period.

Their practice of bathing is once a week—their Baths are very hot.

The Empress gives three Ranks to Officers that come into Siberia & serve six years—2 while out from Petersburg & one on their return. It has two important effects; it civilizes Siberia, & is a prostitution of Rank & Honour, which in a Government like this is a prostitution of every thing—This is not [p. 8] Hypothesis, I have before my eyes the most consummate Scoundrels in the Universe of a Rank that in any other civilized Country would insure the best virtues of the heart & head, or at least common

101. Bracketed word is insertion from the Forman transcript.

102. In 1708 the old Slavonic alphabet was simplified; the new style was followed in all lay publications.

honesty & common decency. The Empress of Russia will be a Bankrupt at this rate to her own Ambition. Siberia is more than half of her Dominions, & it is professedly a Nursery of the most infamous Characters in her Dominions. The Succession of those characters is every 6 years, & the number annually increasing. at present there are 6,000 of those Officers in this province only,[103] without estimating the extra annual increase this in 6 years furnish 36,000 Scoundrels—of full proof.

[p. 9] The Yakutee here take their children out in the Evening & teach them the names of the principal Stars—how direct a march by them—how to judge of the weather. Astronomy is an early Science.

The Russ & Yakutee appear to live together here in harmony & peace, & without any difference as to national Distinction, or of Superiority and Inferiority. I know but of one Circumstance (but alas it is a great one) wherein the Yakutee are not on an equal footing with the Russ—They have no Office civil or military.

The Russians have been here 250 years & the Yakutee Tartars under the Russian Government since that time;[104] yet have [p. 10] the Yakutee made no alteration in his manners or Dress in general: The Russians have conformed themselves to the Dress of the Yakutee. There are but very few of the Yakutee who have embraced the Christian Religion & those who have perform its duties with a species of sarcastic Indifference that is very curious. In this respect particularly, the Tartar whether in Asia or America acts up to that Excentricity & singularity of Character which distinguishes them from any other people—Religion of any kind, & professed by any other people than the Tartars is always a matter of a serious contemplative & important nature & forms at least as strong a Trait in their several Characters as [p. 11] any circumstance of Art or Science—But it forms no part of the character of a Tartar—I have not in my mind the Christian System particularly; its Doctrine are indeed a Mystery to the

103. Ledyard was probably referring to the namestnichestvo of Irkutsk, which included Yakutsk.

104. Under the Russian government for around 150 years; Yakutsk was established in 1632. See also n. 87 above.

greatest minds & the best hearts—to a Tartar they must surely be more so, & the surprize is less why it forms no part of his Character. But the Mahometan System, for example, which courts the Senses & fascinates the passions of Man, it has operated on the Tartar no otherwise than to induce him to shave his Head—there it stops—it does not enter it—nor the heart.

The Tartar is a Man of Nature—not of Art—his Philosophy therefore is very simple—but sometimes very [p. 12] sublime—let us enumerate some of its virtues—He is a lover of Peace[105]—no Helen, & no System of Religion has ever yet disturbed it. He is contented to be what he is. never did a Tartar I believe speak ill of the Deity, or envy his Fellow Creatures. He is hospitable & humane—He is constantly tranquil & cheerful—He is Laconic in Thoughts Word & action—They do not prostitute even a Smile or a Frown any more than an European Monarch.

This is one reason (& I think the greatest) why they have been constantly persecuted by nations of another Disposition & why they have always fled from before them & been content to live any where if they could only live in Peace. Some have attributed [p. 13] this conduct solely to a Love of Liberty: I can only observe that I believe their Ideas both of Peace & Liberty to be very different from ours, & that a Tartar if he has his dear Otium would be as likely to call it Liberty as Otium.[106] There is much liberty in England,[107] for Example, but I think it would be less agreable to a Tartar to live there than in Russian Siberia where there is less Liberty. They indeed think differently in most things from the people of Europe & indeed of Africa.

If the planters in the state of Virginia were to give their Negroes large commodious houses to inhabit instead of poor huts & encourage them otherwise to do so, I believe the African would think like the Virginian [p. 14] Planter & very gladly accept the proposals. The same thing exactly has been offered the Yakutee

105. Here the Forman transcript adds: "No Lawyer here perplexing natural rights of property." Helen: Helen of Troy.

106. Otium: leisure.

107. The Forman transcript reads: "They talk much of Liberty in England . . ."

here by the Crown, & they have besides much greater Inducements to accept the proposals than the African, but they have not & they will not; & there is no expence attending the acceptance; but rather contrary wise. they will inhabit the Yoort.

The Yoort or Hut as we generally call it, or as the American Tartars call it pretty generally Wigwaum is in this Country a Substitute for a Tent: in milder Climates it is made either with Skins, Canvass, or Bark of Trees, of Sedge or some other kind of Grass: & in cold Climates it is made also of Skins if they are sufficiently plenty; and in any of those cases it is always of a conical form, [p. 15] not divided into apartments: an Aperture in the Top & in the Center & the fire made in the Center: round the side of the Yoort if they are only temporary ones are placed their Baggage & Furniture; if not temporary then are round the Sides Seats to sit or sleep on.

Here [in the neighbourhood of Russian Settlements][108] the Yoorts are made a little different; they are sunk two or three feet in the Ground; square; divided into apartments—the frame of wood—the Sides plaistered with Mud—a flat Top & covered with Earth. They have the fire in the Center & a slight little Chimney—They have 2 or 3 little Windows, in Summer of Talc, in Winter of Ice, & like the Scotch Highlanders one Apartment of the Yoort is for the Cow, Ox, or [p. 16] Horse, if they have them —these resemble not a Tent—but remote from Towns all the Tartars have Tents either of Skins Bark or Grass.

The Commandant shewed me to day a Man descended of a Yakutee Father & Russian Mother & the Son of this Man. I remark that the Colour of the first descendant is as fair as that of the second, & that this Colour is as fair as the Russian Mother. I conclude therefore that after the first descent, the Operations of Nature by Generation have little or no effect upon the Colour, & I remark also that whenever this change in the Colour by generation takes place that the alteration is from the darker to the lighter Colour much oftner than the Reverse. The Colour of the Hair & the Eyes also incline to be [p. 17] light, but do not always

108. Insertion from the Forman transcript.

accompany the change in the colour of the Skin. My general remark is that Nature with respect to the colour of Man, inclines to a colour fairer than the Negro & the Indian—(Nature is so inclinable to the fair Colour that she does her Business at once) I have caught her sporting in this as in other cases. I have in my Memoranda at Irkutsk mentioned an instance of it, wherein 4 Children descended of a Tartar & Russian Parents were alternately fair & dark complexioned—it was the most curious Circumstance of the kind I ever saw.[109] Upon the whole with respect to the difference of the Colour of the Indian and the European they appear to me to be the effects of natural Causes. I have given much attention to the Subject on this [p. 18] Continent: its great, its vast extent, & variety of Inhabitants affords the best field in the World in which to examine it, & I again remark that by the same gentle gradation in which I passed from the height of civilized Society at Petersburg to incivilization in Siberia, I passed from the Colour of the fair European to the Copper-coloured Tartar. I say the Copper-coloured Tartar, but there is the same variety of colour among the Tartars in Siberia as among the other Nations of the Earth. The Journal of a Russian Officer which I have seen here informs me that the Samoiede (amongst whom he lived 2 years) are fairer than the Yakutee who are of a light Olive & fairer than the Tonguse or Buretti who are Copper coloured; [p. 19] & yet the three last mentioned Tribes are all Mongul Tartars.—General Remark is that far the greatest part of mankind compared with European Civilization are uncultivated & that this part of Mankind are darker Coloured than the other part *viz* European. There are no white Savages & few uncivilized people that are not brown or black.

Among other remarkable circumstances that distinguish the Tartars is the form & features of the Face. It is perhaps the most remarkable circumstance. It invites me to a field of observation that I am not able to set bounds to. neither my Travels nor my

109. See above, under the date August 16. The "Memoranda at Irkutsk" must have eventually been incorporated into the body of the journal.

knowledge of their history are sufficient for the purpose, & indeed to [p. 20] do justice to the Subject I should be able to describe the face anatomically. I cannot do it—I remark that it is not an European Face but very remote from it; it is more an African Countenance. The Nose is the most remarkable Feature in the human Face. I have seen some Instances among the Calmucs where the Nose, between the Eyes, has been much flatter & broader than the Negroes, & some few instances where it has been as flat & broad over the Nostrils, but the Nostrils in any case are much smaller than the Africans. Where I have seen those Noses they were accompanied with a large Mouth & thick Lips, & these people were genuine Calmuc [p. 21] Tartars. Universally the Nose protuberates but little from the face & is shorter than that of the European. The Eyes universally are at a great distance from each other & very small, & over each Corner of the Eye the Skin projects over the Ball—the part appears swelled.[110] The Mouth in general is of a middling size, & the Lips thin. The next remarkable Features are the Cheek Bones; These like the Eyes are very remote from each other, high & broad, & project a little forward. The Face is flat. When I regard a Tartar en profile, I can hardly see the Nose between the Eyes, & if he blows a Coal of fire when I view him in profile [p. 22] I cannot see the Nose at all.[111]—Their Eye is straiter: the Lid has not the European Curve—The Forehead is narrow & low. They have a fresh Colour & on the two Cheek bones there is a good ruddy hue. There is not a variety of expression in their Faces,[112] I think the predominating one is Pride: but whenever I have viewed them they have seen a Stranger.

110. The following lines appear here in the Forman transcript: "the eyelids go in nearly a strait line from corner to corner. In the act of closing the eye, the two corners draw in from the centres by which the lids are enabled to meet. When opened the eye appears as in a square frame."

111. The Forman transcript adds here: "The face is then like an inflated bladder."

112. The Forman transcript has here the following footnote: "With but few objects to contemplate the mind must be supposed to be generally without employment of course the face without expression."

The generating cause does not operate so completely in producing a change of Features as of Complexion between the Tartar & the European. I have seen the third Descent lineally & the Features of the Tartar predominated over the [p. 23] European Features.

General Remark is that the Tartars from time immemorial (I mean the Asiatic Tartars) have been a people of a roving, wandering disposition—That they have ever been more among the Beasts of the forest than among men, & when among men it has been only those of their own Nation. That they have ever been Savages averse to Civilization, & have therefore never until very lately & now rarely have commixed with other Nations That whatever cause might originally have given them those remarkable Features the cause why they still continue is that they have not commixed with any other People, but [p. 24] I doubt the originality of their Features because by commixing with Europeans they have changed into those of Europeans. I am also ignorant how far a people constantly living with Beasts may operate in changing the features of the Face.[113] I am not insensible how far a cultivation & non-cultivation of the Mind alters the Features. I even observe in Europe that Mechanics of different professions have different Faces.—I know of no Nation, no people on Earth among whom there is such an uniformity of features except the Chinese, the Negroes & the Jews as there is among the Asiatic Tartars. They are distinguished by different Tribes, but this indeed [p. 25] is only nominal—Nature has set a Barrier to this Distinction & to all Distinction among them that marks them wherever found with the indisputable signature of Tartar: No matter if in Nova Zembla,[114] Mongul in Greenland, or on the banks of the Mississippi they are the same, & form the

113. The Forman transcript has here: "but am persuaded that this circumstance together with an uncultivated state of mind if we consider a long and uninterrupted succession of ages must account in some degree for this melancholy singularity. I have thought that even in Europe medical employments having been continued among the same people for a length of time has had a considerable influence in uninforming [*sic*] their faces."

114. Novaya Zemlya.

most numerous, & if we except the Chinese the most ancient Nation in History—& I myself do not except the Chinese because I have no doubt of their being of the same Family.

So strong is propensity of the Russians to Jealousy that they are guilty of the lowest faults on that account; the observation may appear [p. 26] trivial to an European: but an ordinary Russian will be displeased if one endeavours to gain the good will of his Dog. I affronted the commandant of this Town very highly by permitting his Dog to walk with me one afternoon—He expostulated with me so seriously about it that I could not believe him in earnest; I told him so, & I told him that whatever declaration he might make to the contrary I *would not* believe it—This is not the only Instance. I live with a young Russian Officer with whom I came from Irkutsk;[115] no circumstance has ever interrupted a constant harmony between us but his Dogs, & they have done it twice & I have been [p. 27] obliged to tell him positively that they shall not do it a third time. A pretty little Puppy has come to me one day & jumped upon my knee; I patted his head & gave him some bread; he flew at the Dog in the utmost rage & gave him a blow that broke his Leg; the Lesson I gave him on the occasion has almost cured him—but I have told him to beware how he disturbs my peace a third time by his rascally passion, & he has done it. I remarked that this observation may appear trivial to an European. I observe also that I am not fond of trivial Observations.

I have observed from Petersburg to [p. 28] this place & here more than any where that the Russians in general have very few moral Virtues, the body of the people are almost totally without. the Laws of the Country are mostly penal Laws; but all civil Laws are but negative instructors; they inform people what they must not do and affix no reward to the Virtue:[116] This in some

115. Probably Laxmann.

116. Here, instead of "no reward to the Virtue," the Forman transcript reads: "the penalty to the transgression. but they do not inform people what they should do and affix the reward to virtue, Untaught in the sublime of morality the Russian has not that glourious basis on which to exalt his nature."

Countries is made the business of Religion & in a few instances of the civil Law. In this unfortunate Country it is a business of neither civil nor ecclesiastical Concern. A Citizen here fulfils his duty to the Laws if like a base Asiatic he licks the feet of his superior in Rank; & his duty to his God if he [p. 29] adorns his house with a set of ill looking brass or silver Saints & worships them.—Sherlock! Tillotson! Sterne! what a Revolution would your Sermons produce among such a people.[117] They have never heard that sweet Truth that virtue is its own Reward & know no more of such an Idea than a New Zealander. It is for this Reason that their Peasantry, in particular are indubitably the most unprincipled in Christendom. I looked for certain Virtues of the heart that are called natural. I find them mot [*sic*] in the most remote & obscure Villages in the Empire but on the contrary I find the rankest vices to abound as much as in their Capital.

[p. 30] The Tonguse are Tatowed—The Ischutskoi are tatowed—The Kuriles, the Alutore, & the Nova Zemblans are also tatowed The Mohegan Tribe in America are tatowed.

I find as yet nothing analogous to the American Calumut[118] except that the Tartars here when they smoke the Pipe give it all round to every one in the Company. The form of the Pipe here is universally the identical form of the Chinese Pipe. I expect to find it the same in America since the Pipe they have on the Tomohawk resembles it. This form intimates Economy & that the original Custom of smoaking the Pipe was a mere Luxury: it [p. 31] holds but a very little. The manner in which the Chinese & the Tartars here use it corresponds with that Idea. They make but one or two draughts from the pipe & these they swallow or discharge thro' the Nose & then put the Pipe by. They say that the Smoke thus taken exhilarates.

I observe that among all nations the Women ornament themselves more than the men: I observe too that the Woman wher-

117. These preachers were probably Thomas Sherlock (1678–1761), bishop of London; John Tillotson (1630–94), archbishop of Canterbury; and Laurence Sterne (1713–68), clergyman and novelist.

118. The calumet or peace pipe.

ever found is the same kind, civil, obliging, humane, tender, being; that she is ever inclined to be gay & cheerful; timorous & modest; that she does not hesitate like Man to do a generous action of any kind. (And yet nature has bestowed more beauty on the Male of every Species [p. 32] of Animal)—The Woman is never haughty, arrogant or supercilious; full of courtesy & fond of Society; economical, ingenious; more liable, in general, to err than man, & in general have more virtue & perform more good actions than him: they have not so great a variety of character as Man & few are above or below this Description. I do not think the Character of Woman so well ascertained in that Society which is highly civilized & polished as in the obscure & plain walks of Life; it assumes an importance here unknown to higher Life.

My general Remark is that Climate & Education makes a greater difference in the Character of Men [p. 33] than Women. That I never addressed myself in the Language of Decency & Friendship to a Woman whether civilized or savage without receiving a decent & friendly answer—even in english Billingsgate.[119] With Man it has often been otherwise.

In wandering over the barren plains of inhospitable Denmark; thro' honest Sweden & frozen Lapland; rude & churlish Finland, unprincipled Russia & with the Wandering Tartar, If hungry, dry cold, wet, or sick Woman has ever been friendly to me and uniformly so. and to add to this Virtue so worthy the appellation of Benevolence; those actions have been [p. 34] performed with so free & kind a manner that if I was dry I drank the sweetest draught & if hungry eat the coarse Morsel with double Gout.[120]

Every body at Yakutsk has two sorts of Windows; the one for

119. Billingsgate: London fish market, notorious for foul and abusive language.

120. Gout: goût, relish. Here the Forman transcript adds: "Those who have been used to contemplate the female character only in Societies highly civilized and polished may think differently from me but having viewed in almost every parcel of the Globe, in the uttermost obscurity in unadorned Simplicity where nature only dictates, and where her page is clear and legible they would agree with me that with less variety of character than man the number is not great that is above or below this discription."

Summer the other for Winter. Those for Winter are of many different forms and materials—those made of the outside [skin] of the paunch of the [beef][121] are the best, but none of them keep out the Frost. This however is of no consequence with respect to the warmth of the Room. The inconvenience is that they are so covered with Frost on the inside that they are not transparent & consequently so far useless. A large Glass Window [p. 35] is covered with 1½ & 2 Inches of Frost, so that it is but a little more luminous than an Ice Window, but you can see nothing without not even the body of the Sun at Noon.[122]

The Asiatic like the American Tartars never change their Dress. They are the same on all occasions, in the field, in the house, on a Visit, at the most dirty work, on a holyday, It is all the same they have never but one Dress, & that is as fine as they can make it.

Those Tartars that live with the Russians in their villages are seldom above mediocrity as to Riches, and discover the same indifference about [p. 36] accummulating more & for the concerns of to morrow that an American Indian doth. They stroll about the Village, & if they can, get drunk, smoak their Pipe or go to sleep. The Gardens of the Russians are cultivated more or less, but theirs lie unmolested. The House of the Russian is a scene of rural occupations filled with Furniture, Women Children, Provisions, dirt & noise: That of the Tartars is as silent & as clean as a Mosque. If the Season admits they are all abroad except an old Woman or Man. Very little Furniture & that rolled up and bound in parcels in a corner of the house, & no appearance of Provisions; If it happens that the[y] profess [p. 37] the Russ religion they treat it with the same indifference, not thinkingly but because they do not think at all about it.

I have not as yet taken any Vocabularies of the Tartarian

121. The words "skin" and "beef" are taken from the Forman transcript; the Beaufoy transcript leaves blank spaces.

122. Here the Forman transcript adds: "The most common is Ice in winter and talc in summer: these afford a gloomy kind of light within which serves for ordinary purposes."

Languages & if I take any they will be very short ones.[123] Vocabularies are very delicate things when taken by a perfect stranger. they constitute a part of the history of the people & men of scientific Curiosity make use of them in investigating questions in philosophy as well as History, & I think too often with too much confidence since nothing of the kind is more difficult than to take a Vocabulary that shall answer such a purpose. The difference [p. 38] in the orthography of [the Languages of][124] Europe is an insurmountable difficulty. The different manner in which two persons of the same language would write a Vocabulary of a new Language would make the Vocabularies thus wrote different the one from the other, so that a Stranger to either of the languages might suppose them to be two different Languages.

Most uncultivated Languages are more difficult to orthographize than the cultivated. They are generally guttural but when not so the inflection of the voice in either case cannot soon enough accommodate itself to the modified Ear of the European to catch the true sound. That must be done in a moment [p. 39] which among ourselves we are not able to do in several years. I catch the accidental moment when I observe a Savage inclined to give me the names of things. I write & he speaks until we both understand that he speaks what I write, & that I write what he speaks. The medium of this conversation are only signs.

The Savage would wish to say head to me & lays his hand on the top of his head; I am not certain whether he says—*the head, my head,* the *top* of the head or perhaps the *hair* of the head—the same of Leg &c[125]

There are other difficulties—The Island of Oonalashka is on the

123. By "Vocabularies" Ledyard meant lists of equivalent words in two or more languages. He had already presented Jefferson with such a comparative vocabulary of North Pacific Indian and English words. A similar compilation was made by Sauer among the different peoples of northeastern Siberia.

124. Insertion from the Forman transcript.

125. Instead of the phrase "the same of Leg &c," the Forman transcript has: "he may also wish to say leg and puts his hand to *the Calf* I am not certain that he means the leg or the calf or flesh."

coast of N. America opposite Asia; there are a few Russian Traders on it; I was there with Captain Cook. I was walking [p. 40] one day on Shore with a Native who spoke the Russ Language. I did not know it. I was writing the names of several things. I pointed to the Ship supposing he would understand that I wanted the name of it: he answered me with the Words Ya Snaiu which in Russ is *I know* I wrote *a Ship*. I gave him some snuff which he took & held out his hand to me for more making use of the Word *Malinko* which signifies in Russ *little*, I wrote *more*.

I think therefore that to judge the analogy of Languages it is best to form an opinion from the tone & inflexion of the voice, from sound only & to give an opinion accordingly without risking a thousand [p. 41] dangers & difficulties that attend the reduction of it to orthography. I think it better for many reasons. It is the surest way because the sound does not vary like the Orthography. Sound was before Orthography: that is nature, the other art. Two persons of different Languages would think more in unison of a third from the *Sound* of it than its *orthography*. There is always more difference in the Sound or pronunciation of different Languages than their Orthography. Living Languages in general are first learnt from their Sound, & are always better spoken when thus learnt than otherwise. The Chinese Language can be learnt much easier from its sound than from its own orthography. Europeans [p. 42] cannot reduce it to their orthography. The sound of any Language is more characteristic of it than it[s] orthography.

Captain Billings's Command from the River Kovyma arrived here the beginning of this month (Novr 1787) & I went to live with him a few days after at his Lodgings as one of his Family & his Friend.

Captain Billings Mistress ill, partly occasioned by a bad air that the Peet gives when the top of it is too soon shut down; it gives violent Head aches & Vomitings.[126] This is the case also

126. Of the "bad air" given off by burning peat in stoves, Steller remarked while at Yakutsk that "if there was a stove it gave out so much

when a house is newly heated & inhabited. She has also an illness about the Navel. This I am informed by Captain Billings is [p. 43] frequent among Women in this Country, & he supposes proceeds from some imperfect conduct of the Midwife at the time of Delivery—*NB*. The Husband delivers the Wife.*[127]

The action of Theft arises from Want either real or imaginary. In savage Society there are no imaginary Wants & I cannot say indeed if there be any real wants unless they affect the whole community & in that case there can be no theft for a Community cannot steal from itself. If in such a Society there are any real wants which affect individuals they must be *few* & *temporary* & that lessens the inducement to steal; but if I consider the principles of hospitality that so generally prevails in [p. 44] such Societies I cannot suppose that there is ever room for want; besides no persons would be at the Trouble to steal if they could have their wants relieved without that trouble. In Savage Societies *theft* when known is not considered as a Crime. Want is not considered as a Crime. the manner of Life they lead subjects the Community as well as Individuals to temporary wants, but it is only temporary, if it was otherwise the Savage would be more anxious about the approaching inconvenience than he is & he cannot be less so & is almost as indifferent about every other future event.—

*Captain Billings has a drawing of this which he showed me; it was taken among the Ukagere Tartars. [p. 45] In a few words it is thus.—The Woman when supposed near the Moment of Delivery is alone except the Husband & one more Woman. a Place like a Gallows is erected in the Room as high as the Breast. The Woman leans herself forward upon it pressingly below her Breasts. The Husband stands behind her & applies his two hands to her Belly pressing the Feetus downward. The Wife stands

---

gas as to cause splitting headaches." Stejneger, *Georg Wilhelm Steller*, p. 112.

127. Here follows an insertion, probably the transcriber's: "(vid: next page an account of this)." By the asterisk at the bottom of transcript p. 44 is written, "vid: mark preceding page."

strideling[128] & before her sits the other Woman with a Skin in her hand waiting the appearance of the Feetus. In the room is hung up near at hand a Bow for the Boy if it prove to be such, & for the Girl a Piece of Embroidery. [p. 46]

Novʳ 24 1787 } The arrival of Captain Billings at Yakutsk is a circumstance that gives a turn to my affairs. I have before had no occasion to write Journialment.[129] I now commence.

Captain Billings is last from the Kovyma River where he has some small Cutter built vessels in which he last Summer made an attempt to pass the Shalatskoi Noss.[130] The Event of this Undertaking & other circumstances relative to the Tour both by Land & Water I am yet uninformed of, perhaps some accounts will be kept secret from me, but as others will naturally transpire in the course of my acquaintance with him I shall write them as they occur. Went out [p. 47] in the Evening to a Birth Day Feast which the Russians in these parts commemorate with the utmost extravagance & debauch. At all these places there is a melange of Character I have seen in no other Society, but this peculiar difference that there is no particle of honesty or honour in the mixture.

Thermom: 34

Novʳ 25 } More of the Command arrived belonging to Captain Billings. we have lately had a Church burned to the Ground in this Town. The time was very favourable or the fire would have burnt the whole quarter where it stood. The Images form almost the whole decoration of the Russian Churches & those melted [p. 48] on this occasion are estimated to have been worth at least 30,000 Roubles. Superstition how long wilt thou continue to debase & to curse my Brethren & my Sisters.

Clean Mercury exposed to the air is now constantly frozen.[131]

128. "straddling."

129. From the French *journellement:* daily.

130. Present-day Shelagski Nos (cape), east of the Kolyma delta, around which Dezhnev sailed in 1648.

131. Mercury freezes at −37.9° F., or at about −31° R., the scale which Billings was using.

Captain B—— has not yet made any experiments on the Coldness of the Air but judges it to be 38 Degrees.

Pennant in his Introduction to his Natural History[132] makes mention of a Disease he calls the *Black Death* which he says once spread itself all over this Country among others. Captain Billings informs me of a horrid disease at this day among the Tartars N.E. of this Place, that [p. 49] well deserves that name. he says it is a kind of Rotteness of If I may so say a Mortification of the whole Frame. The Flesh putrifies & falls off from the Bones &c. I have not as yet had a particular Description of it, if I get one will insert it. He once ordered a Physician to endeavour to cure one of the Tartars thus afflicted. The Physician began a Salivation: The Tartar from the operation of the Mercury supposed the Remedy worse than the Disease & run away in that condition without affording the Physician an Opportunity of continuing his Experiment.[133]

Novr 29 } The Witch of Injeginsk is a tale yet untold & for which I leave a Blank[134] [p. 50]

[p. 51] I find that Mr Pennant does not take notice of the Rocks in his description of Coasts—They are a naked, detached, high, craggy rock & situated inland, in the form of Towers, Pyramids &c The most remarkable I ever say [*sic*] or heard of are on the banks of the Lena

132. Thomas Pennant (1726–98) was an English traveler and naturalist from whose writings on natural history Ledyard gained much information on Siberia. See n. 37 above.

133. The mercury used to remedy this unidentifiable disease caused the saliva to flow excessively. Regarding the nature of this disease, Abulgazi, writing of Siberian natives in general, makes the following comment: "As the Nourishment which they are accustomed to take is very unwholesome, and for the most part crude, they are grievously tormented with scorbutick Distempers, which eat the Parts infected like a kind of Gangrene, and infect one Part after another till it kills them. . . . the most of them search after no Remedy, and very patiently see themselves rotting alive, because they say they have no Knowledge in Physick" (*A General History of the Turks, Moguls, and Tatars,* 2:646–47). According to Sauer, the only diseases that Billings came across before his encounter with Ledyard were smallpox and venereal disease among the Yukagirs and scurvy among his own men.

134. Page 50 of the transcript has been left blank.

The Asiatic Tartars have different methods of hunting the Moose & such kind of Game, but the most prevalent is that used by the Americans of forming an Ambuscade. They even hunt Ducks in that manner at the mouth of the River Kovyma. The Otaheitans catch Fish sometimes in the same Manner. It is simple, universal & antient. The uncivilized part [p. 52] of Mankind war against each other in the same way.

Question—Is the Light-coloured or the dark-coloured Eye the most predominant among white coloured people? It strikes me that in drawing the line between the Fair, the brown, & the black of the human species that this Feature considered would be of particular Service.

No Sea Otter Skins have ever been seen in either Hudsons or Baffins Bay, or any of the Eastern Coasts of America. How far is this a proof that no Commercial Intercourse has ever subsisted (tho' supposed by Captain Cook) either with the Hudsons Bay Company or Indians or with the eastern Indians of America. Does not this Circumstance tend to [p. 53] invalidate the Authenticity of several pretended Voyages & Discoveries on the N.W. Coast of America? Why should Captain Cook & the Russian Voyagers be the only ones who found them; others have not even made mention of them, & yet they are not only very plenty with the Natives, but we with Captain Cook also saw them frequently in the Waters of the Coast alive.—

I understand from Captain Billings Journal that the universal Method among the Tartars N.E. of this, in the Ceremony of Marriage, is for the Man to purchase the Woman that he demands in Marriage or make presents to her Parents which I consider as the same thing.[135] It is also customary for the young Man, the Groom, to come & [p. 54] serve a stipulated time with the Parents of the Bride. In case of disunion afterwards which is done without passion, the presents made are returned. In case of death either party marries as soon as convenient & the sooner the better they say because the Loss ought not to be

135. The *kalym* or bride-price was a custom especially common among the Buryats, Yakuts, and Tungus.

lamented if it can be repaired. This sentiment is peculiar to the Tartar both here & in America (& so indeed are the above mentioned Ceremonies) & demands Reflection. I suppose myself that Love in this case is infinitely below that which existed in the Bosoms of Eloisa & Abelard; & I suppose the Philosophy as infinitely superior to that which Eloisa & Abelard discovered, as the Love is below it.—Speak of a medium between the two—[p. 55] if they are extremes—I confess I cannot oppose the Tartar Sentiment at all, if I make my appeal to Reason; its Logick alone is invulnerable. If I appeal to my passions I should love like Abelard. The Feast on the occasion like all the Feasts among the Children of Men is a Sacrifice to the Passions, which among all Savages is carried to a greater degree of Extravagance than elsewhere. In the number of the lesser Ceremonies which form parts of the Ceremony I find nothing that appears remarkable indistinct from being the Customs of a strange People. Formality I have already observed takes place in every transaction in Life among every savage people & is more or less minute & complicated [p. 56] in proportion to their incivilization; there are therefore numberless Ceremonies on this occasion. The best that can be said of them is that they are succedaneous to[136] pleasure which among these people have too little of intrinsic Virture to exist with them & that they are therefore justifiable in making use of them by our own mode of thinking They reflect no analogical Light on any historical or any other Subject that I recollect.—Religion forms a part of the Ceremony—A Priest with a Male attendant is present. They are exactly like those described by the unfortunate Carver in the interior parts of N America[137] indeed like most or all other priests from him who taught the Magic Art in Egypt to [p. 57] the one I speak of, the most accomplished Jugglers. Captain Billings who was, with all his Officers, present on this occasion, & who had read Carver told me he had from a

136. "succedaneous to": a substitute for.

137. Jonathan Carver (1710–80) explored the upper Mississippi valley and Lake Superior region in 1766–67. The first editions of his travels appeared in 1778 and 1781. In spite of his publications, he died penniless in England and was buried in paupers' ground.

[*sic*] determined if possible not to be deceived like Carver in the Story of the Bean flung into an Indians Mouth, placed himself & his Officer in such a manner as could best detect any of the Arts of the Priest on this Occasion; but the Priest deceived them all. The Circumstance in which he thus triumphed was plunging a Knife into his Bosom & vomiting Blood: I cannot dwell in detail on such a Subject. It answers my purpose as it did the Priests—that *every body present were deceived.* The Priest gives his *Benediction* & receives his Reward. [p. 58] It is remarkable that he was the *first* served & the *best* served on every occasion.

I remark that all the Tartars like the Americans coincide in this Sentiment of Religion *viz* "that there [is] a great God, & that he is so good as that they have no occasion to address him for the bestowment of any Favours, & that being they good he will not do them any injury. But as they say they certainly meet with Calamities, so they say there[138] must be a God distinct from the other; that he must be very powerful because they have many Calamities; to this Deity they therefore sacrifice; not affirmatively to bestow good, but negatively not to do harm."[139] Their Priests (Shamants) have therefore nothing to do with [p. 59] the good God: their Business is solely with the other whom they divid[e] into a plurality of Character having a Subordinate evil Spirit presiding over each Evil; this affords the *Shamant* an opportunity of playing the Devil in the extraordinary manner they do, with the same success that the introduction of *Saints* & *Images* & *Angels* have afforded to Priests of I leave this Blank for him to fill up that can do it without blushing: & the following vacant Page I leave a blank for the animadversions of an honest Man on the religious Sentiment above-mentioned informing such at the same time that the sentiment affects immediately all the Religions of Savage America & [p. 60] savage Asia, & collaterally that of every untutored human being.[140]

138. The Forman transcript has the following insertion here: "is another God the source of evil and that he."

139. It is not known whom Ledyard is quoting here.

140. A blank space of one line has been left in the transcript.

The more I reflect on the Circumstance the more it appears to demand Reflection & of course attention, even to others. I declare frankly that appearances have alone given birth to the Sentiment. I have already made some observations with regard to the difference of Colour in the human Species. The Result is that I think this difference is the mere effect of natural Causes, & of the most [powerful] of these, that of Generation.

But my other Sentiment is that which respects the still more remarkable Circumstance in the Human Species, viz, the Anatomy of the [p. 61] Face?—I have not time nor even abilities to amplify. I humbly ask. To what a degree can exterior objects operate on the Feetus or any other Circumstance? Mr John Hunter[141] has made or is making some Anatomical Strictures on the Head of a Negro[142] which it is said exteriorly at least resembles that of a *Monkey*. If I could, I would send him the Head of a Tartar who lives by the Chace and is constantly in the Society of Animals who have high Cheek Bones; & perhaps in his Strictures on this he would also find an Anatomical likeness to the Fox, the Wolf, the Dog, the Bear &c.

I began a Thermometrical Diary at Yakutsk & continued untill the [p. 62] latter end of November. I had a Mercurial Thermometer, & found according to the observations made by others that the Mercury froze at 32½ degrees below 0 by Reaumur. Captain Billings has also found the same in his N. East expedition—He has there had frequently 42½ Degrees by a Spirit Thermometer the coldest 43¾.[143]—Strong French Brandy in well corked Phials thickened like coagulated Blood but did not become hard. We have here no Spirit Thermometers. Two ounces of pure Quicksilver freezes here every Day in December quite hard so as to be cut with a Knife like lead. This quantity has

141. Dr. John Hunter, English anatomist and surgeon who helped promote Ledyard's journey.

142. The context suggests that "strictures" refers to Hunter's critical remarks. Hunter describes the head of a Negro in his posthumously published *Essays and Observations* (London, 1861), 2:3.

143. By Réaumur −43¾ degrees is about −65° F. The average January temperature around Yakutsk is below −40° F. Oymyakon, 400 miles east of Yakutsk, in 1963 recorded a maximum low of −96° F.

froze by a Watch here in fifteen Minutes. Good French Brandy exposed openly coagulates; I suppose therefore that at Yakutsk we have [p. 63] 40 Degrees of Cold. These severe Frosts are uniformly attended by a thick Mist over the surface of the Earth about the height of a common Fog & almost of an equal Density with the thickest Fogs. It is dangerous to be much abroad at such times on account of the quick & subtle operation of the Frost The Houses & Rivers keep a continual Cracking & all Nature groans beneath its Rigour.

Mr Pennant observes that the Scythians scalped their Enemies.

Pray is there not an analogy between the custom of scalping & that of taking the Foreskins of the Enemy as among the Philistines.[144] I have ever thought since my Voyage with Captain Cook [p. 64] that the same Custom under different Forms existed throughout the Islands in the Pacific Ocean. It is worthy remark that though the Indians at Owhyhee[145] brought a part of Captain Cook's head, yet they had cut off all the Hair, which they did not return to us. I have also frequently observed the Islanders to wear great quantities of false Human Hair. All savage Nations however have ever been fond of preserving some badge or testimony of their Victory over their Enemies of *this kind.* In the time of Sampson, *Foreskins* were in Repute. Whether this means the *Prepuce* or the skin of the *Forehead* I know not.

Among the antient Scythians the *Scalp,* & so among the Aborigines [p. 65] of America. Among the Islanders in the Pacific Ocean Teeth & Hair are in Repute—They have all given the Preference to some part of the head—except the Izraelites

I dined Yesterday with a Turkish Lady who told me that the Peasantry of Moldavia tatow themselves & that among them it is a mark of Friendship to wear the same Marks[146]

144. This refers to 200 Philistines slain by David, whose foreskins he presented to King Saul as dowry for the hand of his daughter. I Samuel 18:25–27.

145. Hawaii.

146. It is unlikely that a Turkish lady would have been in Yakutsk at this time of year; this was probably written in Irkutsk.

Informed to day by a German Gentleman who commanded a Russian Regiment in the last War that the Janizaries tatow.[147]

Informed also that the Custom of staining the Nails of the Fingers of [p. 66] a Scarlet Colour is common on the Caspian & black Seas.—I saw one instance of it myself near Kazan. This is a Custom among the Cochin Chinese. I saw it at the Island of Perlo Condor myself.[148]

The Custom among the Russians of calling John the Son of John: Alexander the Son of Alexander &c is a Custom as antient as the antient Jews.

The Scripture Phrase at the Death of a Patriarch is, "& he gathered himself up & died"—"& he was gathered to his people".[149] A Corps at Sandwich Islands is always gathered up, & in the form of some Feetuses in the Womb. &c—Abraham was buried in the Cave of Macpelah, the American Indians also bury their Dead in *Caves.* [p. 67] The artful Custom of dreaming among the American Indians when they want to gain any thing corresponds with Jacobs Dream about the speckled Sheep. Sir William Johnson tells a good Story of this Kind[150]—The Americans are much given to pretended Dreams & both Jacob & an Indian of America have had Impudence enough to father such Dreams upon their Gods.

It is very remarkable that both the Asiatic & American Tartars have the same chaste or superstitious notions of Women during the Menstrual Illness that Laban had in omitting to search for his Silver Gods when hid under Rachel who feigned the Menstruals.[151]

[p. 68] Jacobs Servitude for his Wives exactly correspond with the same Custom universal with the Asiatic & American Indians.

147. The Russo-Turkish War of 1768–74. Janissaries were infantry units that comprised the main fighting force of the Turkish army.

148. Ledyard visited the island of Pulo Condor, off the coast of Cochin China, in January 1780.

149. Genesis 35:29, and 49:33, in reference to the deaths of Isaac and Jacob.

150. Sir William Johnson (1715–74) was the superintendent of Indian affairs in colonial New York.

151. Genesis 30:34–35.

The first particoloured Coat mentioned in History was Joseph's.

The Russians use the word *Benanite* by way of Reprobation. The Child Lot had by his youngest Daughter was called *Benani*[152]

The Story of Cain's murdering Abel is as true as others of the kind—God said he would put a Mark on Cain. What mark could this have been? It must have been something very distinguishable since those whoever it might be (as well me as another) that met with should know him; but where are his Offspring God has marked them in Vain.

[p. 69] The Otaheite word *Tata* or *Taata,* (since at Otaheite they cannot sound the Letter R,) is analogous in Sound & Orthography to the word *Tartar.* The former signifies Man in the Otaheite language & in the Tartar language the latter is I think expressive of the same Idea.[153]

I wish I could assert upon better authority than my own Suspicions that Wampum works contain Hieroglyphics. The Scoundrel Chevalier Karamyschew of Irkutsk was the first that I have seen who coincided with me in that Idea. I had purposed to have procured Drawings of the Asiatic & American Wampum but I am I know not how a prisoner to her Majesty of Russia.[154] I have seen the Initials of a Tartars name worked among the [p. 70] Wampum on the borders of his Garment. A people so attached to their Ancestors as the Tartars would[155] also place the

152. Genesis 19:38. Here the transcriber, JWL, has given the correct spelling in parentheses: "(*Ben-ammi JWL*)."

153. "Tartar" in old Turkish means "inhabitant of the region north of China."

154. His calling Karamyshev a scoundrel at this point suggests that his former host was involved in his arrest.

155. After this word, the Forman transcript substitutes for "also place . . . It gives me.": "naturally endeavour to preserve some memorials of them My anxious hopes are once more blasted, the almost half accomplished wish! what secret machination has there been? what motive could direct to this? but so it suits her royal Majesty of all the Russians and she has nothing but her pleasures to consult she has no nation's Resentment to apprehend, for no State's, no Monarch's Minister am I, but travel under the common flag of humanity. Commissioned by myself to serve the World at large, and

name of their Fathers there also. Detained at every Town I pass thro' by one idle Rascal or another, & the Snuff box Serjeant that guards me now more than any other— —"take Physic pomp"[156]— loose your Liberty but once for one hour ye who never lost it that ye may feel what I feel. It gives me. Altho' born in the freest Country in the World, Ideas of its exquisite Beauties & of its immortal Nature that I had never before. Methinks every Man who is called to preside officially over the Liberty of a free People should once—it will be enough—actually be deprived *unjustly of his Liberty* that [p. 71] he might be avaricious of it more than of any earthly possessions. I could love a Country & its Inhabitants if it was a Country of Freedom & for no other reason than because it was a Country of Freedom. There are two kinds of People I could anathematize with a better Weapon than St Peters;[157] those who dare deprive others of their Liberty, & those who could suffer others to do it. Methinks if I was a victorious Prince I would never keep any Prisoners if the People I was at War with fought for Liberty.

The Russian Female Head Dress is Asiatic & of the Turban kind. The Russ Dress is all Asiatic: It is long, loose & of the Mantle kind covering almost [p. 72] every part of the body. It is a Dress not originally calculated for the Latitudes they at present inhabit. Within Doors the Russian is an Asiatic & without an European.

The Words Turk & Tartar might have been of the same origin. The Turk was a Bucarian roving Tartar.[158]

I am now at Kazan. It is 9 Months since I left it, & I am 9 times

---

so the poor, the unprotected, wanderer must go where sovereign will ordains. If to death why then my Journey is over sooner and rather differently from what I had contemplated. If otherwise why then the Royal Dame has taken me rather much out of my way but 'I may take another route—' The rest of the world lies uninterdicted." The phrase "I may take another route" may refer to Catherine's opening statement in doc. # 6.

156. King Lear III, iv, 33: "Take physic, pomp": cure yourselves, you great men.

157. Excommunication by the Church of Rome.

158. The Forman transcript has "*Buccanneering* roving Tartar." "Bucarian" refers to Bukhara, a Central Asian khanate at that time.

more fully satisfied [than I was before][159] of some circumstances mentioned in my Diary in June last[160] because fond of the Subjects I have been in pursuit of I was jealous that I might have been rash & premature in some of my Opinions, but I certainly have not been & I feel a double satisfaction in saying [p. 73] so because I have ever thought that the first Ideas of things were the best.

One circumstance alluded to in my Diary is the cause of the difference of Colour in the human Species. I must speak decisively of it—I am fully convinced of its being solely the Effect of natural Causes. I have never extended my opinion & do not to the Negros. I cannot give publicly an opinion of them; but privately I think of them as I do of the other two Classes of Man which I call in the common Language, the *White people* & the *Indians.* There are many excellent reasons that rise collaterally from my present Voyage to induce me to think so but yet I still wish to have better, because I think they exist as well in Africa to [p. 74] render the Negro blacker than the Indian as in Asia to render the Indian darker than the European, or in Europe to render the European fairer than the other two: or in other Words that the principal Causes exist no where locally, but as much in one quarter of the Globe as another.

The other circumstance alluded to is particularly that national or genealogical connexion, that remarkable affinity of person & manners which exists between the Indian on this & on the American Continent. Of this I must speak equally decisive, & I declare without the least hesitation, with the most absolute conviction, that the Indians on the one & on the other [continent] are the same people as far as I have seen either. It also respects [p. 75] the origin of the great Tartar Nation & their present history considered as a People of this Continent. I at present feel myself justified in supposing that neither their origin nor present extent as a Nation clearly & remarkably distinct from any other has

159. Insertion from the Forman transcript.

160. See Ledyard's comments on the causes of human color and physical differences and on the customs of Tartars in Asia and America, pp. 144–45.

been ascertained or even well thought of. Albugassi[161] who was himself a noble Tartar has said much the most & best of their origin & something of their extent but not half enough particularly of their extent which in fact he did not know. Like a Soldier he has wrote a kind of Muster Roll of his Country men. I do not remember any thing like Philosophic Research or Information in his History, tho' I read him with Avidity not twelve months since. Among the Voyagers in this [p. 76] Country even the most modern, I have instead of more still less Information. A few vocabularies to lead astray those who would wish to find real Information. & a relation of a few Customs without any remarks upon them is the amount of the whole.

I find nothing material said about this great people by any Writer whatever. The late contest about the contiguity of Asia and America has accidentally struck out a few observations remotely consequential & one now & then finds something Philosophically said of them, but very unphilosophically placed, among Quadrupeds, Fish, Fowl, Plants, Minerals & Fossils.—I am sensible that many reasons are assignable for this neglect both among [p. 77] Travellers & Men in general, but not one or all of them together would be sufficient in my opinion to justify the former; with half the Abilities of the least accomplished among them I should blush to be of the number. Steller ought to have been hung and Le Bruyn burned.[162] Such Travellers in Countries of such immense extent and replete with those circumstances that lead boldly into the most remote History of Man & of Nature have only furnished matter to feed the pampered Vanity of Buffon & of airy Hypothesis.

When the History of Asia & I will subjoin America because it is the latter part of the former, is as well known as that of Europe it

161. Abulgazi-Bagadur, khan of Khiva from 1643 to 1663, was known for his *History of the Turks,* in nine volumes, which was translated into several Western European languages, including English (1729–30).

162. Georg Wilhelm Steller (1709–47), German-born natural scientist who traveled on Bering's second expedition and on Gmelin's expedition. Cornelius de Bruyn (1652–1726), also known as Le Brun, traveled from Archangel to Astrakhan via Moscow in 1701–03.

will be found that those who have written the History of [p. 78] Man have begun at the wrong End.

March 12 } I am on my Road to Poland & 220 Versts from Moscow—Thank Heaven a Petticoat appears! & thank God the Glimmerings of other Features! How nice this Gradation is & yet as plain as the simplest thing in Nature. But Wampum, or if you will, Beads, Fossils,[163] Rings, Fringes, & easter[n] Gewgaws, are as much here as in Siberia. I find on the borders of Poland[164] that they bury like the Tartars near Kazan among a Tuft of Trees. Women are the Harbingers of an alteration in manners in approaching new Countries.

I am at the City of Neeshna,[165] in a vile, dark, dirty, gloomy, damp Room; it is called quarters; but it is a miserable Prison. The Soldiers who [p. 79] guard me are doubly watchful over me when in a Town tho' at no time properly so thro' their consummate Indolence & Ignorance, for every day I have it in my power to escape them[166] if I chuse it. I was very ill Yesterday. I am emaciated. It is more than 20 days since I have eat & in that time have been dragged in some miserable open Kabitka 5,000 Versts.[167] Thus am I treated in all respects (except that I am obliged to support myself with my own Money) like a vile Convict. Was I guilty of any the least thing against the Country or any thing in it, or was there even a Crime alledged against me, I could suffer with some patience or at least resignation; but when I reflect upon my Innocence not only as to any [p. 80] Injury, done or thought of not only to this Country, or to any

163. For "Fossils" the Forman transcript has "Tassels."

164. At the beginning of the journal Ledyard described the country around Tobolsk as formerly belonging to the Poles (p. 143). Either his sense of geographical orientation was still faulty, someone misinformed him, or this entry in his journal was chronologically out of place. It should be noted that in Ledyard's time adequate knowledge of Russian geography was quite uncommon in England and the West.

165. Nizhni Novgorod; for discussion see p. 46.

166. Instead of "if I chuse it." the Forman transcript has: "but tho' treated like a felon, I will not appear one by flight."

167. By present-day routes, Nizhni Novgorod (Gorki) is about 4,800 versts from Irkutsk, Moscow about 5,190 versts.

other, or against human Nature itself,[168] I consider Resignation as Cowardice, nor will I set the base Example, debase my honour, or sin against the Genius of my noble Country. They may do wrong & treat me like a Subject of this Country, but by the Spirits of my great Ancestors, & the ignoble Insult I have already felt they shall not make me one in Reality.[169]

[p. 81] I had left Moscow in the manner related in some scattered paper in my Port Folio on the 10th of March.[170] It was the time of the equinoxes with them. The Gales were from the East attended with heavy Snow falls three Days. I had them in the Rear as I travelled West. They blew me almost to the City of Polosk which I hoped would have been the End of my unfortunate Voyage as a Prisoner without a Crime—it was not.[171] General Passek to whom I was sent was not there, he was at the City of Mogaloff, 200 Versts (as I imagined) S.E of Polosk.[172] I could see nor be informed of any thing. The General at Moscow[173] did not know where General Passek was [p. 82] or General Passek was where he ought not to have been. I suspect the former, be it

168. Here, with the following lines, the Forman transcript ends: "it might not make me contented indeed but I suppose it would make me resigned but to be arrested in my Travels at the last Stage but one in these dominions where the severe Laws of the Climate and season had unhappily detained me, both of which however I should have braved but for the Restraining courtesy of the Governor [the commandant]. seized imprisoned and transported in this dark and silent manner with no cause or accusation but what appears in the mysterious wisdom which is pictured in the face of my Serjeant of course without even a guess at my Destination: treated in short like a Subject of this country. In such a case Resignation would be a crime against the noble Genius of my dear native country."

169. The rest of page 80 in the Beaufoy transcript has been left blank.

170. March 21, N.S., the first day of spring. The "scattered paper" has been lost.

171. Polotsk is located on the Western Dvina River, which was then the boundary between Russia and Poland.

172. Pëtr Bogdanovich Passek (1736–1804) was then governor-general of the Belorussian provinces, Polotsk and Mogilëv. The town of Mogilëv was about 170 miles by road southeast of Polotsk.

173. This general was perhaps the civil governor of Moscow, Maj. Gen. P. V. Lopukhin, who served as such from 1783 to 1793. *RA* (1886), Bk. 1, p. 167. I could not determine who in early 1788 was the military general-in-chief in Moscow.

which it will it matters not as to the manner of doing business in this Country & the Character of its Officers. The General slumbers on the pillow of Rank & so does the Serjeant; & to know their rank is to know their duty & their Duty their Rank; & ne plus ultra. When the Kabitka stopt in the Street at Polosk I was so weak & ill with fatigue (for the first time in my life) that I fell asleep as I lay, & although carried out of the City to the first post (15 Versts) on the road to Mogaloff over a very bad road I knew nothing of my Fate until I arrived at the Post. When I understood from the Serjeant that I had to go 200 Versts to seek Genl Passek I was frantic; my want of [p. 83] Information left me ignorant of any other Subject to vent my rage against except the one called Fate which I never could comprehend & could therefore never gain any kind of satisfaction of, but from habit & the custom of Europe I cursed it wherever it was. I was never before sensible of a weakness of body. I fell down in my rage on the floor & slept until daylight.

Pursued my Journey next day & the following I arrived at Mogaloff.

My reception, detention & departure must be a Subject hereafter.

I left Mogaloff on the 18 of March and arrived at the Barrier Town 90 Versts the same evening—waited in the Street half an hour before called in to the [p. 84] Majors—from there conducted to the Directors house—alone in an anti-room there half an hour.—At last the dear moment came that I was conducted over a Bridge across a little River,[174] across the Barrier into the little Village Tolochin in Poland.—O Liberty! O Liberty! how sweet are thy embraces! Having met thee in Poland I shall bless that Country; Indeed I believe it wants the blessing of every charitable mind. I was conducted for quarters to the house of a Jew. not being permitted to enter the Dominions of a people more destitute of principle than themselves they hover about its boundaries here in great numbers. It was a large dirty house filled with dirt & noise & children. When my Baggage was

174. The Drut River.

brought in, I found I had been robbed of 5 Roubles that were in a Bag [p. 85] in my Portmanteau. I discovered it to the Russian Lieutenant who instantly set about seeking for it. It was found in the Boots of the Russian Postillion, & as the Russian Soldier was guard over me & my Property & was drunk, at the moment (tho' not before) I suspected him to be an accomplice. I wrote so in my letter to General Passek. The Russian Officer did me the Satisfaction, without asking or thinking of it myself, to strip & flog the Postillion before me. Thus was my Voyage in Russia finished as it was begun. I was robbed at Moscow on my setting out of 50 Roubles, which I lost entirely, & from that time to this at different times whether in Russia or Siberia I have constantly had something stolen from me. For the third time only since my confinement I slept without my Clothes this Night [p. 86]

March 20 } This morning I had a hot bath prepared for me. Very dirty, & fond of the Russian hot Bath it was a great Luxury to me. I was reanimated after half an hour spent in it.

I received as a present of the Commandant of the Russian Frontier Village 4 Bottles of a small Wine of some kind, & from the commanding Officer of the Russ Guard 6 Lemons & some white Bread; which was a friendly present here, where the bread is very black & coarse, & what is worse very dear: indeed other things are so also. I had not time to ask the reason. It is the uncertain boundary of a Queen on the one hand, whose rapacity of Empire is boundless, & on the other by a People who I strongly suspect of all the Vices of Indolence & Vanity. It is besides almost solely inhabited by Jews who [p. 87] are ever nuisances except in places totally Commercial. The Company drank some Wine & smoaked a Pipe with me. The manner of my Deportment toward the Director of the Russian Barrier Village, in my own Empire, as I called it, visibly mortified him, the vain Russian, for his (I will not say his ungenteel but) beastly haughtiness, disdain & impertinence to me the Evening before: but mark the pliability of a genuine Russian—He choaked me with congratulations on my Deliberation from Confinement; bowed, smiled, complimented, lyed, swore, & protested with all the ease & grace of his Predecessor Sinon[175]—In the Evening I contracted with a Russian Trader with the Precautions of writing & signing & taking his Passport in my own possession to carry me from this place to Konigsberg [p. 88] in Prussia 600 Versts for 40 Roubles. I received also from General Passek, by express, who had not yet left his generous Solicitude for me, a young Man, as a Servant to interpret for me, & to serve me as long as I pleased having discharged [him] from his own Family expressly for the purpose.

March 21st } In the morning I set out, but still weak & low—we went 50 versts & I stopped in the Evening. I slept in my Kabitka, tho' I wanted much to be in a house that I might undress myself which I find in my weak state is a great refreshment to me, but the Stage houses are not fit for such or hardly any repose.

22d } The Russian Birch Forests have left me. I have at present well grown Pines, Alder, & a few poor Oak Trees. [p. 89] The few Rocks that are scattered above the Snow are Granite. I passed 20 odd round Hillocks 15– to 30 feet high, situated in a Cluster & without Order, between the Skirts of a Wood & the borders of a Rivulet.[176] The Country hitherto is a plain covered with Forests, a few detached houses, & about every 25 or 30 Versts a Town. The Inhabitants are almost [all] Jews, who keep little, very little miserable Shops in them, & they also keep the Stage houses on the Road. The Villages here are as miserable receptacles as the Russian ones on the desart of Barabanskoi.[177] I never saw more poverty nor much more dirt. It is however a proper situation for them; they ought to be placed between the borders of every Nation. I believe it is curious that I am so often exposed to the small Pox without taking it. I was surprized [p.

175. Sinon: the Greek who induced the Trojans to bring the wooden horse into Troy.

176. These hillocks were nomadic burial mounds; see p. 144, n. 6.

177. The Baraba steppe, almost 400 miles in extent, lies between Omsk and Kolyvan. Sauer stated that about ten years before this time the Empress "built villages all over it at the distance of 20 to 25 versts. . . . The inhabitants of all the villages are convicts." *Account of a Geographical and Astronomical Expedition*, p. 8.

90] to day as I have been several times before in this Country by being in the same Room where it was in its full force.

23[d] } We have rain & the roads are gone, we have taken to our wheels. I have been waiting ever since my first arrival at the Frontiers of Poland to be determined if the poor Devils of Peasantry I there meet with were a sample by which I could judge of the whole. The pleasure I have in seeing a good Peasantry is an uniform Ingredient in the pleasures of my Voyage. Besides my Malice against the Empress of Russia & to the wish I had of seeing a good Peasantry here. Without knowing what he was or his people, I became a partizan of the King of Poland, the moment I entered his Dominions.[178] They afforded me Shelter from the persecutions of an unjust & insolent Tyrant. [p. 91] I said to myself in my wrath that supported by such a Peasantry as I supposed the King of Poland had, that I would joyfully fight the best Corps of Beasts the Empress has; but alas with the Peasantry I have Seen I should be content to be King of Poland whatever he is. If their united Efforts will keep me from starving until I can hurry out of the Country I shall be satisfied. They are without exception, not only the poorest Peasantry but the poorest men I ever saw; surely there are better. Those I have seen are wretchedly diminutive and ill formed, ill fed, ill clothed & ill looked. 5 Feet 2, 4, or 5 Inches is the average height of those I have seen; bandy-legged, splay-footed, & knock-kneed; slender built, effeminate Voices, & unanimated Faces. Their Dress is like the Russ [p. 92] except the colour of their Frock which is white. They have the Hair shaved from the head except the Crown. The domestic Animals I have hitherto seen are equally wretched. I wish since there are such Writers in Europe that when they want to expatiate on the history of little men that they would not fly with such malicious illiberality among the Samoiedes & Esquimaux without acknowledging at least one exception to their general System, in their own dear dominions. Reasoning from Theory downward to facts has exceedingly injured truth. Buffon

178. Stanislas Augustus Poniatowski, king of Poland from 1764 to 1795.

is a well made Athletic Frenchman: how would he look to meet with thousands among the Laplanders Samoiede & Esquimaux that would foil him in any of the manly Exercises, & more I doubt with his Burgundy [p. 93] to boot he should make his appeal to the talents of the mind he would come off, any better. Good Sense is more the result of undisturbed contemplation than of reading, & I leave mankind to draw the comparison between the French and Samoiede in this respect.—I have passed to day above 50 of the same round Hillocks mentioned yesterday only larger these were situated without order in a wood between two little Villages & not more than ¼ of a mile from a burying Ground which is like the Mahometan Tartars as I have before observed. These Hillocks must have been the Tumuli of some people. I have remarked also in some parts of Russia. On the road I passed on the Strait Elsineur[179] to Stockholm in Sweden they are very numerous. In some Instances I suppose them to be the [p. 94] remains of deserted Villages as in Russia, tho' there are also some there that are Tumuli in other Instances as in Sweden I suppose them to be the receptacles of slaughtered Armies. The Grove burying Places have uniformly accompanied me since my arrival on the confines of Poland.

24th March or 4th April N.S. } The Parts of Poland I have hitherto passed constitute a close, thick, wooded Country; little bad Roads & no cultivation except a few small fields round the Houses. I now & then see a Polish Gentleman's House.—Misery!—Oppression how many forms wilt thou assume to lull the wretched to Submission & to harden the hearts of Tyrants! God grant a part of the Christian System at least to be true & that an hereafter shall rectify the absurd Situation in which daring Villainy, & base Temerity have [p. 95] placed my Brethren & my Sisters in this world with respect to each other. I dare not trace this Custom back of one Moses tyrannizing over thousands, for the honour of human Reason I fear it is of very remote Date.

The Insignia of Catholicism are as disgustful here as in Dane-

179. The Sound, or Øresund, separating Denmark from Sweden.

marc.[180] A miserable Jesus made with a Hatchet, some old Rags hung round it: the Crucifix yclipt with pincers, a hammer, Nails, spear, a long Pole with a Spunge, & a number of such things carved in Wood & some things that Jew or Gentile never knew. Why is Christ thus rendered the theme of Scandal & Mahomet not—These however are pitiable Weaknesses, but Russian Impudence in professing the Christian Religion & the Worship of a God when they are as arrant Idolaters as history affords—any account [p. 96] of it is still more offensive.

The Jewish Women I observe as I pass along to be very handsome, cheerful, & free, but very filthy.

Having stopped early this Evening, I have an hour of Day light with which I amuse myself in relating my reception with General Passek.

When I arrived at the Generals Door I was in my Kabitka half an hour or more before I was sent for (it was about 4 in the afternoon) I was conducted by an Officer thro' several plain, decent Apartments to his Bed room, & found him sitting in Bed a little indisposed, with a Romish Parson on a Sopha by his Bed conversing with him. The first rencontre of his Eye gave me his Character, & ascertained my Fate.—[181] I am interrupted by the noisy Worship of [p. 97] the Jewish Family where I am. They have lighted their 7 Candles & begun their hymning. They must be obstinate Dogs to repeat with such perseverance a formula that appears to be so very tedious and insipid to them—they yawn, & loll, and stretch themselves, & are very uneasy, but still they will go on. Now I declare that was I to worship as Jew or Gentile, Greek or Barbarian I would worship not, without it was

180. Ledyard surely saw few signs of Catholicism during his short stay in Denmark.

181. The French traveler Caron de Beaumarchais who in May 1788 visited Passek in Mogilëv, described his first encounter with him as follows: "General Passek was five feet eight inches tall and of a Herculean build; he had a proud glance and during the time he was silent, judging by the expression of his face, one might think that he was intelligent; he was about 66 years old, however he spent two hours each day before a mirror, although his entire toilet consisted of putting on his wig, already curled beforehand." *Russkaia Starina,* 22 (1878):330.

a pleasure to me & no longer than it was a pleasure to me. Thanks be to them they have stopped their Mouths with some Fish Soop—Eat Sons of Jacob & be happy; if I judge right of your appetites by your actions you like eating better than praying; Eat, it is there we all think & act alike.

As a Traveller sees many things, so he thinks of many things & thinks [p. 98] of them in the careless order he sees them. Seeing a Jewess lift up her Eyes in Devotion before the Seven Candlesticks while the others are chanting I am thinking how universally the Element of Fire has constituted a part of the Ceremony of divine Worship. I question if any other Custom will be found so universal. None can be more antient if the Burnt-Offerings of Cain & Abel is the most antient part of human History.

The General received me with a most endearing politeness, begged me to sit by his Side, & asked if I would take some Tea, Coffee, or any other Refreshment. I made choice of some Tea. He addressed me in French & observed to me that the orders of his Sovereign were that I should be conveyed out of the Empire into Poland, & that I was forbid ever to enter it again without permission [p. 99] & that I had hardiment[182] passed thro' it. It was his business to have said how this or something else he had in his Letter must have constituted my Crime—but it seemed by chance that he mentioned the Circumstance of passing *hardiment* thro' Russia. I had motives the most just to demand a full explication of the reasons for the conduct of his Sovereign. If indeed the Empress had treated me with as much politeness as injustice she would have ordered me a copy of a Crime so considerable as to send for me 6000 versts to transport me out of her Dominions & with the insulting Charge never to enter it again without permission.

My Motives were stimulated too by an Indignation I did not hesitate to discover. I told the General that his were the last hands I should pass thro' [p. 100] & if her Majesty had not ordered him to inform me of my Crime she had added an Insult

182. French for impudently or boldly.

to the rest of her Conduct to me, he said I thought too rigidly of the Affair, & went on to tell me by complimenting his Mistress, as the most wise, amiable, prudent, & humane Sovereign in Europe & concluded for the moment with this most condoling & sensible Remark; that whatever Reasons her Majesty had for her proceedings she had only politely told me that my Visit to her Dominions was disagreable & desired me to discontinue it. "had I not been waited on to the place of my destination *by a Guard*"? You have not been prisoner; you have not lost your Liberty &c &c. & then begun in Proverbs to tell me "that Sovereigns had long Arms"—I could no more—I rise—Yes by God M^r le General yours are very long Eastward; If your [p. 101] Sovereign should stretch the other Westward she would never bring it back again entire, & I myself would contend to lop it off.

March 25th } I am troubled with Floods, Rivers & bad Roads.

26 } I want about 50 Versts or 10 Polish Miles of half my distance to Konigsberg. The Country begins to be more peopled & more cultivated, & the Inhabitants to appear a *little* more personable, but I have not yet seen one Instance of an *approach* to Beauty in either Sex. The Jews form a very curious Contrast with the Poles in this respect, the Women particularly, I have seen but two or three Women that were unhandsome—But they were very much so; The Jewish Women have beautiful Complexions. A fine Skin & as happy a Mixture [p. 102] of Colour as ever I saw; long black Hair which among the Demoiselles hangs down behind in one & sometimes two plaits, the rest is hid, as the Married Women do all theirs under one or more Handkerchiefs. They have large full Jet black Eyes which like all others of that Sort rather surprize than convince me into the Idea of Beauty. They have good Teeth & some very pretty Features. But I am disgusted the Moment I view a horrid clumsy, large coarse dirty Hand; this added to their uniform filth, & now & then the Itch—I know nothing of their shapes; I regret it, but they are disguized under a vile Eastern Dress. The Child of damned Jealousy or damned Superstition called into existence

expressly to turn the Eyes of Man from viewing a Work of Nature as expressly formed to attract Attention, Admiration [p. 103] Esteem & Love.—There is a remarkable Gradation in Dress from the East to the West as in other Customs. The tout ensemble leads to a supposition of a very formidable Nature & gives to understand at least that Mankind have long been acquainted together—to say no more about it—There is a *Melange* of Dress here & so of other Customs. The effects of the Geographical situation of its Inhabitants between the Eastern & Western World this is with difficulty described. The Jews are entirely in the Eastern Stile, if I should say *Mosaic* I believe it would be still more proper, & if the antient Izraelites were Slovens as gross as the modern it ought not to prevent my Remark, & I have no doubt they were, for real Cleanliness is ever a Concomitant of real [p. 104] Genius & Science, speaking nationally & almost always so when the observation is applied to Individuals. This leads me to make a bold inference, that the Moderns have more of Genius & Science, than the Antients which I suppose is true. The Poles on the other hand (if I include the Ladies, who I am apt to think are the best judges & examples of Dress & Cleanliness) have more of the European than Asiatic about; but both the Dress & Manners of Europe sit ill upon them. I speak of the Country People of Condition & what they call Nobless, some of whom viz 2 Ladies & 2 Gentlemen are at Dinner at the Table where I am writing.[183] I suppose I do right to take those people & those below them as a standard to judge by, tho' I should be glad to take those of more Fashion, since the Nobless I have seen join another species of Awkwardness to the one already [p. 105] intimated being mere down right Rustics on whom it is probable that the Asiatic Dress would sit as badly. This however little affects the observation when I see huge, coarse Ear-rings, Rings, Bracelets, a dozen strings of coarse Wax Beads of a dull *red*, (the favourite Colour of a rude People) hang about their Necks; Fingers of both hands loaded

183. These were members of the Polish landed nobility, or *szlachta*, which comprised about 8% of the population at this time.

with coarse Rings, Pieces of Coin or Medals round the Bosom & in short all the Trinkets of one of Solomon's Mistresses.—Indeed there is a rude, unfinished, capricious fantastic Taste that divides both Poland & Russia from the Genius of Europe; & that any one may understand me I will illustrate my observations by remarking that full seven eights of the Merchandize imported (for Russia has hardly any Manufactures except Images [p. 106] in Iron & other Metals, & Poland I believe none at all) into these Countries are of the flimsy, tawdry kind and mostly from France. A Pedlar from thence will make his Fortune in these Countries with his well painted Gewgaws & the refuse of a French Toyship, when an Englishman would starve with an Assortment of the best goods in Europe; & France particularly fits out her Caravans for these parts in the same manner she does her Ships for the Coast of Africa, or the English their's for Hudsons Bay.

27th } Passed many more of those Hillocks.

28} I arrived to day at the City of Vilna, which is the Capital of the province of Lithuania.[184] The first Salutation was by two dirty wretched looking Soldiers from a decayed smoaky [p. 107] log-built Guard house, who wanted to know if I had any Merchandize in my Kabitka—being answered not—they then wanted to know if I had any money to spare. It seems to me that there is a most wretched Discipline in all the parts of the North where I have passed except in Russia In Denmark I have had the Centinels round the Royal Palace as well as elsewhere carry their Arms to me & at the same Moment ask money of me. In Sweden I never had my Trunk examined if I would convey a sixpence or a Shilling into the hands of a Soldier, & here I have no doubt I could have passed for the same trifle with my Kabitka full of Goods or even with the Grecian Horse.

Vilna begins a new Country; from an unvariegated, miserable, sickly plain my Eye is relieved by Groups of fine [p. 108]

184. Vilna in 1788 had around 20,000 inhabitants (*Entsiklopedicheskii slovar'*, 11:384). From the 17th to the 19th centuries it was the principal seat of Jewish culture in Europe.

romantic Hills & well cultivated Vallies, but it does not compensate for the number of Beggars that surround me. I had one Coup d'Œil[185] at a Group, to day, of Hills that I will visit tomorrow. I am constantly thinking about Hills, or something else of the Kind & as my thoughts are all my own I write what I think without knowing whether it is of Importance or not & leave others to judge of it being convinced only of this that I ought to write if I think so, & that it is better to write many pages in vain than that one of Service to Mankind should not be written.—I make this remark once for all to inform my Friends that I am sensible of my humble Genius but not ashamed of it, & to intimate to them that I wish them to deal with me with the same honest careless freedom I do [p. 109] with them. to be damned is no torment to the Guilty, & to enjoy fame is no happiness to him who is not convinced he merits it

Remark.—I have observed on this as well as all the other Continents I have visited that on approaching the Confines of Land & Sea the surface of the Earth is covered with smooth round Rocks or Stones. The Superficies having apparently been rendered smooth & equal by other causes than mere length of time or its various effects in the situation in which they are & that there is a great Affinity if not a perfect one between Rocks & Stones (thus described) situated at certain Distances on Land from the Sea & those situated at certain Distances in the Sea from the Land: Those on the Land appearing to have had their Superficies formed from the Effects of Water; from the Movement [p. 110] of the Sea; the wash of the Sea; from Currents or Tides.

I do not remember to have observed this on any of the Islands I have visited except new Holland, where however I did not go far enough inland to make the Observation compleat.[186] I must confess that in travelling thro' the interior parts of Countries in a

185. Glance.

186. New Holland is an old name for Australia. Ledyard visited its southern tip in January 1777.

Centrifugal direction, I should as soon recognize them for Marks of an approaching Sea as in coming from Sea towards Land, Sea-Weed for a Land mark & sooner. The observation like most of my others has obtruded itself upon me & has been tormenting me for several Years to take Notice of it; which I confess I do not like & have therefore given it a place here.

Remark—The Beds of large Rivers near their Sources as I view [p. 111] them intimate to me that they have never changed their positions that the Rocks & mountains which confine & direct their Courses now have always done it & that the Chasms in which they run were not caused by the Rivers; the Chasms being Antecedent or at least coeval to them, & that one cause produced the two effects & perhaps at the same time. If Rivers could not form those deep Chasms what could? Why is the peaked, ragged Mountain peculiar to the central parts of Land & why are they Scarrified in the manner they universally are?—The *Flood*

All Rivers are most rapid at their Source & an Eye accustomed to it will from the rapidity of its Waters & from the elevation of the surrounding Land very nearly Judge his distance from [p. 112] their Source & what sort of Rivers they are Rivers do not meander much near their source; those whose Waters are muddy are very serpentine

Where Rivers begin to wind they begin also to shift their Beds, form & destroy Islands & plains, & conceal & reveal by turns the Fossil World. Nothing is more capricious than their Currents. It requires great Sagacity to trace their deserted Tracks; & a cautious observer often doubts at first view what upon a review he is thoroughly convinced of; their operations are very extensive & in Countries where they are large & numerous they fairly change the Face of Nature. In Siberia I have remarked something like this that I cannot account for—nay more than I have mentioned; for whether they are the [p. 113] cause or not they are certainly the longitudinal boundaries of Climates.—Every River from the Lena to the Wolga is more or less a proof & an example of the last Observation; some of them very positive ones particularly the Yenissy; There even the Vegetable Kingdom is divided & as the Chevalier Karamyschew very pertinently observed to me. There also is the *natural* boundary between Russia & Siberia. The Tomsk[187] is the next instance & after that the Oby: The others are not such Striking Instances but still worthy of remark. I do not for the moment recollect one general & positive Law that those wandering Districts are subject to that however they meander or digress their ultimate courses shall be towards the Poles or if not directly to the Poles, the inclination shall be north & south & vice versa. There are few exceptions [p. 114] to this general Rule & almost all those Rivers which are such, rise under the Equator which I supposed easily accounted for:—I remark also as a Circumstance that appears merely curious to me, that Rivers which have a Northern & Southern course have almost universally the highest Bank on the East Shore, & that those which run E & W have the high bank on the South shore.[188]

As fishing constitutes a part of the Chace a Savage if he has any fixed abode forms it on the banks of Rivers & so will the new settlers of a new Country. Most of the Russian Cities & Capital Towns that lay on the Rout eastward thro' their dominions beginning at Kazan the first after Moscow to Yakutsk the last to the Pacific Ocean, having been first Towns [p. 115] of Tartars are almost all built on the old & present banks of great Rivers. The City of Tobolsk is partly on an old Bed & partly on the high eastern Bank adjoining it at the conjunction of the Irtys & Oby. The Town of Tomsk, exactly like it on an old bed & Eastern Bank of the river Tomsk, in those places the Rivers are very wide. At Yakutsk on the borders of the Lena the River reckoning from an old Bank West to the present high Eastern one has occupied a bread[th] of 15 English Miles, & this one change it is plain to be seen has been formed not by gradual process, but three different

187. The Tom River, a tributary of the Ob.

188. If Ledyard had traveled through southern Russia, he would have observed that of the Dnieper, Don, and Volga each has the highest bank on the western shore.

Changes somewhat sudden; The Town of Yakutsk being situated on the middle Bed formed by the three Changes & has been built [p. 116] near 200 years. The River here is also full of Islands & appears very wide, therefore tho' its true Channel is but 2 or 2½ English Miles over. This remarkable change in the Lena here is as I have intimated before because it here *winds much* & forms that great & unfortunate turning from N.E. easterly, in which direction it would have joined the Pacific south of the River Anydirskoi[189] to a course NW & N where it looses its useless Stream in an Ocean still more useless than itself.—I must remark however one thing in favour of it, that at its Mouth & the Islands & Sand Banks there formed by the repercuration[190] of an endless variety of tides & currents it affords a rich Endroit[191] to the curious in the fossil Way; after meandering thro' various Countries & Climates with a Depth & Strength of Water [p. 117] sufficient for the purpose, it here leaves a part of whatever it has found in its Way & rolled along with its Stream or forced hither by the Ice; whether Sand, Rocks, Trees, large Mounds of Earth, wrecks of Houses &c.

It is so also with the other Rivers in this Country the same; their united operations in this respect has rendered the confines of the frozen Ocean & the borders of what Naturalists term with the most Philosophic Propriety the Arctic Flats; a repository of Fossils unequalled elsewhere in extent & I doubt not in variety since those Fossils already found by a few very slight visits have given rise to enquiries of the most interesting Nature, Enquiries that Fossils found in Rivers however extensive which roll longitudinally only cannot be supposed to produce, since a difference of Latitude is the greatest cause of a difference of Climate [p. 118] & objects in natural history known, or supposed to be general or peculiar to certain climates, found reposited in Climates different from them, form a Contrast, & this forms En-

189. The Anadyr River flows into the Pacific north of Kamchatka.
190. "repercuration": a repeated crossing.
191. Place, or spot.

quiry; & this Enquiry is not about the Epoch of an inglorious Sovereign, nor the change of Empire but the history of Man at large, the Globe itself, & the Ways of God to Man.

It is singular that the Kovima River which is not more than half the Magnitude of the Lena or Yenisey which has its source & which empties itself in Regions still more remote should notwithstanding more abound in Fossils than those two Rivers.

I am much obliged to Captain Billings for this & many other accounts from that quarter, & had not the unprincely Malice of the Empress of Russia impeded [p. 119] my Travels I should have had many more The Circumstance alluded to of the Kovima Fossils affects very much the Argument of a General Deluge in my poor Opinion, I dare not say how much yet; I will however say upon the whole that I am led independent of Opinion & with a very moderate share of self Love to this. Idea viz. "That all parts of the Earth have at some period unknown to me enjoyed the same Climate, that they have consequently [been] accessible to universal and uninterrupted Migration, & that the Fossils found in Climates we now call frigid were natural to them when those Climates were not frigid"; & that the reason why we have only fossils to support the Argument is that the Period when this alteration took place is so remote that nothing else remains which has not lost its form in the unfashioned particles [p. 120] of matter & that Substances the least subject to decay are the Fossils we find; I observe it in the parts of Bones we find, the flinty Shin Bone of the Elephant & the Teeth are almost the only parts that are found & many of them almost gone. The Head of a Rhinoceros added to the rich fossil Cabinet of the Empress of Russia by D[r] Pallas is the only material exception that I know of, & that is very curious indeed. I could not take my Eyes from it when I saw it; the form is almost minutely entire even to the Skin & the Hair. It is from Siberia the place where it was found, & some Mem[da][192] respecting it are among my unfortunate papers at Yakutsk nei-

192. Memoranda. Concerning this rhinoceros see Ledyard to Jefferson, # 26.

ther must I forget to mention several horns in a tolerable state of preservation in Captain Billings [possession] from the Kovyma, but so miserably are [p. 121] we both accoutred in the Knowledge of such things that we could only suppose what Animals they are parts of Viz—the Buffaloe.

They were composed of a Substance black & grey intermixed resembling the colour of Whale Bone & strips of it hanging detached from the Horn, elastic like Whale Bone; the forms of them not particularly different in any respect, as I conceived, from the Horn of an European ox of good size.

It is a pity Men of Science will not or cannot travel themselves & that Fate should so whimsically ordain to sally forth such as I am for example for the purpose of adding to natural Knowledge, & it appears very demonstrable to me that they ought to be hung for staying at home as much as I do for going abroad, & that both should be done.

[p. 122] I suppose the history of Fossils to be very interesting; since we find the Subject of it at least in as great abundance in our highest excursions North as in the lower ones South: why not pursue the Enquiry, the research; particularly N.E. from the Ischutskoi Dominions in NE Asia to the contiguous coasts of NW America. Would it not affect the historical Analogy of those remarkable portions of Earth so much the theme of every Species of Philosophy—but the right—(for I feel it in my heart to be impertinent) which is travelling. On whom do I reflect when I say that parts of our Globe altogether accessible to discovery are less known in strict truth than are parts of the Moon since the Optical Improvements of Dr H[unter] & yet we will affect to reason of them in a style of as much familiarity as [p. 123] Hunter with a Skeleton before him.

April 9th } I have been out to see the City of Vilna; it is about ¾ of a Mile in Diameter each Way, situated in a Vale having both within & without a number of round hills; those within have houses on their Tops & those without Castles, now in Ruins. The City has been laid out in the Style Militaire, with its inner & outer Departments—but the whole was dismantled by a Russian Visit[193]—Some of the Houses are very old & one or two Churches, but not a trait in Architecture (in which by accident I have a smattering kind of Knowledge) worth remark. The Style is grecian.[194] It is watered within by a pretty little Stream,[195] is decently built, & for the season of the year & its situation remarkably clean.

[p. 124] I was extremely pleased in my Walk to meet what they call the Directeur of the Town making his rounds personally to superinspect its Affairs. He was on Horseback in a plain Polish Dress & a plain Sabre by his Side & one Horseman in his Suite, he appeared intent upon his Business like a good Officer & a good Citizen. To the expence of Russia & the honour of this Country I declare that a Russian Officer in the same Office (if he went himself) would never have gone on this or any other Duty without his Coach, the exact number of Horses tied to it whether dead or alive & the exact number of attendents his Rank entitled him to, & then he [would] have drove Phaeton like over every thing he met & returned with the same Information he set out with, but he had been *seen* tho' he saw nothing himself it was enough for a Russian Officer. Vive l'ecclat!

[p. 125] The Jews here have in appearance for I do not think it worth While to ask any questions the sole management of all kinds of Traffick & as there is no kind of Manufacture here as I am accidentally told I leave as a thing disagreable to examine how people support themselves.

What a Pity it is after having seen the Directeur that I have seen three full dressed Polish Ladies–France has marred the Faces of half Mankind & done more mischief with its Rouge than

193. Russian troops then in northeastern Poland entered Vilna in 1788, presumably before Ledyard's arrival.

194. The Town Hall, begun in 1786, and the Cathedral of St. Anne, restored after 1783, were designed in classical style by the architect Wawrzyniec Gucewicz. For these buildings Vilna was often called "the Athens of the Poles." Other notable buildings dated back to the 14th century.

195. The Wilja (or Neris) River.

its politics—Their Dress was a bad imitation of the French. With all my eager Glances not one handsome Face have I seen, & but very few well looking Men.—Their Carnival is at hand & I could wish to see it as among their Joan & Darby Nobless[196] one might rencontre at least with something Buxom.

[p. 126] At the town of Yakutsk there are a great number of Russia Merchants or Traders: they are very enterprizing, hardy Men. It is the most remote Russian Town in the North of Siberia & on that Account particularly is the resort as well as residence of those Men from every known Corner of that Country. I was much in their Company. some had been at the mouth of the River Yenesey, others the Lena & others the Kovyma. Among them all there was hardly any place in the North or East where they had not been. They all agreed in the Voluntary accounts they gave me of the great quantities of Drift Wood at the mouths of the Lena & Yenesey. At the Kovyma there is hardly any. their accounts of this matter were that there was almost constantly a thick crowded Mass of Trees [p. 127] floating on the Borders of the Icy Sea & that it extended out for many Versts some said 50 & others more. As an instance of their simplicity for they did not mean it as a compliment, they have often asked me where I thought so much Wood came from since there was none that grew on the Coasts. They also told me that old Russian hunters or Fur Traders for in Siberia those Epithets are indiscriminately used that were then living said that since their Memory the Sea had retired many Versts to the North, in some places 100 Versts, & that those forsaken plains were overspread with old trunk of Trees buried in the sand.[197] A rich, intelligent Merchant there called Popoff & brother to the Popoff mentioned I think in the preface to Dr Pennants Synopsis[198] gave me also the same ac-

196. By this term Ledyard is referring to the Polish landed gentry, who lived as rustically and humbly as the English couple Darby and Joan, described in the poem of that name by St. John Honeywood (1763–98).

197. This alludes perhaps to a delta such as that of the Lena, which today extends about 100 miles into the Arctic Ocean.

198. Ledyard's memory is faulty here; Pennant does not mention Popoff in the Preface of the first edition of *Synopsis of Quadrupeds* (Chester,

counts & added also others the result of his [p. 128] Travels to the Eastward on the American Coast & also among the Kurile Islands on the Coast of Korea & the River[199]

The number & the magnitude of the Rivers in the Russ Dominions which empty themselves into the Icy Sea produce very great changes, & as a change begun by them continually increases until they loose their existence as Rivers in the frozen Ocean so is there the greatest Change because the last. If I had information sufficiently particular I would dwell on the Subject & go so far as to estimate first of all the quantity of fresh Water they roll into the Mere glaciale, & then the quantity & quality of Earth & vegetable Substances they carry & deposit there. There is but one River in Northern Russia (viz. the Wolga which goes into the Caspian) that does not empty itself immediately or [p. 129] collaterally into the Northern Sea, & as most Rivers have Connections with Lakes so have those, & there also of course numbers of Lakes which also pay their Tribute in the same line to the Icy Sea & the princely Baikal among the others. The Column of Water that goes into that Ocean from the Continent by these Conveyances alone would of itself in 12 months form an Ocean equal in solid Contents to the shallow one that at present barely covers the Earth beyond the Latitude of 70 North.—. Also the circumstance of such a quantity of fresh Water in that Ocean I should suppose would merit the attention of the curious since it naturally leads to a reflection on the quantity of Ice there, of its cause, duration, formation, diminution &c Men have supposed that Ocean to be supplied with Ice from those Rivers [p. 130] but if I had not positive proofs to the contrary I confess I should attribute the cause of the quantity of Ice there to the quantity of fresh Water there, which I believe has not been yet thought of

1771) or of the second, *History of Quadrupeds* (London, 1781). The Popoff brothers are perhaps two merchants from Lal'sk, Vasilii and Ivan Popov, who were active in sending out fur-trading voyages from Kamchatka in the 1760's. See Efimov, *Iz istorii russkikh ekspeditsii na Tikhom okeane*, pp. 302–5.

199. The river: probably the Amur.

except collaterally by Captain Cook whose few observations on the Subject I admire as much as I did his Abilities & good Sense. accustomed to think for himself & rely upon his own Opinion it rendered him equally penetrating, cautious & bold, & without any particular knowledge of the Circumstances I allude to could nevertheless assert that the Waters of that Ocean froze & that it did not receive its Ice from Rivers, & he assigned a very excellent reason for it which is that Ice formed in Rivers floating in that Ocean must necessarily bring along with them Vegetable Substances of some kind. If his [p. 131] Information would have carried him so far as to say that at the Mouths of every great River in Siberia emptying themselves into that Ocean there were Islands, Spits, & Bars of Sand across them that rendered a Communication of Ice to or from the Sea impracticable his Observations would have been perfect. The Mouths of the Kovyma are in 69 & 69.30 N [Latitude] by Captain Billings observation & by his Journal the Ice was 4 & 5 feet thick only. I was induced to think from this Circumstance when first informed of it that it was the effects of a frost for a Season only which made thus thick & no thicker the Ice; but finding on Enquiry both among the Russ & Yakutee that they never saw any Ice thicker (meaning solid transparent Ice) it obliged me to change my Opinion; Join the [p. 132] observations I had made in my own Voyages with theirs & reason about it in the following manner. Having never reflected on the circumstance of Congelation generally & particularly of the thickness of Ice, those observations above alluded to strike me the more forcibly. Born in one[200] of the NW States[201] of America & having also travelled to the NW among our cold Lakes & Rivers in the Winter[202] I do not remember ever to have seen Ice of a greater if so great a solid thickness either on Lakes or Rivers. Northward of the Streights of Bellisle I have seen the

200. "one" is repeated in the transcript.

201. It is doubtful that Ledyard would have considered Connecticut a northwestern state. Perhaps this is a mistake in the transcript.

202. Ledyard is probably referring to the winter of 1772–73 that he spent in the area around Dartmouth College, living among the Indians.

high Sea Ice, & so much for America.[203] In Sweden, Lapland, Finland & at Petersburg I never saw any thicker if so thick. Among the Cakes of Ice cut out of the Neva River at Petersburg for the Icehouses I do not think the Ice exceeds this [p. 133] thickness if so thick. At Yakutsk the Ice (for they cannot carry Water) that they bring on their Sledges from the Lena for domestick use in large Casks was not thicker. The Ice Windows there are taken from the Lena & are nothing but clear solid Ice, they are not more than 12 Inches—but then they are cut out in the fore part of Winter. Therefore I do not remember to have seen or heard of any Ice thicker than that at the Kovyma in nearly 70° nor Ice in any other cold Latitude (particularly where the cold approaches towards the fixed degree of Congelation viz. 32½) but what had nearly or for aught I know for certain the same thickness with the Kovyma where by the best observations made by [p. 134] Captain Billings there during a Winters Residence the degrees of Cold were 38°, 40° & so high as 43¾ Deg^{r}[204] Except Ocean Ice I have not seen or heard of any but what is about the same thickness in the Countries I have mentioned. Now if the Ice (for Example) on the Neva at Petersburg in 59°½ N is 4 feet thick only & at the Mouths of the Kovyma in 69°½ N. is 5 feet thick only, & if that is the proportional Difference of Cold in 10° difference of Latitude that difference will be an increase of one Inch & the fractions of two[205] in the thickness of Ice to each Degree of Latitude. But I can draw new Inferences from this. I pursue the Idea & say that if this proportion does in sort exist that the [p. 135] thickness of the Ice in a River near the Pole would be only 20 Inches thicker, but what can be inferred from this—That Ice in different situations is of different thickness but that the thickness of Ice formed by Congelation *only* in any place whatever is confined to 4, 5 or 6 feet and that all beyond is adventitious accumulation not owing to Frost only, but to Snow

203. Ledyard could have been north of Belle Isle Strait, separating Newfoundland from Labrador, only on his passage to England in 1775 or upon his return to America in 1782.

204. These measurements on the Réaumur scale approximate −53°, −58°, and −65° F., respectively.

205. This is 1.2 inches.

Hail, Sleet & far to the Northward heavy mists which fall on it & add rather a coagulated than a frozen conjunctive Mass—It appears to me that an Answer to those Doubts requires rather a comparative Detail of a number of facts to ascertain their Merit or Demerit than a *Coup d'esprit,* or perhaps a Coup d'esprit would destroy them entirely, and let its will be done. [p. 136]

April 10th } To day after Dinner I left Vilna whose Environs on the West Side are very pretty—it is surrounded by the prettiest little Hills & in the prettiest manner I have seen any where I remark some Instances of Country Houses in imitation of the English manner, but I quit it gladly for the Godlike Regions of the West. If I had believed from Information I never could have formed any adequate Idea without the little Tour I have made of the inferiority of the Eastern to the Western World & that so vast a difference could be found in the qualities of the Hearts & even of the Minds of men. If cultivation can produce such effects I see nothing romantic in supposing that the Men of the West may become Angels without the Ceremony of dying for it. I have a [p. 137] most horrid post house this Evening, not because it is filled with Smoak, Dirt & noise but a band of Polish peasantry, which word, by the by signifies in every Country that makes use of it entirely to express the lowest order of People *Slaves,* & I cannot bear the sight of one it becomes the occasion of as much uneasiness to me, as Liberty of Happiness. I become interested to think & act for him, & I have not time to do either.

April 11th } Charming Weather for the Season. I cannot find any thing that interests me among the Poles; perhaps it is because I am stupid or inattentive, & I wish as good an apology in their Favour might exist but in my Soul I doubt it. The Jews marry very young here. I saw an Instance to day of a pair the Female 12 & the Male 14 had been [p. 138] two years married from that time and had no Children.

The Custom of the Young Women or Virgins wearing the Hair hanging down & the Married hiding it is very curiously adhered to by the Jews who are tenacious in all their Customs, so that if they had originally been a good People they would now be the best on Earth. The same Custom is also Universal among the Poles, Russians & Tartars. This is another of those Eastern Customs the offspring of Eastern Jealousy. The Moment a Woman is married among them she becomes marked as we do a Horse we have bought. To hide the Hair is to have it cut off & to have cut off the Ears for the same purpose would not have been more ridiculous. Thus has that inoffensive & endearing part of the human Race been ever Used by Man; [p. 139] in the early & uncivilized parts of Society. The general observation that Complaisance to that Sex is the truest test of the degrees of civilization is true, but no one thinks it a sentence of Gallantry. There is not a maxim in Rochefaucault nor a Sentiment in Montesque more just

April 12 } I have not before to day approached an open cultivated Country. Roads exceeding bad, only 25 Versts to day.

13th } Roads excessive bad; if all extremes are not incommodious, the extremes in travelling certainly are. I find that 2 or 3 Versts an hour fatigue as much as flying post 12 or 14. It is however an unfortunate reflection as it respects me for until since my Imprisonment I never knew what this kind of fatigue was & hardly sensible of any other. To day I saw the borders of the Baltic The Jews here have certainly the most of [p. 140] an uniformity of Beauty I have seen. It may be prudently said that they are all handsome. This uniformity only is undoubtedly the consequence of their not commixing with other people; but how they became so uniformly handsome I cannot conceive.—I walked over a burying Ground to day on one of those Hillocks I have so often mentioned. It was an old Burying Ground, remote from a Village, 20 feet high, a grove of trees on it & a great Number of *Graves*. read the 2d book of Kings: Chap: 23—[206]

Mankind have universally agreed in one Sentiment with respect to the dead which is that of tenderness. however agreably this fact may at first strike one, yet examined with Candour it is rather a proof of human Infirmity which in every Age has been

206. In II Kings 23:16, Josiah took bones out of the sepulchres on a high place with a grove on it and burnt the bones.

equally exhibited by the Wise & foolish. Ask a Philosopher in Europe if it is a matter [p. 141] of Indifference with him whether he is inhumed after Death & whether so with respect to his best & dearest Friend, It is connected with the Idea of Death itself with many the Ideas are Synonimous. The greatest proof of this Infirmity is ever found like other Infirmities among the least informed of Mankind: If we in Europe doubt this Weakness & particularly of ourselves, let us go where our poor Prejudices will not follow us & appeal to the Customs of the uninstructed Savage we shall there find the Infirmity so great as to produce this most Shameful contradiction, viz "That men take greater care of each other when totally incapable of taking any than when they were capable of doing just the reverse.["] A Misanthropist might very well say that the Circumstance afforded him a proof of consummate Villainy in the Character of Man; I should be fonder of living after Death than an [p. 142] Englishman should I be content to loose one hour of Happiness while living for all that Mankind united could do for me after Death, & think the Man a knave that would excuse himself paying me a Guinea while alive by saying that he would not forget to do it when I was dead; It is like the Conduct of those mighty good & sensible people who are content to see a friend while living appear with a long Beard & a coarse Shirt on, & the moment he is dead send (for the first time) for a Barber & a Ruffle Shirt. Fortunately however our Weakness goes no further.

The Savage is not content with the same Weakness, he carries it much farther: he decorates, inters, & afterwards takes up his dead Friend from the tranquil Couch of Corruption where he lay; carries him however putrified on his [p. 143] back to some place many days Journey distant & reinters him; if occasion afterwards requires it he again repeats the same Ceremony. Dr Bancroft & Mr Carver[207] both give very curious accounts of the

207. Edward Bancroft (1744–1821), Massachusetts-born politician and naturalist, settled in Dutch Guiana in 1763, where he practiced medicine. In 1769 his *Essay on the Natural History of Guiana . . .* was published in England. See also above, p. 16. On Jonathan Carver see p. 191, n. 137.

matter: the former in Guiana & the latter among the interior Indians of the Northern Parts of America. I have yet never seen anything of the kind so extraordinary. However irrational this Conduct it has been productive of Events as remarkable & interesting as the most rational in the history of Man. He who has seen an Egyptian Pyramid has seen a Monument of human Weakness as well as power. What squabbles has the same weak Sentiment occasioned at different periods among all the antients and particularly the old Scythians, Battles, Triumphs & the Lord knows what.

[p. 144] It is however fortunate that the extremes of Virtue & Vice are so nearly allied; this Vice like others of its Magnitude is productive also of its Virtues. It taught the Scyths the Art of War. Their attention to their dead in various Ways, was what partly occasioned their Retreats, Ambuscades, & Counter-excursions It besides taught them to be more careful of the living & not expose to a rash decision the fate of a Battle, & the lives of Men. Alexander was embarrassed & baffled by this Circumstance. It gave also Courage to the Scyths, a people whose Ideas after Death were only about the Care that should be taken of their Bodies, having this removed by the great confidence they placed in the Survivors had a Stimulative to Valour that a more complicated System of Philosophy [p. 145] or Religion could not give to Armies however it might to a few Individuals: they could never say that Conscience made them Cowards—If the above is an Apology that pleads in its Favour, there is also another Circumstance that pleads in its Favour with me much more. It seems to be intimately connected with the Idea of an after Existence, & as universal as antient is the Custom of extending kindness to the Dead so is the belief of an after existence & I suppose I may say of immortality. The various forms in which those Sentiments have appeared in action operate in no manner against the original Idea. Time itself which produces effects so different in other Matters is here an Argument against itself & strengthens the Idea that I hope will at last destroy it. It had however effects different [p. 146] than the mere weaknesses I have mentioned. It produced among the Scyths also the most abominable Crimes, the same which exist at present among their descendants in America. It rendered their Wars the most bloody cruel & unrelenting among themselves particularly, & cruel Wars beget Wars. It is the black Soil in which Revenge receives its full Vigour; the whole heart became corrupted. Extent of territory, Riches or choice of Pasturage or Grounds for the Chace became at length only pretexts for Wars which had their foundations in mere Revenge & since they are the first people who *eat* their Enemies I see nothing forced in the supposition that should lead me to think it also the Child of Revenge alone. The War Songs to this Day sung among the American Indians [p. 147] have always in them such language as this[208]—"We will eat the Flesh of our Enemies & drink their Blood—The Bodies of our *unburied* Friends call out to be gathered up & inhumed."

15th} I this Morning quitted my Russ Conductors whose horses were fatigued & embarked with my demi-gentilhome, demifrizeur & the distressed Girl of Dantzic.[209] I had taken under my protection on board (for the[y] resemble Chinese Junks) some Prussian Waggons. I passed a barrier Town between the very unfortunate or very despicable King of Poland & those of the Rex Borussorum.[210] If human imbecility will have Kings to govern in Gods name let them be men of Genius. The breath of Frederick like the Dew of Heaven has fallen on [p. 148] these parts & I suppose on the whole of his Dominions. The quick Transition I have made of late from Kingdom to Kingdom with a kind of passive attention to their different manners has so habituated me to take notice of every thing I see & ruminate upon them that I believe in my heart nothing escapes me; the most delicate traits are familiar to me, & like an old American Indian Hunter I have Eyes & Ears peculiarly adapted to my

208. "this" is repeated in the transcript.

209. The city of Danzig.

210. King of the Borussi, or Prussians; Frederick II had died in August 1786 and was succeeded by Frederick William II (1786–97). The border between Prussia and Poland at that time was about halfway between Vilna and Königsberg.

Situation. If inspiration was not already a prostituted Theme I should fairly consent to think myself visited with it, & lay aside that rigid mode of thinking & conclusion that Philosophy demands. In the other parts of my Voyage the transition has been so gentle from the different Characters of People different to each other that I sometimes [p. 149] lost the Gradations. A second visit to the same places has convinced me of the Error & I have as well as I could rectified it. There also were others quite abrupt but none of them were so when I compared to the change I mark to day in entering the Dominions of the late King of Prussia: on the Confines of every other Kingdom there has been a Melange of Character of considerable extent within each, forming a kind of Suburb. It has not been so to day I have within the Space of 3 English Miles leapt the great barrier of Asiatic & European manners; from Servility, Indolence, Filth, Vanity, Dishonesty, Suspicion, Jealousy, Cowardice, Knavery, Reserve, Ignorance, Bassess d'Esprit & I know not what, to every thing opposite to it, busy Industry, Frankness, Neatness, well loaded Tables plain good manners, an obliging attention [p. 150] Firmness, Intelligence, &, thank God, Cheerfulness, & above [all] Honesty, which I solemnly swear I have not looked full in the Face since I first passed to the Eastward & Northward of the Baltic. Once more welcome Europe to my warmest Embraces. God the Source of honour can only know my feelings for I cannot describe them: but I remember that after being absent 9 years from my Mother whom I almost adore I did not meet her with greater Raptures than I do thee.

I do not know where to fix the Philosophic Geography of the other parts of Europe, but if my Vanity should ever tempt me to do it I should be sure of one spot to fix the foot of my Compass. There is something singularly decisive in the limits here [p. 151] marked by the great Frederick. I wish to God he had been a Tartar; his rich Genius would not have cursed all Asia with the useless Conquests of the half formed Zengis Chan, but would have chased from that ignominious & almost useless quarter of the World with equal address & vigour the baneful Sources of those Vices which have even to this very day retarded the bold & noble advances made by the Sons of Europe to a state of Society only worthy of mankind, & if I dare to subjoin the approbation of God.—I know not whether this is digression any more than I am certain whether I ever wrote a Line regularly; but this change in manners is also accompanied by that of Dress which has this singularity attending it, that it has an Analogy more extensive than [p. 152] of manners, & more easily traced; at least equally striking is the change of Features & of Person. There is a Delicacy of Feature peculiar to the Asiatic, it is almost uniform; the European variety is not more remarkable. Perfect Beauty is undoubtedly among both; but an Incongruity of Feature is not among the Asiatics. The Arabian Horse in the Subordinate Scale of beings is not a more distinct Species of Animal compared with the multifarious Species of that Animal among us than the Asiatic & European Man. To make the change I speak of more striking I am among the people most commonly known by the national appellation of Dutch,[211] who compared with every other people I have seen are in strict Justice grotesque & humbly [p. 153] & who have a common Character more different from the Asiatic than any of their European Neighbours. The Analogy between the Mind & Body forms the most excellent Data to reason from of human manners, & I can easily conceive why an infinite Variety of Features should exist among a people whose Education, pursuits, Enjoyments, & Thoughts are as various, & I can as easily assign those reasons for the difference between the European & Asiatic. When I speak comparatively of the Whole there are not two persons in Europe who think, & act, & live alike & their Features are as different & so are their Bodies. In Asia the Causes & the Effects are reversed. I have, for example remarked the uniformity of manners among the Jews (who are here Asiatics) & I have also remarked an [p. 154] uniformity of Beauty among them—why do I leap so suddenly among the humbly Dutch, & a variety of Knowledge, Pursuits &c &c

Death is the most remarkable and interesting Event in the

211. "Dutch" meaning *deutsch*, German.

history of Man & all the Animal Creation. Whatever the Ideas of Man have been respecting it or whatever Customs have followed from those Ideas they are the most to be depended on as Guides that will not deceive us or mislead us in investigating the Character of Man, or our Researches into other parts of Philosophy. Life which is but an opposite Event will not furnish more matter for such a Subject, indeed I believe not so many. It is only a circumstance that gives birth to the other & the beginning or Cause of [p. 155] which we have no proofs so positive as of Death, & for this & other reasons it becomes if not less interesting more the Subject of Ceremony. If we take the Date of our Existence from the History of Adam (& we are fond of doing it) we shall find but one remarkable Ceremony antecedent to the circumstance of Death which gave immediate existence to Millions this was the Ceremony of Sacrifice; but this the moment Death appeared lost its Independence & became a tributary Ceremony to it.—

But I am a poor Peasants' Son
uninstructed—& I write alone
I have none to help me.

There seems to have been very little difference in point of Knowledge among Men before the Epoch of the Deluge & [p. 156] a long while after & the most informed among those were very ignorant; & yet this little difference in the possession of a better kind of Ignorance rendered the Objects of it sometimes Objects of adoration to others. This Sentiment compared with ours of learned Men at this Day will shew the difference between the Knowledge of the present Epoch & those remote ones. The comparison will not only be curious but [will] afford a Data for interesting Investigations. Customs that existed before the Deluge as well as since are now in full force. They originated in times of profound Ignorance, Error & Superstition & like an old Disease are not shook off even in Europe. Many give literal Credit to antedeluvian Tales & like an Epicurean Fop are willing to suffer [p. 157] the excruciating pains of the Gout because their

Predecessors did the same, Inspiration (for instance) was a custom of thinking of certain great Men before the Christian Epoch or the harbingers of that Event, an argument that first afforded refuge to Villainy or ingenious Despair, and afterwards like other things, said to be divine; I wish it may be true that God ever inspired Man, & I also wish that Man had not inspired himself first.

It is a mortifying Reflection that the farther back we trace a custom, the greater proofs it gives us of the antient Ignorance & Weakness of Mankind. We see Genius sometimes in our earliest history, but its operations like a misguided Tempest ruined itself by its own [p. 158] force & the same Talents that should have mounted & conversed with reason at the feet of God—descended as far below & lost themselves in a contrariety of mere puerile Riddles. The present cultivated State of the human Mind in Europe is a proof that this reversed Situation of the Understanding at the period mentioned might have been, without the intervention of some unnatural Cause, or of a cause supernatural, for in truth I cannot conceive how any other could produce such an effect any more than I can conceive that the Sublime Points of knowledge of the present European can be the sole effects of natural Causes. God did not create the mind of Man so imperfect as its earliest operations declare it to be, or its operations would not be so perfect as [p. 159] they at present are. Did God at any period withdraw his assistance from Man in the pursuits of Knowledge; if he did was that the reason of his Ignorance. Has man sinned as mentioned under the Moral of the Apple in Eden. How could any Man in a State of Ignorance know himself to be so. We say at present that to be sensible of our Ignorance is to know to a Negative Exactness how wise we are; which is a proof of our Wisdom. could Moses reason thus? He has wrote thus & yet we know that he was uninformed, *beastly*, & Savage, was this Inspiration.

In leaving Vilna the Postillion begged I would not . . . . the young Woman I had with me in the Kabitka [p. 160] for if I did the Horses would certainly be taken with Sickness—One of the many Instances of Russian Superstition & let me subjoin that after all, this is a Thief & robbed my Portmanteau of 2 Roubles—& this at the moment of departure from him, & the last View I had or ever wish to have of a Russian was of a Thief; & a man void of all principle because I had but a few hours before dealt generously by him, & also, which forms the strongest Trait in a Russian Character; a Man whose power to dissemble can only be equalled by his Countrymen for at parting he came uncovered before me with all the good Wishes & good Looks of sacred Honesty & Charity. This good Christian also who carried his [p. 161] Images with him and worshipped them at every post, this good Catholick[212] also who would not suffer a starving Lutheran or any one else to cut his Bread during Lent with a Knife however cleaned that had touched Flesh.

Let no European put entire Confidence in a Russian of whatever Condition and none at all in the lower & middle Ranks of People.

212. It is unlikely that this Russian postillion, who carried his images with him, would have been anything other than Orthodox.

Letters and Other Documents Written after the Order for Ledyard's Arrest Was Issued December 18/29, 1787–1821

34. From the Diary of A. V. Khrapovitskii

[Dekabria] 18. [1787]	Amerikantsa Dzhona Lediarda, probiraiushchagosia iz Okhotska v Ameriku, prikazano ottuda vyslat'; on byl v gardemarinakh pri slavnom Kuke.

Translation:

[December] 18. [1787]	It is ordered to send back the American John Ledyard, making his way from Okhotsk to America, from that place;[1] he was a naval cadet with the famous Cook.[2]

"Dnevnik Khrapovitskago" (Khrapovitskii's Diary), *RA* (1901), Bk. 2, suppl., p. 34. A. V. Khrapovitskii was Catherine's personal secretary (*stats sekretar'*) from 1783 to 1796.

1. This suggests that Catherine presumed Ledyard had already proceeded as far as Okhotsk, not realizing that he had been stalled in Yakutsk and later in Irkutsk.

2. Catherine may have learned of Ledyard's accompanying Cook on his third voyage from such sources as Jefferson's letter of Feb. 9, 1786, to Lafayette (#2) and Ledyard's petition (if we accept as Ledyard's the memoir mentioned by Golder), both forwarded to St. Petersburg by Grimm.

35. Martin Sauer's Account of Ledyard's Arrest

At Yakutsk we found, to our great surprise, Mr. Ledyard, an old companion of Captain Billings, in Cook's voyage round the world; he then served in the capacity of a corporal, but now called himself an American colonel, and wished to cross over to the American Continent with our Expedition, for the purpose of exploring it on foot.

. . . The guns, medicines, sailors' clothing, &c. weighing upwards of 100 tons, still remained at Irkutsk, where they had lain ever since last winter.

Captain Billings resolved to go himself to Irkutsk to see these articles forwarded down the Lena so soon as the river should open in the spring. Accordingly, on the 29th December, he set out with carriages on sledges, which we had made on purpose. Mr. Ledyard, Robeck, Leman, his first mate, and I, accompanied him; the Russian secretary and several necessary hands were ordered to follow with all possible speed.

We arrived the 16th January 1788, and I took up my abode with my friend Brigadier Troepolski.

The Captain began making preparation for transporting the guns, &c. and sent to build vessels on the Lena at Katshuga, where they were deposited.

In the evening of the 24th February, while I was playing at cards with the Brigadier and some company of his, a secretary belonging to one of the courts of justice came in, and told us, with great concern, that the Governor-General had received positive orders from the Empress, immediately to send one of the Expedition, an Englishman, under guard to the private inquisition at Mosco; but that he did not know the name of the person, and that Captain Billings was with a private party at the Governor-General's. Now, as Ledyard and I were the only Englishmen here, I could not help smiling at the news, when two hussars came into the room, and told me that the Commandant wished to see me immediately. The consternation into which the visitors were thrown is not to be described. I assured them that it must be a mistake, and went with the guards to the Commandant. Here I found Mr. Ledyard under arrest. He told me, that he had sent for Captain Billings, but he would not come to him. He then began to explain his situation, and said that he was taken up as a French spy, whereas Captain Billings could prove the contrary; but he supposed that he[1] knew nothing of the matter, and requested that I would inform him. I did so; but the Captain assured me that it was an absolute order from the Empress, and he could not help him. He, however, sent him a few rubles, and gave him a pelisse;[2] and I procured him his linen quite wet from the wash-tub. Ledyard took a friendly leave of me, desired his remembrance to his friends, and with astonishing composure leaped into the kibitka, and drove off, with two guards, one on each side. I wished to travel with him a little way, but was not permitted. I therefore returned to my company, and explained the matter to them; but, though this eased their minds with regard to my fate, it did not restore their harmony. Ledyard's behaviour, however, had been haughty, and not at all condescending, which certainly made him enemies.

Sauer, *Account of a Geographical and Astronomical Expedition,* pp. 99–101.

1. Billings.
2. Pelisse: a fur-lined coat.

36. Gavriil A. Sarychev's Account of Ledyard in Eastern Siberia (English Version)

There was at this time in Jakutsk, an English traveller of the name of Ledyard, whose eccentric conduct excited considerable attention. He was known to Mr. Billings, from having been with him in the capacity of a corporal in Captain Cook's last voyage; after which he is said to have been a colonel in the army of the United States during the war. He had formed the design of going round the world in the literal sense of the word,[1] and for that purpose went to Petersburg, in order to begin with Russia; and on reaching the eastern boundaries of Asia, to wait for some vessel in which he might pass over to the English settlements. The absurdity of this enterprize is sufficiently manifest, from the circumstance of his intending to travel through a civilized country, without money or letters of recommendation; and afterwards to cross those boundless tracks on foot, thinly clad in winter, through which we had laboured with infinite difficulty on horseback, and in the warmest clothing. Where would he have found an opportunity of being conveyed over the water to the place of his destination? and supposing that he could have ingratiated himself with the savages, yet what endless mountains and deserts lie between Russia and the single inhabited coast in those regions! He was relieved from the necessity of walking as far as Jakutsk, by the civility of the Russian travellers, whom he met on the road, who carried him from place to place without any recompence. Here he met with still greater kindness, being admitted to the house and table of the commander, and receiving as a present from him a warm dress, more fitted for the cold season, which had commenced: and yet, the only return which Mr. Ledyard made for this extraordinary hospitality, was to calumniate and abuse every one; and finally challenge his benefactor for remonstrating with him on the impropriety of his behaviour.[2] The arrival of Mr. Billings, at this moment, prevented any farther serious consequences from this affair, by his taking this man with him to Irkutsk on his departure for that place. The commander wrote a letter of accusation against him to the governor-general, in consequence of which he was taken into custody on his arrival at Irkutsk, and sent from thence to St. Petersburg, on the charge of disorderly conduct.

Sarytschew, *Account of a Voyage of Discovery to the North-East of Siberia* (1806), pp. 42–43. The Russian version, somewhat altered in places, is in Sarychev, *Puteshestvie po severo–vostochnoi chasti Sibiri* (1952 ed.), p. 92n. Gavriil Andreevich Sarychev (1763–1831) in 1788 was a naval lieutenant in Billings' expedition. Sarychev arrived at Yakutsk Nov. 24, 1787, and left in early January 1788 (soon after Billings' departure for Irkutsk), proceeding to the mouth of the river Mai. Sarychev worked on his account during the years 1794–1800 and had it first published in St. Petersburg in 1802.

1. The Russian version has here: "His intention was to walk around the world on foot." Cf. Catherine's reference to this: "jamais il n'y a eu de compagnie ambulante" (# 6).

2. The Russian text has here: "finally, after a reminder of decency to him, he dared to challenge the commandant to a duel."

37. Andrew Kippis' Account of Ledyard's Journey (June 1788)

This corporal Lediard is an extraordinary man, something of whose history cannot fail of being entertaining to my readers. In the winter of 1786, he set out on the singular undertaking of walking across the continent of America; for the accomplishment of which purpose, he determined to travel by the way of Siberia, and to procure a passage from that country to the opposite American coast. Being an American by birth, and having no means of raising the money necessary for his expenses, a subscription was raised for him by Sir Joseph Banks, and some other gentlemen, amounting, in the whole, to a little more than fifty pounds. With this sum he proceeded to Hamburgh, from which place he went to Copenhagen, and thence to Petersburgh, where he arrived in the beginning of March, 1787. In his journey from Copenhagen to Petersburgh, finding that the gulph of Bothnia was not frozen over, he was obliged to walk round the whole of it, by Tornæo. At Petersburgh, he staid till the 21st of May, when he obtained leave to accompany a convoy of military stores, which at that time was proceeding to Mr. Billings, who had been his shipmate in Captain Cook's voyage, and who was then employed by the empress of Russia, for the purpose of making discoveries in Siberia, and on the north-west coast of America. With this convoy Mr. Lediard set out, and in August reached the city of Irkutsk in Siberia. After that, he proceeded to the town of Yakutsk, where he met with Captain Billings. From this place he went back to Irkutsk, to spend a part of the winter; proposing, in the spring, to return to Yakutsk, in order to proceed in the summer to Okotsk.

Hitherto, Mr. Lediard had gone on prosperously, and flattered himself with the hopes of succeeding in his undertaking. But, in January last, (1788,) in consequence of an express from the empress, he was arrested, and, in half an hour's time, carried away, under the guard of two soldiers and an officer, in a post sledge, for Moscow, without his clothes, money, or papers. From Moscow he was conveyed to the city of Moialoff in White Russia, and thence to the town of Tolochin in Poland. There he was informed, that her majesty's orders were, that he was never to enter her dominions again without her express permission. During all this time, he suffered the greatest hardships, from sickness, fatigue, and want of rest; so that he was almost reduced to a skeleton. From Tolochin he made his way to Konigsberg; having had, as he says, a miserable journey, in a miserable country, in a miserable season, in miserable health, and a miserable purse; and disappointed of his darling enterprise. Mr. Lediard informs Sir Joseph Banks, to whom he sent from time to time, a full account of his transactions, that, though he had been retarded in his pursuits by malice, he had not travelled totally in vain; his observations in Asia being, perhaps, as complete as a longer visit would have rendered them. From his last letter it appears, that he proposed to return, as speedily as possible, from Konigsberg to England.[1]

Andrew Kippis, *A Narrative of the Voyages Round the World Performed by Captain James Cook; With an Account of his Life*, 2 (1830): 126–27nn. Kippis' Preface is dated June 13, 1788. (Originally published as *The Life of Captain James Cook*, London, 1788.) On Kippis, see above, p. 23, n. 39.

1.This letter, probably written in Königsberg to Banks, I could not locate.

38. Henry Beaufoy's Description of Ledyard's Siberian Journey

Proceedings of the Association, from the Time of Its Establishment, to that of the Departure of Mr. LEDYARD.

The Association for Promoting the Discovery of the Interior Regions of Africa was formed on the 9th of June, in the year

1788; and on the same day a Committee of its Members was invested with the Direction of its Funds, the Management of its Correspondence, and the Choice of the Persons to whom the Geographical Mission should be assigned.

Naturally anxious for the speedy attainment of the important object thus recommended to their care, an object made doubly interesting by the consideration of its having engaged the attention, and baffled the researches of the most inquisitive and most powerful nations of antiquity, the Managers proceeded with the utmost ardour to the immediate execution of the Plan.

Two Gentlemen, whose qualifications appeared to be eminent, proposed to undertake the Adventure.[1]

One of them, a Mr. LEDYARD, was an American by birth, and seemed from his youth to have felt an invincible desire to make himself acquainted with the unknown, or imperfectly discovered regions of the globe. For several years he had lived with the Indians of America, had studied their manners, and had practised in their school the means of obtaining the protection, and of recommending himself to the favour of Savages. In the humble situation of a Corporal of Marines, to which he submitted rather than relinquish his pursuit, he had made, with Captain Cook, the Voyage of the World; and feeling on his return an anxious desire of penetrating from the North Western Coast of America, which Cook had partly explored, to the Eastern Coast, with which he himself was perfectly familiar, he determined to traverse the vast Continent from the Pacific to the Atlantic Ocean.

His first Plan for the purpose was that of embarking in a vessel which was then preparing to sail, on a Voyage of Commercial Adventure, to Nootka Sound, on the Western Coast of America; and with this view he expended in sea stores, the greatest part of the money which his chief benefactor Sir Joseph Banks (whose generous conduct the Writer of this Narrative has often heard him acknowledge) had liberally supplied. But the scheme being frustrated by the rapacity of a Custom-house Officer, who had seized and detained the vessel for reasons which on legal inquiry proved to be frivolous, he determined to travel over land to Kamschatka, from whence, to the Western Coast of America, the passage is extremely short. With no more than ten guineas in his purse, which was all that he had left, he crossed the British Channel to Ostend, and by the way of Denmark and the Sound, proceeded to the capital of Sweden, from which, as it was Winter, he attempted to traverse the Gulph of Bothnia on the ice, in order to reach Kamschatka by the shortest way; but finding, when he came to the middle of the sea, that the water was not frozen, he returned to Stockholm, and taking his course Northward, walked into the Arctic Circle; and passing round the head of the Gulph, descended on its Eastern side to Petersburgh.

There he was soon noticed as an extraordinary man. Without stockings, or shoes, and in too much poverty to provide himself with either, he received and accepted an invitation to dine with the Portugueze Ambassador. To this invitation it was probably owing that he was able to obtain the sum of twenty guineas for a bill on Sir Joseph Banks, which he confessed he had no authority to draw, but which, in consideration of the business that he had undertaken, and of the progress that he had made, Sir Joseph, he believed, would not be unwilling to pay. To the Ambassador's interest it might also be owing that he obtained permission to accompany a detachment of Stores which the Empress had ordered to be sent to Yakutz, for the use of Mr. Billings, an Englishman, at that time in her service.

Thus accommodated, he travelled Eastward through Siberia, six thousand miles, to Yakutz, where he was kindly received by Mr. Billings, whom he remembered on board Captain Cook's ship, in the situation of the Astronomer's Servant, but to whom the Empress had now entrusted her schemes of Northern Discovery.

From Yakutz he proceeded to Oczakow,[2] on the coast of the Kamschatka sea, from whence he meant to have passed over to that peninsula, and to have embarked on the Eastern side in one of the Russian vessels that trade to the Western shores of America; but finding that the navigation was completely obstructed by the ice, he returned again to Yakutz, in order to wait for the conclusion of the Winter.

Such was his situation when, in consequence of suspicions not hitherto explained, or resentments for which no reason is assigned, he was seized, in the Empress's name, by two Russian soldiers, who placed him in a sledge, and conveying him, in the depth of Winter, through the Desarts of the Northern Tartary, left him at last on the Frontiers of the Polish Dominions. As they parted they told him, that if he returned to Russia, he would certainly be hanged; but that if he chose to go back to England, they wished him a pleasant journey.

In the midst of poverty, covered with rags, infested with the usual accompaniments of such cloathing, worn with continued hardship, exhausted by disease, without friends, without credit, unknown, and full of misery, he found his way to Koningsberg.—There, in the hour of his uttermost distress, he resolved once more to have recourse to his old Benefactor, and he luckily found a person who was willing to take his draft for five guineas on the President of the Royal Society.[3]

With this assistance he arrived in England, and immediately waited on Sir Joseph Banks, who told him, knowing his temper, that he believed he could recommend him to an adventure almost as perilous as the one from which he had returned; and then communicated to him the wishes of the Association for Discovering the Inland Countries of Africa.

LEDYARD replied, that he had always determined to traverse the Continent of Africa as soon as he had explored the Interior of North America; and as Sir Joseph had offered him a Letter of Introduction, he came directly to the Writer of these Memoirs.[4] Before I had learnt from the note the name and business of my Visitor, I was struck with the manliness of his person, the breadth of his chest, the openness of his countenance, and the inquietude of his eye. I spread the map of Africa before him, and tracing a line from Cairo to Sennar, and from thence Westward in the latitude and supposed direction of the Niger, I told him that was the route, by which I was anxious that Africa might, if possible, be explored. He said, he should think himself singularly fortunate to be entrusted with the Adventure. I asked him when he would set out? "To-morrow morning," was his answer. I told him I was afraid that we should not be able, in so short a time, to prepare his instructions, and to procure for him the letters that were requisite; but that if the Committee should approve of his proposal, all expedition should be used.

Such is the history, and such were the qualifications of one of the persons whom the Committee engaged in its service.

Proceedings . . . for Promoting the Discovery of the Interior Parts of Africa, pp. 17–26.

1. The last name of the other was Lucas. According to the *Dictionary of National Biography* (12:242), his first name was probably William. Nevertheless a letter of Sir Joseph Banks written to Lucas states his first name as Simon (*The Banks Letters*, ed. Dawson, p. 557). Lucas left England in August 1788 for Tripoli. His attempt to reach Fezzan from there was thwarted and he returned to England the next summer. See also doc. # 39, n. 20.

2. Beaufoy evidently confused Ochakov, a Turkish fortress on the Black Sea, with Okhotsk. Ledyard, of course, never reached Okhotsk.

3. Sir Joseph Banks.

4. Henry Beaufoy.

39. Ledyard to Isaac Ledyard

[London, early June] 1788.

To Monecca.

I was last evening in Company with Mr Jarvis of New York[1] who I accidentaly met in the city & invited to my lodgings: when I was in distress in Paris he behaved very generously to me, & as I do not want money at present tho no doubt I shall some other time, I had a double satisfaction in the recontre & invitation I gave him, being equaly happy to see him & to pay him 100 livres which I never expected to be able to do & I suppose he did not think I ever should himself:[2] [[but in this mortal life one is always dissappointed & beriddled some way or another]]. If he goes to N York as soon as he told me he expected to do I shall trouble him with this letter to you & some others to your address for my other dear friends. The Last time I wrote you was from hence two years ago nearly: but I suppose you heard from me at Petersburg by a Mr Franklin of N York—indeed I think I wrote you from Petersburg: I ought to have done it.[3] I promised to write you from the remote parts of Siberia: I promise every thing to those I love & so does fortune to me sometimes but we reciprocaly prevent each other from fulfiling our engagements & she left me so poor in Siberia that I could not write you because I could not franc the Letter. You are already acquainted with the intent of the voyage I have been 2 years past engaged in: the history of it I cannot give you nor indeed the world: parts of it, both would comprehend, approve, & I suppose admire, & parts of it are incomp[r]ehensible because undescribable: if I had you by the hand it would however not be so: we have a language of our own, & you so well know my soul that should language fail in the communication you would still understand me.

I had penetrated thro Europe & Asia almost to the Pacific Ocean: but in the midst of my career was arrested a prisoner of state to the Empress of Russia by an express sent after me for that purpose: The motives of the Empress in arresting me are found upon examination to have been a mixture of jealousy envy & malice. I passed under a guard a part of last winter & spring: was banished the Empire, & conveyed by a guard to the frontiers of Poland 6000 miles[4] from the place where I was arrested & this journey was performed in 6 weeks: cruelties & hardships are tales I leave untold.[5]

I was dissappointed in the pursuit of an object on which my future fortune entirely depended, as well as my immediate existence. I know not how I passed thro the Kingdoms of Poland & Prussia or from thence to London where I arived the begining of the present May.

Dissappointed, ragged, penniless: and yet so accustomed am I to such things I declare my heart was whole. My health for the first time had suffered from my confinement, & the amazing rapidity with which I was carried thro the unlimited wilds of Tartary & Russia—but my liberty regained, & a few days rest among the beautifull daughters of Israel in Poland re established it & I am now in as full bloom & vigour as 37 years will afford any Man—Jarvis says I look much older than when he saw me at Paris 3 summers ago which I readily believe, an american face does not wear well like an american heart.

From my acquaintance in London my arival was anounced to a Society of Noblemen & Gentlemen who had for some time been fruitlessly enquiring for somebody that would undertake to travel through the continent of Africa.[6] I was asked & consented to undertake the tour. The society have appropriated a sum of 1500 guineas to defray the expences of the Journey. I dine with them collectively this day week, finish the affair & within the month shall be on the move. My route lays from here to Paris, to Marseilles, across the Mediterranian to Alexandria, to Grand Cairo in Egypt & to Mecca on the Red sea:[7] beyond is unknown & my discoveries begin; where they will terminate or how you shall know if I survive.

As we have now at London no Embassy & as I know of no certain medium of conveyance I cannot certainly promise you letters from Asia or Africa: I can only say that I will write you from grand Cairo if I can find a conveyance

Should Mr Jarvis conclude on going to Am[erica] before I leave town I shall send you some tartar curiosities: if not, I am not Certain that I shall have that pleasure. If I can (& I shall strive hard for it) I will also send you a transcript of the few rude remarks I have made in my last tour: with respect to the history of man, the hints I have given from circumstances & facts that have come within my personal knowledge you would find totaly new & extremely interesting: they form an excellent data for investigation: but are better in my hands than any others because no other Man has seen as much of Asia & America, & the analogy of the histories of these two continents form one of their greatest beauties: they would be charming additions to the happy retirement Mr Jarvis tells me you lead on long Island: & your abilities might also improve them into an importance with Mankind: now if I should not send them after saying so much of them it would be a pretty commence & if Jarvis goes not it is most probable I shall not.

My seeing Jarvis has been as good almost as a visit to N York: his account of our family & friends has been minute & faithfull as far as he knows them, & he is pretty well acquainted with them. Nothing in the history of them all has affected me so much as the mercantile misfortunes of your worthy brother & my dear cousin B:[8] surely the race is not to the swift or the battle to the strong:[9] did the pyramids of Egypt w[e] I shall soon see, cover hearts as worthy as his I should no more stile them monuments of human imbecility: I should worship before them. M[r] Jarvis has not been able to give me an exact acc[t] of his situation: I only understand that he has failed in business & retired to Jersey where I think he ought to stay for the world is absolutely unworthy of him: I do not say this because he is my cousin & shared with you the earliest attachments of my heart: these are things I feel, & that the world has nothing to do with any more than it ought to have with him. They are compliments his enimies would make him if he had any. I never knew so much merit so unfortunate. I cannot reflect upon his fate unimpassioned; & unprejudiced against the world. He should retire: if barely comfortable it will be enough for he cannot go from dignity. Embrace the brave fellow for me, & my cousin his wife & her dear little ones—God bless them. Remember me to all my Jersey friends. I am a bankrupt not to them alone: I am one even to myself: but I am not without hopes that a liqu[i]dation on all sides may take place.

I am at present somewhat known to fame & by accident to money: it is but little yet, & whether it will be more or less—to make use of English wit is more or less uncertain. My heart is on your side of the Atlantic. I know the charms on Long Island: the additional ones your residence on it adds to it:[10] & the sweet accordance of recubans sub tegmine fagi.[11] do not think that because I have seen much & must see more of the World I have forgot America: I could as soon forget you,—my dear Ben—myself—my God.

My Travels have brought upon me a numerous correspondance which added to the employments of my new enterprize really embarrass me. I am alone in every thing and in most things so because nobody has ever been accustomed to think and act in Travelling matters as I do. If I should not be able to send you any transcript from my Travels you will please to accept of these two observations of mine, they are the result of extensive and assiduous enquiry and entirely my own; and they are circumstances that will perhaps afford you some satisfaction and such of your curious and learned friends as you may please to communicate them to. They are with me well ascertained facts. The first is that the difference of colour in the human Species, as the observation respects all but the Negroes (whom I have not yet visited) originates from natural causes. The next is that all the Asiatic Indians called Tartars, & that all the Tartars that have formed the later armies of Zingis Khan together with the Chinese are the same people; and that the American Tartar is also of the same family: the most ancient and numerous people on Earth; and what is very singular the most uniformly alike—I have been to Day with Mr Jarvis and he leaves London in three Days time the consequence of which is I can send you no transcripts from my writings: I shall [send] you however by him my Siberian Dresses—they are such as I have worn thro' many a scene and glad to get them—I send them to you to remember me by: if you choose to present them or any of them to your Society of Arts and Sciences do so.

The Surtout coat marked N° 1 is made of the Rein deer skin & edged with the dewlap of the moose: perhaps you will wear this yourself in winter: it is made for a riding coat & I have rode both horses & deer with it—but you are some how strangely like the english not fond of fur dresses. The Cap N° 2 is made all of the Siberian red fox & is also a traveling cap. the form is entirely Tartar The Cap N° 3 is a Russian made cap consisting of white ermin & bordered with blue fox skin: it cost me at Yakutsk on the banks of the great river Lena 25 roubles which is 4 guineas & one rouble.[12] The surtout cost 70 roubles. the fox skin cap 6 roubles: the gloves marked N° 4 are made of the feet of the fox & lined with the Tartar hare & cost 5 roubles. The Tartar froc N° 5 is the only one of the kind ever brot to Europe: the form & stile is truely Tartar: it was made a present to me and comes from the borders of the frozen ocean at the mouth of the River Kovima Lat^d 69–39. N.[13] it is made of a spotted Rein deer calf (& the surtout is also the calf) the dark border is a dark skin & as they are rare among the Rein deer so it is there put for ornament the edging is the same as the surtout: you will observe on the inside of the skin a number of spots: these were occasioned by a small insect bred there from the eggs of a species of fly & which together with the vast numbers of musquestoes obliges this charming animal to migrate annualy N & S. as the seasons require & particularly [for] the conveniencies of bringing forth its young. The boots N° 6 are made also of the Rein deer skin & ornamented with European cloath. The form is Tartar they cost 8 robles: the socks for the boots N° 7. are made of the old rein deer skin: they are worn the inside of the boots with the hair to the feet; with or without stockings: these were made a present to me & came from the borders of the frozen ocean: the cloak N° 8 which they are wrapt up in was made in London I traveled on foot with it in Danemarc Sweeden Lapland Finland & the Lord knows where: in opulence & in poverty I have kept it slept in it, eat in it, drank in it, fought in it, negociated in it: it has been thro every scene my constant & faithfull servant from my departure to my return to London & to give it an asylum for I have none here I send it to you—lay it up. as soon as I can I will call upon you for it & lay myself up with it. I have mentioned the prices of the above articles to give you an Idea how dear fur dresses are even in the remotest parts of the vast dominions of Russia.

These cloaths were not all that I wore last winter in Siberia: I wore many more & froze my nose & ears after all. You have no Idea of the excessive cold in those regions. by experiments I made at Yakutsk (which by the by I desire you to be geographicaly acquainted with) I found on Novr 19th my mercurial Therm^r froze. In December I found by observations repeated that 2 ounces of clean quicksilver openly exposed froze hard in

15 minutes by a watch: strong coniac brandy coagulated. by a Therm^r graduated by Reaumer & filled with rectified spirits of wine I had 39½ deg.[14] On the borders of the frozen ocean a Capt Billings had the winter before last 43¾ deg by the same Therm^r

I observed in those severe frosts that the air was condensed as it is with you in a thick fog: the Atmosphere is frozen respiration is fatiguing: all exercise must be as moderate as possible. ones confidence is placed alone on the fur dress it is a happy law of nature that in such intense colds there is seldom any wind: if there is it is dangerous to be abroad: those who happen to be, lay down on the snow & secure themselves so. In these seasons there is no chace. the animals submit themselves to hunger & security & so does Man. There are no wells at Yakutsk by experiment they freez 60 feet deep. People of these regions are therefore obliged to use Ice or snow: they have also ice windows: glass is of no use to the few who have it. The difference of the state of the air within & without is so great that they are covered on the inside with several inches of ice & in that state are less luminous than ice: the timber of the houses splits & opens with loud cracks. the rivers thunder & open with broad fissures—all nature groans beneath the rigorous winter Just at the turning of this cold season I travelled last winter 2,600 versts about 1950 english miles on the river Lena.[15]

I am sorry Mr Jarvis goes out of town so soon to day is saturday & he calls on me on tuesday to take the things for you & to take leave of me. I have not time to do any thing & it happens that just at this moment I am the busiest with the African society: among other things, I want to send you a copy from my Sweedish Portrait at Somerset house[16]—I have one by me, but it is an old stupid devil of a thing [[& looks exactly like Avery the taylor on Groton bank]] it was taken by a boy, who is as dumb & deaf as the portrait—he is however under the patronage of Sr Joshua Reynolds the English Raphael. The boy was sent to me by a country Squire who accidentaly got acquainted with me at an Inn where I lodged in London & who has taken a wonderfull fancy to me & begs to hang me in his hall— —this one is yet unfinished, & so is the one for the Squire—they are done in water & are mere daubings

Jarvis says our Trumbull[17] is clever & advises me to get him to copy the Sweedish drawing which is not only a *perfect* likeness but good painting—If I do according to his advice it cannot be soon & indeed I should not trouble you or myself about this shadow of Josephus was I persuaded of presenting him to you hereafter in substance[18]

I shall not have time to settle my affairs, before Jarvis goes if it is to morrow for to Morrow I must be with the African Committee —I must tell you what this African Committee is. Some few weeks only before my arival now at London a number of Gentlemen had been tallking somewhat in earnest about exploring the Continent of Africa. My arival has made it a reality. An Association is formed & a Comittee balloted from it last week for the management of the affairs of it. The Comittee chosen are a Mr Cerke a Mr *Beaufoy*, Lord Rawdon Sir Joseph Banks & the Bishop of Landaff.[19] The Society consists at present of 200 Members. It is a growing thing, & the King privately promoting & encouraging it will make its objects more extensive than at first thought of. The king has told them that no expence should be spared: the subscriptions are then altered from any fixed sum to such sums as exigencies may require; & one or two other Gentlemen are going in behalf of the Society to travel in & about the dominions of civilization in Africa[20]—exclusive of myself who nobody will follow—& to tell you the truth cannot. Mr Jarvis is this moment going

adieu yrs always

JOSEPHUS

NB Mr

Jarvis will not

take the 100 livres of me

I believe you will hear from me again soon

First and third parts of the letter from original in NYHS; the paragraph beginning "My Travels" on pp. 245–46 from transcript in JLP. JLP contains all three parts of the letter; NYHS possesses only the first and third sections.

1. Probably James Jarvis, an American merchant, who in December

1787 had arrived in London from New York. Jarvis had evidently met Ledyard while in Paris during the spring of 1785.

2. As Ledyard had by this time agreed to undertake the expedition for the African Society, he was probably subsidized by some of its members.

3. There is no record of such a letter. Ledyard's latest known previous letter to Isaac was written in London and dated November 1786 (# 19).

4. This figure is incorrect, for 6,000 miles equals 9,000 versts. The journey from Irkutsk to Mogilëv was little more than 6,000 versts.

5. Ledyard reached the Polish frontier on the evening of March 18/29; six weeks before this date would have been February 16 (N.S.).

6. This acquaintance was probably Sir Joseph Banks, who introduced Ledyard to the Association for Promoting the Discovery of the Interior Parts of Africa.

7. Ledyard must not yet have been certain of the exact route his expedition to the Niger River would follow.

8. Ledyard's cousin Ben (Benjamin), who was then living in New Jersey. The second and third letters of "Ben" are crossed out in the MS.

9. Ecclesiastes 9:11.

10. Here the following passage has been crossed out: "the necessity of a few pence."

11. "Stretching out at your ease under the shade of a beech tree" (Vergil, *Eclogues* 1:1).

12. In other words, four guineas equals 24 rubles.

13. This was probably the pelisse given to him by Billings which Sauer mentions (# 35).

14. About −57° F.; −43¾° R. equals −65° F.

15. By Ledyard's calculations a verst equaled .75 miles; moreover, his itinerary (# 29) gives the distance of the Lena from Kachuga to Yakutsk as 2,357 versts (about 1550 miles).

16. According to Sparks: "Soon after [1828] . . . , it was ascertained that a portrait of Ledyard existed in Stockholm, painted by Breda, an artist of celebrity, who had known Ledyard in London. The picture was seen at Stockholm, by an American traveller, in possession of the artist, who was then far advanced in life. It is doubtless the same that is mentioned by Ledyard as His 'Swedish portrait,' and which he pronounces to be 'not only a perfect likeness, but a good painting.' An effort was immediately made to procure this picture, or a copy; but, on inquiry, it was found that the artist had died, his pictures had been sold and dispersed, and no one could tell into whose hands this portrait had fallen" (*Life of John Ledyard,* 1864, pp. 4–5).

The Swedish painter Carl Fredrik von Breda (1759–1818) had arrived in London in 1787, where he studied under Sir Joshua Reynolds. Augur explains: "The association had had a Swedish painter do a portrait of Ledyard, which was then hanging in Somerset House. It showed the explorer standing with a half-open map in his left hand, a finger of his right pointing . . . to Africa" (*Passage to Glory,* p. 266).

17. John Trumbull (1756–1843), well-known Connecticut painter.

18. According to Sparks: "Neither the portrait nor a copy was sent. The original was taken to Sweden by the artist, where it has been lost" (*Life of John Ledyard,* p. 380n).

19. According to *Proceedings . . . for Promoting the Discovery of the Interior Parts of Africa* (p. 16), in addition to Rawdon, Llandaff [Richard

Watson], Banks, and Beaufoy, a Mr. [Andrew] Stuart was elected to the committee. The name of Mr. Cerke does not appear here.

20. One of these gentlemen, the Englishman Lucas, was commissioned to explore the Sahara Desert from Tripoli to Fezzan.

40. Ledyard to Isaac Ledyard

June 1788

To Monecca

I suppose that my Letters & curiosities sent by Mr Jarvis are now half way over the Atlantic. This is a little postcript that I leave to the care of his brother in town. Inclosed with it is a poor portrait of me taken by the dumb boy mentioned in my other Letter: if it was any thing like painting I would desire you to keep it: as it is I beg you to send it to my mother who will be as fond of it as if done by Guido:[1] it is the only thing I ever presented the dear woman who gave me being & presided over my infancy. I would have sent it framed if the opportunity permited me to do so.

[[I also send you a penciled sketch of coats of arms. N° 1 are arms that I think I remember to have seen on Grandfathers old Chaise—I remember the motto well: that, however is arbitrary. As my god fathers & god mothers advanced me, I saw on Aunt Seymours mantle tree peice arms somewhat like them to the name of Ledyard. In the Heraldry books here they are to the name of Legar—or as it would be in french le Gar. But there is no kind of historical analogy between the crest & motto, which is very beautifull. N° 2 are the arms of the Ledyard—or Lediard (for I can find no such name as Ledyard) & of the Sutton family of the english county of Wilts: joined by some circumstance the scollop quarters being the Sutton. N° 3 are the Ledyard or Lediard arms indistinct from the Sutton: field sable: cross pattee in gold with gules or stars: the crest a silver ½ Lion with gules in his right paw—it is good & honorable: difficilia et pulchra might be wrote under such a crest with propriety

I know not how the orthographical difference of Ledyard &

Lediard has arisen: it is but little, & if a french name easily accounted for, as we use the y very often where the french use the i. It is a french name by its orthography & in french would be wrote le diard. I think I remember in a conversation between grand father & Aaron Bull about pumpkin beer that the former said the faimily (meaning ours) came from Normandy in france: the name is in france & England: in the former it is spelt Lidiard: here Lediard. why with us Ledyard I know not: be it which it may I am right in being yrs]]

*Let y[e] postscript come in here

JOSEPHUS

P.S.* June 29th 1788.

I set out to Morrow morning
for France. Adieu!

NYHS (original). On the letter jacket are written the words: left at London/ to the care and/ friendship of/ M[r] Jarvis. Addressed: Isaac Ledyard Esq[r]/ New York/ North America.

1. Probably Guido Reni (1575–1642), Bolognese painter.

41. Ledyard to ———

London June 1788

I had proposed in my last Tour to go round the World by Land which you know. I have not been able to effect it, not from any natural Difficulties, for I had made the worst half of the Journey but from the unprincely malice of the Empress of Russia who made a prisoner of me when I had almost got out of her vast Dominions and banished from her Empire. I have seen and suffered a great deal but I have my health and Spirits & in the greatest perfection.

JNO LEDYARD.

JLP (transcript).

42. Ledyard to Jefferson

M[r] Ledyard presents his compliments to M[r] Jefferson—he has been imprisoned and banished by the Empriss of Russia from her dominions after having almost gained the pacific ocean. he is now on his way to Africa to see what he can do with that continent. he is ill with a cold & fever or he would have waited on Mr Jefferson with Mr Edwards.[1] he is with perfect respect & affection Mr Jeffersons most humble & ob^{t} servant.

Hotel d'aligre
rue d'orleans
4 Juilet

MS 787900.1: Archives, BL (original). Addressed: A Monsieur/ Monsieur Jefferson/ Ambassadeur from les etats uni/ de l'amerique.

1. Probably Alexander Edwards of South Carolina, to whom in London in early 1788 John Adams had given a letter of introduction to be presented to Jefferson.

43. Ledyard to Jefferson

To his Excellency Thomas Jefferson Esquire
Embassador for the United States of America

[Paris, early July 1788]

Sir

When men of genius want matter of fact to reason from it is bad, though it is worse to reason without it: it is the fate of genius not to make, or to misapply this reflexion, and so it forms theories: humble minds admire these theories because they cannot comprehend them, & disbelieve them for the same reason

Simplify the efforts & attainments of all the antient world in science & it amounts to nothing but theory: to a riddle: the sublime of[1] antient wisdom was to form a riddle: & the delphic god bore the palm: Men had then great encouragement to do so: they were made priests phrophets, kings & gods: & when they had gained these distinctions by riddles it was necessary by riddles to preserve them.

Men have since tho but very lately & not yet universaly sought impartialy for truth & we now a days seek truth not only for its own enchanting beauty, but from a principle tho not more valuable yet more generous viz the pleasure of communicating it to one another. The soothsayers, magicians phrophets & priests of old would think us as errant fools as we think them knaves

In my travels I have made it my rule to compare the written with the living history of Man, & as I have seen all kinds of men so I have not hesitated to make use of all kinds of history (y^t^ I am acquainted with) in the comparison: & I give in many cases as much credit to traditions as to other history: implicit credit to none nor implicit credit to inferrences that I myself draw from this comparison except rarely; & then I am as sure as I want to be. Thus I know & feel myself above prejudice: Moses, Albugassi[2] & the writers of the last 20 years are all alike to me as to what I am seeking for: I would only understand if I could what Man has been from what he is: not what he may be hereafter tho all mention the tale. I would also know what the earth has been from observing how it is at present: not how it may hereafter be, tho all mention also this tale. You know how ignorant & plain a Man I am, but I declare to you that in this temper of mind & from the information incident to the extent & nature of my travels I find myself at my ease concerning things which some cannot & others will not believe that are of considerable importance; & I will tell you in a very few words what some of them are—I wish I had time to mention them all, or if I do that it was more in detail.

S^r^ I am certain (the negroes excepted because I have not yet personaly visited them) that the difference in the colour of Men is the effect of natural causes.

S^r^ I am certain that all the people you call red people on the continent of America & on the continents of Europe & Asia as far south as the southern parts of China are all one people by whatever names distinguished & that the best general one would be *Tartar*

I suspect that *all* red people are of the same family. I am satisfied myself that America was peopled from Asia & had some if not all its animals from thence.[3]

I am satisfied myself that the great general analogy in the customs of Men can only be accounted for but by supposing them all to compose one family: & by extending the Idea & uniting customs, traditions & history I am satisfied that this common origin was such or nearly as related by Moses & commonly believed among all the nations of the earth. There is a transposition of things on the globe that must have been produced by some cause equal to the effect which is vast & curious: whether I repose on arguments drawn from facts observed by myself or send imagination forth to find a cause they both declare to me a general deluge

I am y[r] Excellencys most humble
& most gratefull friend
LEDYARD

Thomas Jefferson Papers, Vol. 41, folios 7081–82: LC (original). On the MS is written in Jefferson's hand: "Ledyard John. rec[d] July 5. 1788. Paris." According to Boyd (*PTJ,* 13:306), this letter was "endorsed by TJ: 'Ledyard John. recd. July 3. 1788. Paris.' SJL [Jefferson's Summary Journal of Letters] Index, which usually carries in the letters-received column an asterisk to indicate undated letters, has an asterisk between entries for 4 July and 15 Aug. 1788; such entries in SJL Index refer to the dates that letters were written, not received, and the appropriate asterisk for an undated letter is usually, but not always, placed in proper chronological sequence in SJL Index. In view of these facts, it is possible that Ledyard, who was in London in May–July 1788, wrote TJ a (missing) letter from that place on 4 July, 1788; that the asterisk for the present letter, received on 3 July, was misplaced; and that the present letter therefore may have been written from some point in Ledyard's trek across Siberia, being received in Paris sometime after Ledyard arrived in London."

Boyd's supposition is not completely correct. Ledyard's "missing" letter of July 4 is actually that written in Paris to Jefferson, in which Ledyard first informed him of the failure of his Siberian journey (# 42). Furthermore, Boyd gives the date that Jefferson received the present letter as July 3. The handwriting is not clear but the curl at the top of the number is similar to that of Jefferson's recognizable "5's," as is the slant of the number upward to the right. Jefferson's "3's," on the other hand, slant upward to the left.

It is most likely that the present letter was written in Paris on or about July 4 or 5, probably as a follow-up or an accompanying letter to Ledyard's note of July 4. (This might well explain Ledyard's unusual omission of date and place.) In this case, the asterisk was not misplaced in SJL Index; and the present letter, received on July 5, was placed chronologically in the Index beween the entry for the note dated July 4 and the entry for Ledyard's letter from Alexandria, dated August 15, 1788. Furthermore, the subject matter in the present letter closely parallels certain observations mentioned by Ledyard in his letter to Isaac of June 1788 (# 39); there is less relationship between these ideas and the train of his thoughts prior to his arrest in Siberia.

1. "of" is repeated in the MS.

2. Abulgazi-Bagadur, historian and khan of Khiva who ruled from 1643 to 1663. See Journal, p. 199, n. 161.

3. Jefferson had discussed the problem of the origin of the American Indians in his *Notes on the State of Virginia* (pp. 96–97) without coming to any definite conclusions.

44. Jefferson to the Reverend James Madison

Paris July 19. 1788.

. . . .

A country man of ours, a Mr. Lediard of Connecticut set out from hence some time ago for St Petersburgh, to go thence to Kamschatka, thence to cross over to the Western coast of America, and penetrate through the continent to our side of it. He had got within a few days journey of Kamschatka, when he was arrested by order of the empress of Russia, sent back and turned adrift in Poland. He went to London, engaged under the auspices of a private society formed there for pushing discoveries into Africa, passed by this place, which he left a few days ago for Marseilles, where he will embark for Alexandria and Grand Cairo, thence explore the Nile to it's source, cross to the head of the Niger, and descend that to it's mouth. He promises me, if he escapes through this journey, he will go to Kentuckey and endeavour to penetrate Westwardly from thence to the South sea.

. . . .

TH: JEFFERSON

PTJ, 13:382. Press copy is in LC. The Rev. James Madison, an Episcopal clergyman, was president of William and Mary College in Williamsburg, Va.

45. Jefferson to William Carmichael

Paris Mar. 4. 1789.

. . . .

I have had a letter from Admiral Paul-Jones dated St. Petersburgh Jan. 31. He was well and just arrived there on the call of the Empress. He has commanded on the Black sea during the last campaign, but does not know where he is to act the ensuing one.—My last accounts from Lediard (another bold countryman of ours) were from Grand Cairo. He was just then plunging into the unknown regions of Africa, probably never to emerge again. If he returns, he has promised me to go to America and penetrate from Kentucke to the Western side of the Continent. I do not know whether you are informed that in the years 1787. 1788. he went from here bound for Kamschatka, to cross over thence to the Western coast of our continent and pass through to the Eastern one. He was arrested, par ordre superieure, within two or three days journey of Kamschatka, conveyed back to the confines of Poland, and there turned adrift. He arrived here last June, and immediately set out for Africa.

. . . .

PTJ, 14:616. Press copy is in LC. Carmichael was American ambassador to Spain at that time.

46. From the Diary of Nathaniel Cutting at Le Havre and Cowes

Thursday 1st. Octr. [1789] . . . I enquired of Mr. J[efferson] concerning an eccentric Genius, Mr. Ledgyard of Connecticut, who a year or two since proposed to pass thro' Russia to Kamtschatka, then to cross over to the North American Coast, and penetrate through the vast Wildernesses of America till he should arrive at some one of the United States. He actually set out on the expedition, and proceeded to within Two hundred miles of Kamtschatka, when he was siezed by order of the Empress of Russia, closely guarded and brought back to Poland, there he was set at liberty; but strictly charged not to presume ever to set his foot in the Russian Territories again. Thus the Caprice of a Woman probably prevented world from receiving some new and important information that would have been the result of this extraordinary Journey had it been compleated. Mr.

Jefferson had put him upon a method of recording certain important observations which he might make, which to prick certain Characters into his own skin with the juice of some herbs which had a knowledge of. These remarks are indelible. It was natural to suppose that if he attempted to carry implements of any kind with him, he would soon be robb'd of them by the savages, and perhaps murder'd for the sake of them. But it was probable they would readily admit a naked and unarm'd man to pass unmolested:—but in this situation how was he to determine Lattitudes, which would be essentiall toward rendering useful any description of Capital Rivers, or Mountains, or Fertile Tracts of Land. For this purpose he was directed previous to leaving Europe, to have the measure of the English Foot mark'd on some part of his Body, say on his arm; as he has attain'd his full growth it is not probable that this mark would become erroneous. When he intended to find the Lattitude of a spot, he was to form a circle on the Surface of the Earth, then placing a strait stick perpendicular in centre, observe where the shadow came to at Sunrise and where it struck at Sunset then dividing this distance on the Periphery would give the Point where the shadow ought to strike at noon:—having thus discover'd the sun's Southing, he was to break a strait stick just to the measure of a Foot which was mark'd on his arm and when he perceiv'd the Sun on the meridian he was to place this stick in a perpendicular position, and mark the length of the shadow which it cast. This he was to record upon his skin in the manner before directed.

Mr. J. also instructed him in a very simple, and tollerably accurate method of measuring the breadth of a River. Find if possible some strait place on the margin of the Water and place a stick in the Ground perpend. as tall or rather taller than to your Eye. Take another strait stick and place across this on a level with you[r] eye, and point the end farthest from you to the edge of the water on the opposite side:—this done, keep the stick as exactly as possible in this position, and turn yourself and it round till the said end strike on the bank where you are, taking particular notice of some object at that Point; Measure the distance between your station and that point, which will give the breadth of the River, within a few yards.

PTJ, 15:492–93. Original MS is in Cutting Papers, Mass. Hist. Soc., Boston. Capt. Nathaniel Cutting of Boston first arrived in France and met Jefferson in late 1787. After Cutting had told what was essentially this same story to John Quincy Adams on June 5, 1797, Adams concluded in his diary that had Ledyard "pursued his north-west road, whatever benefit his success might have procured to mankind, his journal upon his skin would not, I think, have been worth much." *Memoirs*, 1:189.

47. An Account of Ledyard in Jefferson's Biographical Sketch of Meriwether Lewis (1813)

. . . .

While I resided in Paris, John Ledyard, of Connecticut, arrived there, well known in the United States for energy of body and mind. He had accompanied captain Cook on his voyage to the Pacific ocean; and distinguished himself on that voyage by his intrepidity. Being of a roaming disposition, he was now panting for some new enterprise. His immediate object at Paris was to engage a mercantile company in the fur-trade of the western coast of America, in which, however, he failed. I then proposed to him to go by land to Kamschatka, cross in some of the Russian vessels to Nootka Sound, fall down into the latitude of the Missouri, and penetrate to, and through, that to the United States. He eagerly seized the idea, and only asked to be assured of the permission of the Russian government. I interested, in obtaining that, from M. de Simoulin, minister plenipotentiary of the empress at Paris,[1] but more especially the baron de Grimm, minister plenipotentiary of Saxe-Gotha, her more special agent and correspondent there in matters not immediately diplomatic. Her permission was obtained, and an assurance of protection while the course of the voyage should be through her territories.[2] Ledyard set out from Paris, and arrived at St. Petersburgh after the empress had left that place to pass the winter, I think, at Moscow. His finances not permitting him to make unnecessary stay at St. Petersburgh, he left it with a passport from one of the ministers; and at two hundred miles from Kamschatka, was obliged to take up his winter quarters. He was preparing, in the spring, to resume his journey, when he was arrested by an officer of the empress, who by this time had changed her mind, and forbidden his proceeding. He was put into a close carriage, and conveyed day and night, without ever stopping, till they reached Poland; where he was set down and left to himself. The fatigue of this journey broke down his constitution; and when he returned to Paris his bodily strength was much impaired. His mind, however, remained firm, and he after this undertook the journey to Egypt. I received a letter from him, full of sanguine hopes, dated at Cairo, the fifteenth of November, 1788, the day before he was to set out for the head of the Nile; on which day, however, he ended his career and life: and thus failed the first attempt to explore the western part of our northern continent.

From the "Life of Captain Lewis," written by Jefferson on August 18, 1813, at Monticello to Paul Allen of Philadelphia and printed in the Preface of Lewis, *History of the Expedition under the Command of Captains Lewis and Clark* (1814), 1:ix–x.

1. Ivan Matveevich Simolin (1720–90) had been appointed Russian minister plenipotentiary to France in 1785.

2. See doc. # 48 for Jefferson's correction of this statement.

48. An Account of Ledyard from Jefferson's *Autobiography* (1821)

In 1786, while at Paris, I became acquainted with John Ledyard, of Connecticut, a man of genius, of some science, and of fearless courage and enterprise. He had accompanied Captain Cook in his voyage to the Pacific, had distinguished himself on several occasions by an unrivalled intrepidity, and published an account of that voyage, with details unfavorable to Cook's deportment towards the savages, and lessening our regrets at his fate. Ledyard had come to Paris, in the hope of forming a company to engage in the fur trade of the Western coast of America. He was disappointed in this, and, being out of business, and of a roaming, restless character, I suggested to him the enterprise of exploring the Western part of our continent, by passing through St. Petersburg to Kamschatka, and procuring a passage thence in some of the Russian vessels to Nootka Sound, whence he might make his way across the continent to the United States; and I undertook to have the permission of the Empress of Russia solicited. He eagerly embraced the proposition, and M. de Sémoulin, the Russian Ambassador, and more particularly Baron Grimm, the special correspondent of the Empress, solicited her permission for him to pass through her dominions, to the Western coast of America. And here I must correct a material error, which I have committed in another place, to the prejudice of the Empress. In writing some notes of the life of Captain Lewis, prefixed to his "Expedition to the Pacific," I stated that the Empress gave the permission asked, and afterwards retracted it. This idea, after a lapse of twenty-six years, had so insinuated itself into my mind, that I committed it to paper, without the least suspicion of error. Yet I find, on recurring to my letters of that date, that the Empress refused permission at once, considering the enterprise as entirely chimerical. But Ledyard would not relinquish it, persuading himself that, by proceeding to St. Petersburg, he could satisfy the Empress of its practicability, and obtain her permission. He went accordingly, but she was absent on a visit to some distant part of her dominions, and he pursued his course to within two hundred miles of Kamschatka, where he was overtaken by an arrest from the Empress, brought back to Poland, and there dismissed. I must therefore, in justice, acquit the Empress of ever having for a moment countenanced, even by the indulgence of an innocent passage through her territories, this interesting enterprise.

WTJ, 1:101–2.

BIBLIOGRAPHY
INDEX

Bibliography

Works on Ledyard

A number of biographies and specialized studies of Ledyard have been written in the nineteenth and twentieth centuries. The starting point for those interested in Ledyard's life has usually been Jared Sparks's biography, *The Life of John Ledyard, the American Traveller,* 1st ed. Cambridge, Mass., 1828; 2nd ed. Boston, 1847; 3rd ed. Boston, 1864. Sparks had access to all the Ledyard papers that were generally known at the time of the first edition. The more recent biographies of J. K. Munford, *John Ledyard, an American Marco Polo,* Portland, Ore., 1939; and Helen Augur, *Passage to Glory: John Ledyard's America,* New York, 1946, lack a balanced, scholarly approach. Several brief sketches of Ledyard's life are unreliable and of poor quality: Samuel Schmucker, *The Life of Dr. Elisha Kent Kane and of Other Distinguished American Explorers,* Philadelphia, 1871, pp. 261–329; Agnes Laut, *Vikings in the Pacific,* New York, 1905, pp. 242–62; Henry Beston, *The Book of Gallant Vagabonds,* New York, 1925, pp. 1–55; and Don Carlos Seitz, *Uncommon Americans,* Indianapolis, 1925, pp. 231–41. The best recent biographical study of Ledyard is that by Sinclair H. Hitchings, which is included in the introduction to Munford's careful edition of *John Ledyard's Journal of Captain Cook's Last Voyage,* Corvallis, Ore., 1963, pp. xxi–xlix.

Among the more specialized studies of Ledyard is a short article by Eufrosina Dvoichenko-Markov entitled "John Ledyard and the Russians," *Russian Review,* 11 (Oct. 1952): 211–22. This focuses particularly on the Siberian journey and Ledyard's encounters with Russians in the North Pacific in 1778–79. Another recent article, by E. M. Halliday, deals almost exclusively with Ledyard's voyage with Captain Cook: "Captain Cook's American," *American Heritage*, 13 (Dec. 1961): 60–72, 84–87. An informative article regarding Ledyard's family and ancestry has been written by Charles B. Moore: "John Ledyard, the Traveller," *New York Genealogical and Biographical Record*, 7 (Jan. 1876): 2–8. The latest study on Ledyard, which centers around the significance and extent of his anthropological observations, is that of Sanford H. Bederman, *The Ethnological Contributions of John Ledyard*, School of Arts and Sciences Research Papers, No. 4, Georgia State College, Atlanta, 1964. Ledyard's year at Dartmouth College has been treated in "A Wayward Freshman," *Dartmouth Alumni Magazine* (Feb. 1963), pp. 9–12ff.

Works by Other American Travelers to Siberia

A small number of important and interesting accounts have been written by Americans who visited Siberia in the nineteenth and twentieth centuries. The first known American after Ledyard to visit Siberia was the Rhode Islander John D'Wolf, who traveled by land from Okhotsk to St. Petersburg in 1807. D'Wolf, a sea captain, followed in reverse the route planned by Ledyard twenty years earlier. Except during his trip from Okhotsk to Irkutsk, he proceeded in haste and made few observations. He wrote up his journey over fifty years later: *A Voyage to the North Pacific and a Journey through Siberia*, Cambridge, Mass., 1861. Also see his narrative in W. H. Munro, *Tales of an Old Sea Port*, Princeton, 1917, pp. 97–201. In the years 1812–14 globe-trotter Peter Dobell traveled from Kamchatka to St. Petersburg. Dobell, born in Ireland, lived during his youth in Pennsylvania, later became a Russian citizen, and died in St. Petersburg. His account of his trip, *Travels in Kamtschatka and Siberia with a Narrative of a Residence in China*, was published in London in 1830. On both Dobell and Ledyard see Albert Parry, "The First Americans in Siberia," *Travel*, 87 (June 1946): 18–22, 32.

Most Americans who visited Siberia in the last third of the nineteenth century were geologists, naturalists, arctic explorers, and during the 1890's a number of overland travelers on the newly built Trans-Siberian Railroad. Brief sketches of these visitors and their accounts (if any) are given in Anna M. Babey, *Americans in Russia: 1776–1917. A Study of the American Travellers in Russia from the American Revolution to the Russian Revolution*, New York, 1938. From the Crimean War (1853–56) to the Bolshevik Revolution three

Americans whose writings were later published stand out as keen observers of Siberia: Perry McDonough Collins, George Kennan, and Jeremiah Curtin.

Collins, a California businessman, crossed the Russian Empire from St. Petersburg in 1856 to voyage down the Amur River and investigate the possibilities of opening up this region to trade with the United States. His account first appeared as *A Voyage down the Amoor: With a Land Journey through Siberia, . . .*, New York, 1860. A recent edition of this is *Siberian Journey: Down the Amur to the Pacific, 1856–1857*, edited by Charles Vevier, Madison, 1962. Collins undertook two subsequent trips to Russia, and upon the last one started negotiations leading to the construction of a telegraph line to be built by Western Union connecting Siberia, Russian America (Alaska), and the United States. In the midst of surveying the proposed route in Siberia, this project collapsed when the Atlantic cable was completed in 1866.

One of the members of Western Union's expedition to Siberia in 1865 was a young telegrapher from Ohio, George Kennan. The most noteworthy and widely read report to result from that unsuccessful venture was his *Tent Life in Siberia and Adventures among the Koraks and Other Tribes in Kamtchatka and Northern Asia*, New York, 1870. Another product of it was Thomas W. Knox's *Overland through Asia*, Hartford, 1870. Kennan returned to Siberia in 1885 to inspect the living conditions of Russian exiles and the operation of the exile system; he then wrote a much larger work entitled *Siberia and the Exile System*, 2 vols. New York, 1891.

The third American to study a specific area of Siberia with thoroughness was Wisconsin-born Jeremiah Curtin. An able linguist, Curtin shared Ledyard's interest in the peoples of Siberia. In 1900 he began his studies of the language, customs, and religion of the Buryat Mongols in the Baikal region; the result was *A Journey in Southern Siberia*, Boston, 1909. Another important study done around the turn of the century was George Wright's *Asiatic Russia* (2 vols. New York, 1902), which contains information collected in traveling through China, Siberia, and Central Asia in 1900–02.

Since the Bolshevik Revolution and the American intervention in Siberia during the Civil War, relatively few Americans have visited Siberia. During the period of the first Five-Year Plan (1928–32) and during World War II a number of American engineers and technicians went to western Siberia to help the Soviet government realize the great industrial potential in the Urals and beyond. For an example see John Scott's account of this experience, *Behind the Urals*,

An American Worker in Russia's City of Steel, Cambridge, Mass., 1942. After the mid-1950's a slow rise in the number of American visitors to Siberia took place. However, these are still few and far between, for Siberian cities are not located on the tourist routes promoted by the Soviets. Only occasionally has an agricultural delegation, a newspaper reporter, a scholar, or a statesman received permission to visit such Siberian cities as Omsk, Novosibirsk, and Irkutsk. Excluding newspaper articles, no significant accounts or books have resulted from these visits.

Eighteenth-century Literature on Siberia

Something should be said here concerning the accounts of contemporary travelers, from which a good share of our knowledge of eighteenth-century Siberia has come. Accounts written as a result of scientific expeditions sponsored by the Russian government hold an important place in the descriptive literature on Siberia. The expedition of 1733–43 under Johann Georg Gmelin engendered extensive writings by the leader and his collaborators. Gmelin was the first to describe fully and precisely the geography, peoples, animal and plant life of Siberia, in *Reise durch Sibirien, 1733–1743,* 4 vols. Göttingen, 1751–52. Of the two German historians on the expedition, Gerhard Friedrich Müller capitalized on the opportunity to investigate local archives and contributed two valuable works on Siberian history: *Opisanie sibirskago tsarstva* (Description of the Siberian Realm), St. Petersburg, 1750, and *Sammlung russischer Geschichte,* 9 vols. St. Petersburg, 1762–64; Johann E. Fischer compiled a comprehensive history of Siberia: *Sibirische Geschichte von der Entdeckung Sibiriens . . . ,* 2 vols. St. Petersburg, 1768. (Not until the 1830's did another historian, P. A. Slovtsov, again take up the study of Siberia. On the historiography of Siberia see Anatole Mazour, *Modern Russian Historiography,* pp. 163–69, and A. N. Pypin, *Istoriia russkoi etnografii,* 4: 351ff.) Stepan P. Krasheninnikov, Russian scholar and explorer with Gmelin, wrote what was to become a noted work on Kamchatka describing the animal and plant world, the customs of the natives, and giving a general account of the history of the peninsula: *Opisanie zemli Kamchatki* (Description of the Land of Kamchatka), St. Petersburg, 1755; English translation: *The History of Kamchatka,* Chicago, 1962. The German botanist Georg Wilhelm Steller produced an important work describing his observations in Kamchatka: *Beschreibung von dem Lande Kamtschatka,* Frankfurt and Leipzig, 1774.

As a result of an expedition in 1767–74 Peter Simon Pallas published a detailed and scholarly work on the peoples, flora, and fauna of Siberia which became the standard reference work on that region: *Reise durch verschiedene Provinzen des russischen Reiches*, 3 vols. St. Petersburg, 1783–86. Several of his collaborators supplemented his work with their own publications. Among these were the Swedish botanist Johann Peter Falck, who traveled as far east as Barnaul and the Altai region: *Beyträge zur topographischen Kenntnis des Russischen Reiches*, 3 vols. St. Petersburg, 1785–86; the German ethnographer Johann G. Georgi, who went beyond Lake Baikal: *Bemerkungen einer Reise im Russischen Reich in den Jahren 1773 und 1774*, St. Petersburg, 1775; the Russian academician Ivan I. Lepekhin, who traveled through the Ural region from south to north: *Dnevnyia zapiski puteshestviia po raznym provintsiiam Rossiiskago gosudarstva v 1768 . . . 1772 godu* (Diary of a Journey through Various Provinces of the Russian Empire in 1768–1772), 3 vols. St. Petersburg, 1795–1814; and another Russian, Nikolai P. Rychkov: *Tagebuch über seine Reise durch verschiedene Provinzen des russischen Reiches, 1766–1771, Riga, 1774*. Also connected with the expedition was Vasilii F. Zuev, whose studies of the Samoeds and Ostyaks along the Ob River were first published as *Materialy po etnografii Sibiri XVIII veka (1771–1772)* (Materials on the Ethnography of 18th-Century Siberia), Moscow and Leningrad, 1947.

From the Billings expedition of 1785–94 have come the accounts of Martin Sauer, Englishman and secretary to the expedition, and Gavriil A. Sarychev, a naval lieutenant on the expedition. Sauer's work first appeared in English as *An Account of a Geographical and Astronomical Expedition to the Northern Parts of Russia, . . .*, London, 1802; Sarychev's, *Puteshestvie po severo-vostochnoi chasti Sibiri, ledovitomu moriu, i vostochnomu okeanu* was first published in St. Petersburg in 1802; English translation: *Account of a Voyage of Discovery to the North-East of Siberia, the Frozen Ocean, and the North-East Sea*. London, 1806. Their value lies in their treatment of the northeastern parts of Siberia; they provide little information on the western and central parts. They are less penetrating than the works of Pallas, Gmelin, and some other trained investigators, being for the most part travelogues; but they are among the few known travel accounts to be written on Siberia during the 1780's. Sauer's narrative is useful to a certain extent in portraying Siberian life at this time.

Another important account of this decade was that of Jean Baptiste de Lesseps, a member of the French naval expedition commanded by Jean de la Pérouse. De Lesseps described his overland journey of 1787–88 from Kamchatka to St. Petersburg in his *Journal historique du voyage de m. de Lesseps . . . ,* 2 vols. Paris, 1790; English translation: *Travels in Kamtschatka during the Years 1787 and 1788,* 2 vols. London, 1790. Unfortunately the greater part of his narrative concerns his winter stay in Kamchatka; because of his haste to return to France, he described little of what he saw in central and western Siberia.

A number of individual travelers and scholars have left valuable accounts of their observations and studies in Siberia. During the reign of Peter I these included the Englishman John Bell; the Swedes Lorenz Lange and Philip Strahlenberg; and the German, Daniel Messerschmidt. In the period 1725–1762, between Peter's reign and that of Catherine II, the historian and geographer Vasilii N. Tatishchev made the only scholarly contribution to the study of Siberia by an individual observer; in 1736 he wrote "Obshchee geograficheskoe opisanie vseia Sibiri" (A General Geographical Description of All of Siberia), currently found in Tatishchev, *Izbrannye trudy po geografii Rossii,* Moscow, 1950, pp. 36–76.

In 1761 the French astronomer, Abbé Chappe d'Auteroche, was sent to Tobolsk by the French Academy of Science to view the transit of Venus. A report of his trip was published upon his return home: *Voyage en Sibérie, fait par ordre du roi en 1761; . . .,* Paris, 1768; English translation: *A Journey into Siberia, Made by Order of the King of France,* London, 1774. Perhaps a more important observer in the 1760's was the Swede, Erik Laxmann, who spent much of his life in Siberia in several different capacities: as Lutheran pastor in Barnaul, as scientific investigator in the Baikal and Altai regions, and as a member of the board of directors of the Nerchinsk mines. His correspondence was later edited by the German scholar A. L. von Schlözer as *Sibirische Briefe,* Göttingen and Gotha, 1769, and by Pallas in *Neue Nordische Beyträge,* Leipzig and St. Petersburg, 1781–96, 3: 159–77; 5: 302ff.; and 6: 252–56.

The Swiss doctor Jakob Fries, who traveled to Irkutsk and Kyakhta in 1776, recorded his impressions and observations in the form of a long letter to his family, recently edited by Walther Kirchner, *Eine Reise durch Sibirien im achtzehnten Jahrhundert. Die Fahrt des Schweizer Doktors Jakob Fries, . . . ,* Munich, 1955. An unknown Polish exile who was sent to western Siberia between 1768 and 1776 also left a narrative: "Poliak-konfederat v Sibiri," *Russkii Arkhiv* (1886), No. 1; this was first published in Warsaw in 1790.

Besides the travel accounts of Ledyard, Sauer, Sarychev, and de Lesseps, only two others are known to me which describe at least some part of Siberia in the 1780's. However, these accounts of A. M.

Patrin and P. I. Shangin, who traveled to Barnaul and to the Altai mountains, respectively, are brief and of little descriptive value; both are in *Neue Nordische Beyträge*, 4: 163–98 and 6: 28–112, respectively.

Brief mention should be made of letters, diaries, and notes made by travelers or exiles in Siberia shortly after the time of Ledyard's deportation. In the early 1790's Johann Sievers, a German of unknown background, wrote a number of letters while in central Siberia and the Baikal region which were published as *Briefe aus Sibirien an seine Lehrer*, St. Petersburg, 1796. In 1791 Alexander N. Radishchev, publicist and writer, was exiled to Ilimsk in eastern Siberia by Catherine. From his journey and confinement of several years Radishchev was able to make many penetrating observations and remarks in his letters and diary on the inhabitants of Siberia, its geography, agriculture, etc. These have recently been collected and edited in Radishchev, *Polnoe sobranie sochinenii* (Complete Works), Vol. 3, Moscow and Leningrad, 1952. A relatively detailed description of life in Irkutsk from 1796 to 1803 has been preserved in the writings of three Japanese sailors who were shipwrecked off Siberia; translated and edited by Stewart Culin in "Across Siberia in the Dragon Year 1796," *Asia*, 20 (1920): 505–12.

After the turn of the century both the number of travelers to Siberia and the volume of descriptive writings increased. Yet it was not until the arrival of the exiled Decembrists in the late 1820's that the study of Siberia began to regain the level it had attained in the days of Pallas. The Decembrists, well-educated men of the Russian nobility who in 1825 had failed in their revolt to secure a constitution for Russia, as exiles became deeply interested in this remote region of their homeland to which they were indefinitely relegated. Some of them, such as M. Muraviev-Apostol, V. I. Shteingel, N. V. Basargin, D. I. Zavalishin, and the brothers Alexander and Nicholas Bestuzhev, pursued investigations on the economy, population, geography, ethnography, and political and administrative structure of Siberia. For a listing and description of their individual works see Mazour, *The First Russian Revolution, 1825*, pp. 224–56.

Primary Sources

MANUSCRIPT COLLECTIONS

Additional Manuscripts, British Museum, London.

Correspondance politique, États-Unis, Archives du Ministère des Affaires Étrangères, Paris.

Jared Sparks Collection, MS No. 112, Houghton Library, Harvard University.

John Ledyard's Papers, original transcripts of the journal and letters made by Forman in the possession of the Ledyard family, Cazenovia, N.Y.; photostat copies are in the Archives of Baker Library, Dartmouth College, and in the possession of Professor and Mrs. Vernon Carstensen, Seattle, Washington. For details, see p. 84.

Ledyard Collection of 28 MS letters and documents, New-York Historical Society.

Ledyard Collection, which includes photostats John Ledyard's Papers (3 bound volumes), the Beaufoy transcript of the journal, and other letters of Ledyard. Baker Library, Dartmouth College.

Papers of the Continental Congress, National Archives, Washington, D.C.

Thomas Jefferson Papers, Manuscript Division, Library of Congress.

PUBLISHED DOCUMENTARY COLLECTIONS

The Papers of Thomas Jefferson, ed. by Julian P. Boyd. 17 vols. Princeton: Princeton University Press, 1950–65.

Russkii Arkhiv (Russian Archives). 123 vols. Moscow, 1863–1917.

Sbornik imperatorskago russkago istoricheskago obshchestva (Collection of the Imperial Russian Historical Society). 148 vols. St. Petersburg, 1867–1917.

The Writings of Thomas Jefferson, ed. by A. A. Lipscomb and A. E. Bergh. 20 vols. Philadelphia: Thomas Jefferson Memorial Association, 1904–05.

BOOKS

Kippis, Andrew. *A Narrative of the Voyages round the World Performed by Captain James Cook; With an Account of His Life.* 2 vols. Boston, 1828–30.

Ledyard, John. *A Journal of Captain Cook's Last Voyage to the Pacific Ocean, and in Quest of a North-West Passage, between Asia & America; Performed in the Years 1776, 1777, 1778, and 1779.* 1st ed., Hartford, 1783; 2nd ed., Chicago: Quadrangle Books, 1963.

———. *John Ledyard's Journal of Captain Cook's Last Voyage,* ed. by J. K. Munford. Corvallis, Ore.: Oregon State University Press, 1963.

[Lewis, Meriwether]. *History of the Expedition under the Command of Captains Lewis and Clark to the Sources of the Missouri,*

Thence across the Rocky Mountains and down the River Columbia to the Pacific Ocean, ed. by Paul Allen. 2 vols. Philadelphia, 1814.

Proceedings of the Association for Promoting the Discovery of the Interior Parts of Africa. London, 1791.

Sarychev, Gavriil A. *Puteshestvie po severo-vostochnoi chasti Sibiri, ledovitomu moriu, i vostochnomu okeanu* (A Journey through the Northeastern Part of Siberia, the Frozen Sea, and the Eastern Ocean). Moscow, 1952. Trans.: Gawrila Sarytschew. *Account of a Voyage of Discovery to the North-East of Siberia, the Frozen Ocean, and the North-East Sea*. London, 1806.

Sauer, Martin. *An Account of a Geographical and Astronomical Expedition to the Northern Parts of Russia, for Ascertaining the Degrees of Latitude and Longitude of the Mouth of the River Kovima; of the Whole Coast of the Tshutski, to East Cape; and of the Islands in the Eastern Ocean, Stretching to the American Coast*. London, 1802.

Secondary Sources

WORKS ON THE NORTHWEST COAST

Bancroft, H. H. *History of Alaska: 1730–1885*. San Francisco, 1886.

———. *History of the Northwest Coast*. 2 vols. San Francisco, 1886.

Chevigny, Hector. *Lord of Alaska: Baranov and the Russian Adventure*. New York: Viking Press, 1944.

Golder, Frank A. *Bering's Voyages: An Account of the Efforts of the Russians to Determine the Relation of Asia and America*. 2 vols. New York: American Geographical Society, 1922–25.

Howay, F. W. "Authorship of the Anonymous Account of Captain Cook's Last Voyage," *Washington Historical Quarterly*, Vol. 12, Pt. 1, Seattle, 1921.

———. "A List of Trading Vessels in Maritime Fur Trade, 1785–1794," *Proceedings and Transactions of the Royal Society of Canada*, 24 (1930): Sec. 2, 111–34.

———, ed. *Voyages of the "Columbia" to the Northwest Coast 1787–1790 and 1790–1793*. Boston: Massachusetts Historical Society, 1941.

Johansen, Dorothy O., and Charles M. Gates. *Empire of the Columbia: A History of the Pacific Northwest*. New York: Harper, 1957.

Okun', S. B. *Rossiisko-amerikanskaia kompaniia*. Moscow and Leningrad, 1939. Trans. by Carl Ginsberg titled *The Russian-Ameri-*

can Company. Cambridge, Mass.: Harvard University Press, 1951.

Schafer, Joseph. "The Pacific Slope and Alaska," in G. C. Lee, ed., *History of North America*, Vol. 10. Philadelphia: G. Barrie & Sons, 1905.

Tikhmenev, P. *Istoricheskoe obozrienie obrazovaniia Rossiisko-Amerikanskoi Kompaniia . . .* (Historical Survey of the Formation of the Russian-American Company). 2 vols. St. Petersburg, 1861.

WORKS ON RUSSIA AND SIBERIA

Abulgazi-Bagadur. *A General History of the Turks, Moguls, and Tatars, Vulgarly called Tartars. Together with a Description of the Countries They Inhabit.* 2 vols. London, 1729–30.

Adelung, Friedrich von. *Kritisch-literarische Uebersicht der Reisenden in Russland bis 1700, deren Berichte bekannt sind.* 2 vols. Amsterdam: N. Israel, 1960.

Akademiia nauk SSSR: Sibirskoe otdelenie. *Sibir' XVII–XVIII vv.* (Siberia in the 17th and 18th Centuries). Novosibirsk, 1962.

Anderson, Matthew S. *Britain's Discovery of Russia: 1553–1815.* London: Macmillan, and New York: St. Martin's Press, 1958.

Andreev, A. I. *Russkie otkrytiia v Tikhom Okeane i severnoi Amerike v XVIII–XIX vekakh* (Russian Discoveries in the Pacific Ocean and in North America in the 18th and 19th Centuries). Moscow, 1944.

Andrievich, V. K. *Istoriia Sibiri* (The History of Siberia). 2 vols. St. Petersburg, 1887–89.

Babey, Anna M. *Americans in Russia: 1776–1917. A Study of the American Travellers in Russia from the American Revolution to the Russian Revolution.* New York: Comet Press, 1938.

Basargin, Nikolai V. *Zapiski N. V. Basargina* (The Memoirs of N. V. Basargin). Petrograd, 1917.

Berg, L. S. *Geschichte der russischen geographischen Entdeckungen: gesammelte Aufsätze.* Leipzig: Bibliographisches Institut, 1954. (Trans. from the Russian.)

Blum, Jerome. *Lord and Peasant in Russia, from the Ninth to the Nineteenth Century.* Princeton: Princeton University Press, 1961.

Bruyn, Cornelius de (le Brun). *Voyages de Corneille le Brun par la Moscovie, en Perse, et aux Indes Orientales.* Amsterdam, 1718.

Chappe d'Auteroche, Jean. *A Journey into Siberia, Made by Order of the King of France.* London, 1774.

Clardy, Jesse. "Radishchev's Notes on the Geography of Siberia," *Russian Review*, 21 (Oct. 1962): 362–69.

Cochrane, John D. *Narrative of a Pedestrian Journey through Russia and Siberian Tartary, from the Borders of China to the Frozen Sea and Kamtchatka.* 2 vols. 3rd ed. London, 1825.

Collins, Perry McDonough. *Siberian Journey: Down the Amur to the Pacific, 1856–1857,* ed. by Charles Vevier. Madison: University of Wisconsin Press, 1962.

Coxe, William. *Account of the Russian Discoveries between Asia and America. To Which Are Added, the Conquest of Siberia, and the History of the Transactions and Commerce between Russia and China.* 3rd ed., London, 1787; 4th ed., London, 1803.

Culin, Stewart, ed. "Across Siberia in the Dragon Year 1796," *Asia,* 20 (1920): 505–12.

Czaplicka, M. A. *Aboriginal Siberia: A Study in Social Anthropology.* Oxford: Clarendon Press, 1914.

Efimov, A. V. *Iz istorii russkikh ekspeditsii na Tikhom okeane* (From the History of Russian Expeditions on the Pacific Ocean). Moscow, 1948.

Florinsky, Michael T. *Russia: A History and an Interpretation.* 2 vols. New York: Macmillan, 1960–61.

Georgi, Johann G. *Description de la ville de St. Pétersbourg et de ses environs.* St. Petersburg, 1793.

Golder, Frank A. *Russian Expansion on the Pacific, 1641–1850.* Gloucester, Mass.: Peter Smith, 1960.

Grigor'ev, Vladimir. *Grigorii Shelikhov: istoricheskii roman* (Grigorii Shelikhov: A Historical Novel). Moscow, 1952.

Kerner, Robert J. *Urge to the Sea: The Course of Russian History.* Berkeley and Los Angeles: University of California Press, 1942.

Kirchner, Walther. *Eine Reise durch Sibirien im achtzehnten Jahrhundert. Die Fahrt des Schweizer Doktors Jakob Fries, ...* Munich: Isar Verlag, 1955.

Lantzeff, George. *Siberia in the Seventeenth Century: A Study of the Colonial Administration.* Berkeley and Los Angeles: University of California Press, 1943.

Lebedev, D. M. *Ocherki po istorii geografii v Rossii XVIII v (1725–1800 gg.)* (Essays on the History of Geography in Russia of the 18th Century, 1725–1800). Moscow, 1957.

Lengyel, Emil. *Secret Siberia.* London: R. Hale, 1947.

Lesseps, J. B., Baron de. *Travels in Kamtschatka during the Years 1787 and 1788.* 2 vols. London, 1790.

Levin, M. G., and L. P. Potapov, eds. Akademiia nauk SSSR: Institut etnografii. *Narody Sibiri*. Moscow and Leningrad, 1956. Trans.: *The Peoples of Siberia*. Chicago: University of Chicago Press, 1964.

Lobanov-Rostovsky, Andrei. *Russia and Asia*. Ann Arbor: George Wahr Publishing Co., 1951.

———. "Russian Expansion in the Far East in the Light of the Turner Thesis," in W. Wyman and C. Kroeber, eds., *The Frontier in Perspective*. Madison: University of Wisconsin Press, 1965.

Maliarevskii, P. G. *Ocherk iz istorii teatral'noi kultury Sibiri* (An Essay from the History of the Theater in Siberia). Irkutsk, 1957.

Mazour, Anatole G. *The First Russian Revolution, 1825*. Berkeley: University of California Press, 1937.

———. *Modern Russian Historiography*. Princeton: D. Van Nostrand, 1958.

Ocherki istorii SSSR: period feodalizma. Rossiia vo vtoroi chetverti XVIII v. Narody SSSR v pervoi polovine XVIII v. (Essays on the History of the USSR: The Feudal Period. Russia in the Second Quarter of the 18th Century. The Peoples of the USSR in the First Half of the 18th Century). Moscow, 1957.

Ocherki istorii SSSR: period feodalizma. Rossiia vo vtoroi polovine XVIII v. (Essays on the History of the USSR: The Feudal Period. Russia in the Second Half of the 18th Century). Moscow, 1956.

Pallas, Peter Simon. *Voyages du Professeur Pallas, dans plusieurs provinces de l'empire de Russie et dans l'Asie septentrionale*. 8 vols. Paris, 1794.

Parry, Albert. "The First Americans in Siberia," *Travel*, 87 (June 1946): 18–22, 32.

Pypin, A. N. *Istoriia russkoi etnografii* (A History of Russian Ethnography). 4 vols. St. Petersburg, 1890–92.

Radishchev, A. N. *Polnoe sobranie sochinenii* (Complete Works), Vol. 3. Moscow and Leningrad, 1952.

Raeff, Marc. *Michael Speransky: Statesman of Imperial Russia, 1772–1839*. The Hague: Martinus Nijhoff, 1957.

———. *Siberia and the Reforms of 1822*. Seattle: University of Washington Press, 1956.

Semënov, Iurii N. *Sibirien: Eroberung und Erschliessung der wirtschaftlichen Schatzkammer des Ostens*. West Berlin: Ullstein, 1954. Trans.: *Siberia: Its Conquest and Development*. Baltimore: Helicon Press, 1963.

Shchapov, A. P. "Sibirskoe obshchestvo do Speranskago" (Siberian Society before Speransky), *Sochineniia A. P. Shchapova* (The Works of A. P. Shchapov). Vol. 3 (St. Petersburg, 1908): 643–717.

Shelekhov, Grigorii I. *Rossiiskago kuptsa Grigor'ia Shelekhova stranstvovanie s 1783 po 1787 god . . .* (The Travels of the Russian Merchant Grigorii Shelekhov, 1783–1787 . . .). St. Petersburg, 1791–92.

———. *Puteshestvie G. Shelekhova s 1783 po 1790 god . . .* (Journey of G. Shelekhov from 1783 to 1790). St. Petersburg, 1812.

Stejneger, Leonhard. *Georg Wilhelm Steller, the Pioneer of Alaskan Natural History*. Cambridge, Mass.: Harvard University Press, 1936.

Tatishchev, V. N. *Izbrannye trudy po geografii Rossii* (Selected Works on the Geography of Russia). Moscow, 1950.

Tooke, William. *View of the Russian Empire during the Reign of Catherine the Second, and to the Close of the Present Century.* 3 vols. London, 1799.

Treadgold, Donald W. *The Great Siberian Migration: Government and Peasant in Resettlement from Emancipation to the First World War.* Princeton: Princeton University Press, 1957.

Witsen, Nicolaas. *Noord en Oost Tartaryen: Behelzende eene Beschryving van verscheidene Tartersche en Nabuurige Gewesten, in de Noorder en Oostelykste Deelen van Aziën en Europa; . . .* 2 vols. Amsterdam, 1785.

OTHER CONTEMPORARY AND MODERN WORKS RELEVANT TO LEDYARD'S JOURNEY AND WRITINGS

Acerbi, Joseph. *Travels through Sweden, Finland, and Lapland, to the North Cape, in the Years 1798 and 1799.* 2 vols. London, 1802.

Adams, John Quincy. *Memoirs of John Quincy Adams, Comprising Portions of His Diary from 1795 to 1848*, ed. by C. F. Adams. 12 vols. Philadelphia, 1874–77.

Banks, Sir Joseph. *The Banks Letters: A Calendar of the Manuscript Correspondence of Sir Joseph Banks . . .*, ed. by W. R. Dawson. London: Printed by Order of the Trustees of the British Museum, 1958.

Brissot de Warville, J. P. *New Travels in the United States of America, 1788,* ed. by Durand Echeverria. Cambridge, Mass.: Belknap Press of Harvard University Press, 1964.

Burney, James. *A Chronological History of Northeastern Voyages of Discovery.* London, 1819.

Carver, Jonathan. *Travels through the Interior Parts of North America, in the Years 1766, 1767, and 1768.* 3rd ed. London, 1781.

Clarke, Edward D. *Travels in Russia, Tartary, and Turkey.* Vol. 1, New York, 1813.

Cook, James. *The Explorations of Captain James Cook in the Pacific, as Told by Selections of His Own Journals: 1768–1779*, ed. by A. Grenfell Price. Melbourne: Georgian House, 1958.

———, and James King. *A Voyage to the Pacific Ocean. Undertaken, by the Command of His Majesty for Making Discoveries in the Northern Hemisphere.* 2nd ed. 3 vols. London, 1785.

Duvall, R. F. "Philadelphia's Maritime Commerce with the British Empire, 1783–1789." Unpublished Ph.D. thesis, University of Pennsylvania, 1960.

Forman, Samuel S. *Narrative of a Journey down the Ohio and Mississippi in 1789–90.* Cincinnati, 1888.

Golder, Frank A. *Guide to Materials for American History in Russian Archives.* 2 vols. Washington: Carnegie Institute of Washington, 1917–37.

———. *John Paul Jones in Russia.* Garden City, N.Y.: Doubleday, Page, 1927.

Gottschalk, Louis R. *Lafayette between the American and the French Revolution* (1783–1789). Chicago: University of Chicago Press, 1950.

Historia sztuki polskiej w zarysie (An Outline History of Polish Art). 3 vols. Cracow: Wydawnictwa Literackie, 1962.

Hunter, John. *Essays and Observations on Natural History, Anatomy, Physiology, Psychology and Geology.* 2 vols. London, 1859–61.

Jefferson, Thomas. *Notes on the State of Virginia.* New York: Harper & Row, 1964.

Jensen, Merrill. *The New Nation: A History of the United States during the Confederation.* New York: Alfred A. Knopf, 1950.

Kimball, Marie. *Jefferson: The Scene of Europe: 1784 to 1789.* New York: Coward-McCann, 1950.

Lafayette, Marquis de. *Mémoires, correspondance et manuscrits du général Lafayette, publiés par sa famille.* 2 vols. Paris, 1838.

Lehmann-Haupt, Hellmut. *The Book in America: A History of the Making, the Selling, and the Collecting of Books in the United States.* New York: R. R. Bowker, 1939.

Life and Correspondence of John Paul Jones, Including His Narrative of the Campaign of the Liman. From Original Letters and

Manuscripts in the Possession of Miss Janette Taylor. New York, 1830.

Lorenz, Lincoln. *John Paul Jones, Fighter for Freedom and Glory.* Annapolis: United States Naval Institute, 1943.

Malone, Dumas. *Jefferson the Virginian.* Boston: Little, Brown, 1948.

Mongait, A. L. *Archaeology in the USSR.* Trans. by M. W. Thompson, Baltimore: Penguin Books, 1961.

Morison, Samuel Eliot. *John Paul Jones: A Sailor's Biography.* Boston: Little, Brown, 1959.

———. *The Maritime History of Massachusetts: 1783–1860.* Boston and New York: Houghton Mifflin, 1921.

Pattee, Fred Lewis, ed. *The Poems of Philip Freneau, Poet of the American Revolution,* Vol. 1. Princeton: University Library, 1902.

Pennant, Thomas. *Arctic Zoology.* 2 vols. London, 1784–85.

———. *History of Quadrupeds.* 2 vols. London, 1781.

———. *Synopsis of Quadrupeds.* Chester, 1771.

Phillips, James Duncan. *Salem and the Indies: The Story of the Great Commercial Era of the City.* Boston: Houghton Mifflin, 1947.

Ségur, L. P., Count de. *Mémoires ou souvenirs et anecdotes.* 3 vols. Paris, 1826–27.

Spaulding, E. Wilder. *New York in the Critical Period: 1783–1789.* New York: Columbia University Press, 1932.

Wagner, Henry R. *Peter Pond, Fur Trader & Explorer.* New Haven: Yale University Library, 1955.

INDEX